CZECH VILLAGE & NEW BOHEMIA

CZECH VILLAGE & NEW BOHEMIA

HISTORY IN THE HEARTLAND

DAVE RASDAL
Foreword by Mark Stoffer Hunter

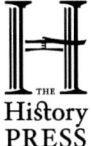

Published by The History Press
Charleston, SC
www.historypress.net

Copyright © 2016 by Dave Rasdal
All rights reserved

Front cover, top: A concrete lion guards a corner of the Bridge of Lions in Cedar Rapids in this photo facing west across the Cedar River toward Czech Village and the carillon tower in front of the National Czech & Slovak Museum & Library. *Photo by Rollin Banderob*; *bottom*: The Karla Masaryk Chorus, founded in 1937 by a group of Czech housewives, performed in native costumes at nearly every special occasion in the Czech community through World War II and into the 1950s. During the war, the chorus made a recording broadcast in Europe by Voice of America. *Photo courtesy of National Czech & Slovak Museum & Library.* *Back cover, left*: The grand reopening of the National Czech & Slovak Museum & Library on July 14, 2012, in Cedar Rapids featured Czech royalty on a colorful float—*from left to right*: Beth Blanko, Miss Czech Slovak Iowa Queen 2010–11; Lisa Volesky, Miss Czech-Slovak USA 2001–02; and Holly Stepanek, Miss Czech Slovak Iowa Queen 2012–13. *Photo courtesy of the* Gazette; *right*: An undated photograph shows workers busy inside one of the early buildings at the T.M. Sinclair & Company packinghouse after it had relocated to the end of Third Street Southeast in Cedar Rapids. *Photo courtesy of the* Gazette.

First published 2016

Manufactured in the United States

ISBN 978.1.46711.761.6

Library of Congress Control Number: 2015956825

Notice: The information in this book is true and complete to the best of our knowledge. It is offered without guarantee on the part of the author or The History Press. The author and The History Press disclaim all liability in connection with the use of this book.

All rights reserved. No part of this book may be reproduced or transmitted in any form whatsoever without prior written permission from the publisher except in the case of brief quotations embodied in critical articles and reviews.

This book is dedicated to the dozens of Czech immigrants and their descendants cited in this book and to the thousands I didn't have room to mention, all of whom helped shape Cedar Rapids into the industrious, progressive and neighbor-friendly community it is today.

CONTENTS

Foreword, by Mark Stoffer Hunter	9
Acknowledgements	11
Introduction: Bridges	13
1. Into the 1870s: Immigration and the American Dream	17
2. 2008: The Great Flood	36
3. The Early 1900s: The Next Generations	43
4. 1918: The Great War—"Free at Last"	72
5. 1930s: The Great Depression	83
6. 1939: World War II	95
7. 1960s: The Mall, Another Flood and Other Things	104
8. 1980s: The Packinghouse Packs It In	113
9. 1995: The Three Presidents	126
10. 2000: Old Becomes New	135
11. Today: Resurgence	146
Appendix: Eat Like a Czech	173
Bibliography	179
Index	183
About the Author	191

FOREWORD

While growing up in Cedar Rapids, I became aware at an early age of the unique character of the areas of the city now known as New Bohemia and Czech Village. I remember taking note of the special architectural details on the historic buildings along Third Street Southeast and Sixteenth Avenue Southwest. Organizational names such as CSPS and ZCBJ were proudly carved in stone on the larger buildings. Cedar Rapids names such as Suchy, Matyk, Barta and Polehna were visible atop the smaller storefront structures. Older generations of Cedar Rapidians would always describe these areas to me as "Bohemie Town." Historically, they had been called the "South Side" or "South End" on the east and "the Avenue" on the west.

As a teenager in the 1980s, I realized through endless hours of research that these neighborhoods have always been critically vital to the history of Cedar Rapids. Renewed appreciation for Sixteenth Avenue Southwest as "Czech Village" began in the 1970s, but community support for restoring the older east-side neighborhood took a long time. The entire area now known as New Bohemia was targeted for demolition in the 1960s as part of an urban renewal plan. Thankfully, that plan was never carried out. In the 1990s, interest began to grow in preserving the old South Side area, especially after the destruction of two landmarks: the 1912 Olympic Theatre (later known as the Strand and the Community Theatre) at the corner of Twelfth Avenue and Third Street Southeast in 1993 and the demolition of the 1873 Monroe School building at 921 Third Street Southeast in 1996.

Foreword

Shortly after 2000, the name New Bohemia was established, and both the "New Bo" and Czech Village areas were listed in the National Register of Historic Places. There was again a brief consideration for demolishing the area after the devastating June 2008 flood, but the Cedar Rapids community rallied behind saving Czech Village and New Bohemia. They have recovered magnificently, as strong as they were one hundred years ago. This area has always been not only special to me but also increasingly special to the entire community, as well as unique on a national level: other cities in the United States may have a "Little Italy" or "Little China," but only Cedar Rapids has a "Little Bohemia."

Mark Stoffer Hunter
Cedar Rapids Historian
The History Center (Linn County Historical Society)
October 2015

ACKNOWLEDGEMENTS

This book wouldn't be what it is without the assistance of so many generous people. Thank you to all, in particular:

The *Gazette*: Zack Kucharski for permission to use the archives and photographs and Diana Pesek for setting me up with a computer to search the electronic files.

Rick Smith, *Gazette* city hall reporter, who brought about my connection with Greg Dumais, acquisitions editor at The History Press. And Greg for being a thoughtful, concise and understanding editor.

Former *Gazette* staffers: Cindy Hadish, who covered Czech Village during the flood recovery; Dale Kueter, an early mentor at the *Gazette* who wrote about the Czech population in Cedar Rapids throughout his career; and Mary Sharp for her expert, down-home encouragement and advice.

The National Czech & Slovak Museum & Library: Gail Naughton for allowing me access to the library and Dave Muhlena for digging up information.

All of the genealogists who compiled family histories and contributed copies to the Czech museum so researchers can grasp the human aspect of immigration and the historical significance of the Czech influence on Cedar Rapids.

Personal interview subjects: Mel Andringa, Bob Chadima, Lijun Chadima, Beth Chacey DeBoom, Bob Drahozal, Jon Jelinek, Donna Merkle and Baron Stark.

A special thank-you goes to Mark Stoffer Hunter, "Mr. History of Cedar Rapids" at the History Center, for his historical knowledge in scanning this original manuscript for accuracy and contributing the foreword.

Acknowledgements

And lastly, you, dear reader, for understanding that this is but a brief history of Czech Village and New Bohemia, for since history is so full and ongoing, no single written account can ever encompass every detail.

Introduction

BRIDGES

A bridge—as does a road—leads somewhere. But a bridge accomplishes much more than a simple road, for it crosses an obstacle—a river, a gulch, railroad tracks, even an ocean.

Sure, you don't see a bridge across the Atlantic Ocean. But if you use your imagination, it's there. From the area known as Bohemia in Eastern Europe to a flat and prosperous land in the middle of America's Heartland called Iowa, that bridge was "built" more than 150 years ago. It has taken adventurous Bohemian or Czech people somewhere—to a new land, to hard work and sacrifice, to family ties and fresh loves, to advanced educations and business opportunities, to realigned loyalties and relief from strife, to adventures unforeseen and to...yes, this symbolic bridge has taken these people to their dreams.

Today, in the Czech Republic's capital of Prague, you can cross the Charles Bridge over the Vitava River. In Iowa's second-largest city, Cedar Rapids, you can cross the Bridge of Lions over the Cedar River. Each bridge takes you past symbolic statues—in Prague they are of historically significant people, and in Cedar Rapids they are lions representing Czech independence. These bridges draw a parallel between old and new.

The Charles Bridge, constructed beginning in 1357, replaced the nearly two-century-old Judith Bridge that had been damaged beyond repair by a great flood.

The Bridge of Lions, erected in 1989, supplanted a weakened 1910 concrete structure that, itself, had replaced a rickety 1875 iron bridge.

Introduction

After just thirty-five years of service and seventy-nine years of service, these bridges across the Cedar River became early examples of the American tradition of "replace rather than rebuild."

The Charles Bridge is magnificent. Its sixteen arched spans that stretch 1,700 feet across the Vitava are covered with cobblestones. It has three large bridge towers with the tower on the Old Town side often described as one of the more significant civil Gothic-style buildings in the world. Along the bridge's rails stand replicas of thirty Baroque-style statues, the originals now preserved and exhibited at the National Museum in Prague.

The Bridge of Lions is functional. Its concrete bed spans seven arches across the Cedar. It provides not only two wide lanes for vehicular traffic but also walkways on either side for pedestrians and bicyclists. On the river's west side stands a tall brick clock tower only twenty years old yet symbolic of the area's Czech heritage. Along the concrete railings, semicircular extensions above the usually lazy river have concrete benches where you can rest, enjoy the scenery of a resurgent Cedar Rapids business district and come face to face with the small statue of a lion.

The Charles Bridge no longer allows anything but foot traffic, hence it becomes crowded with street venders, artists and walking tourists on a daily basis. In its early days, this bridge was significant not only because it connected the two areas of Prague but because it served as the major economic gateway from western Europe to Eastern Europe.

Likewise, the Bridge of Lions connects east and west, albeit on a significantly smaller scale. On the east side of the Cedar River, the New Bohemia area of Cedar Rapids was settled a decade before the American Civil War by Bohemians who left their country after the revolution of 1848. On the west side, Czech Village is a business district originally settled by immigrants of a multitude of nationalities until the burgeoning Czech population crossed the bridge and claimed the area as its own.

It is these neighborhoods of Cedar Rapids—the New Bohemia settlement from 150 years ago and the Czech Village district that came about in the early 1900s—that provide the focus for this brief historical perspective. It is an area that ebbed and flowed through most of the twentieth century until a handful of visionaries in the 1990s planted seeds for a vibrant future.

A well-traveled person would never mistake the quaint Czech Village/New Bo in Cedar Rapids, Iowa, for the huge commerce and markets of Prague in the Czech Republic. But the connection is here and always will be—a bridge between two communities that today resonates as strong as ever with the National Czech & Slovak Museum & Library appropriately located

INTRODUCTION

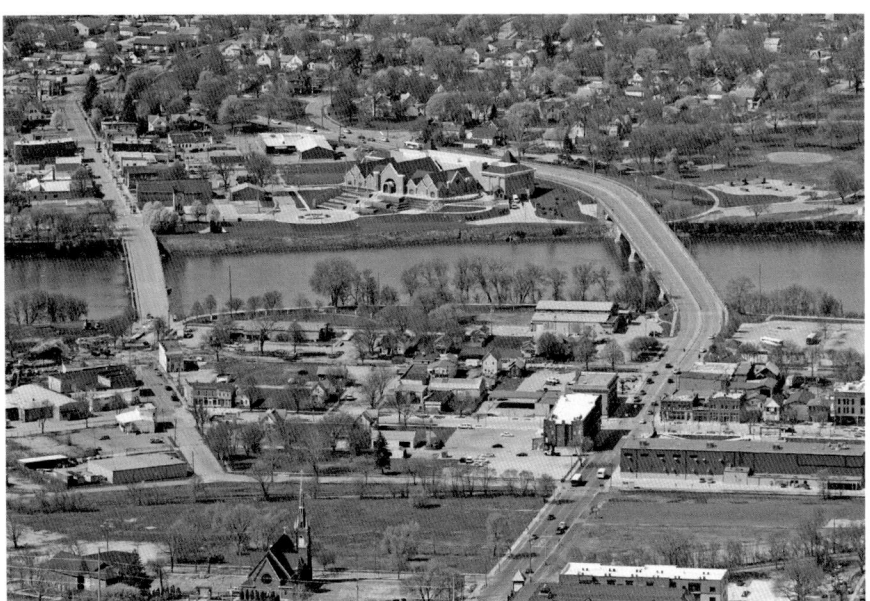

The National Czech & Slovak Museum & Library, upper center, sits on higher ground away from the Cedar River five years after historic flooding in Cedar Rapids forced it to relocate. At left, the Bridge of Lions (Sixteenth Avenue) connects the New Bohemia area in the lower part of the picture to the Czech Village business district in the upper part. At right, the Twelfth Avenue Bridge has connected the areas since 1974. *Photo courtesy of the* Cedar Rapids Gazette.

in the heart of the Czech Village/New Bo area. This neighborhood and its world-renowned museum serve as a testament to the accomplishments realized by arduous work, an appreciation for preserving deeply held Czech traditions and, yes, even more than a century and a half later, the challenging yet magical pursuit of human dreams.

1
INTO THE 1870s

IMMIGRATION AND THE AMERICAN DREAM

In 1870, just twenty-four years after Iowa became a state, its fledgling government spent $30,000 to convince restless Europeans that "the Beautiful Land" between two rivers could make their dreams come true. The 106-page brochure published in a multitude of languages, however, said nothing about the arduous journey required to reach what today has been dubbed "the Heartland" of America.

Frank Peremsky, who came to Cedar Rapids in 1856 by himself before his twentieth birthday, would have told of an ocean voyage long and lonely.

Thomas Korab, seven when his family dragged him across the continent in 1854, told tales of hunting wild rabbits for food and leading ox-driven carts through dangerous rivers and streams.

And Frank Svec, a twenty-something-year-old veteran of war in Bohemia when he arrived in the mid-1860s with his bride, Rose Kventensky Svec, and their two very young sons, Frank Jr. and Joseph, undoubtedly learned that cutting down trees to fuel steam-driven locomotives was as difficult as working the metal mines in his homeland.

For early Bohemian immigrants to Cedar Rapids and the surrounding area, life wasn't a leisurely and wealthy fantasy. But it held promise.

In 1846, when Iowa became the nation's twenty-ninth state, it had few roads and fewer bridges. The first pioneers of 1837 followed rivers and streams, if they didn't actually float handmade rafts on the waters, to their new homes. Those who came later, like Korab and his family, crossed flowing rivers at their own peril, for often, if someone built a rudimentary bridge, high water soon washed it away. Often these pioneers waited days for a river level to subside so they could ford it. A short journey today required an eternity then.

"The trip took twelve weeks," recalled Thomas Korab who published a diary in 1925 about his family's immigration from Moravia to farmland southeast of Cedar Rapids.

> *It was a stormy voyage and it made an impression, not only on me, but upon my parents.*
>
> *When we finally arrived in New York my father saluted the boat in tribute to it for bringing us safely here. We arrived at the Lorences, who lived in Racine, Wisconsin…in November, 1854. They were harvesting corn. We could go no further because it was too late in the year. We lived in a log cabin; three families lived there. My father cut wood in the forest.*
>
> *As soon as spring arrived, my uncle came, by foot, to act as our guide from Wisconsin to Iowa. We bought a wagon and oxen and departed. The trip took two weeks. With us, in two other wagons, also came the Dostals and Lorences. It was the latter part of April, there was no grass, roads were bad, and it was very frosty. While the others went on, I was sent to one farm to buy something to eat and I got a loaf of bread fresh from the oven…My uncle had a gun and whenever he saw a rabbit, he shot it. After a while, we finally came to the Lorences and Zvaceks, east of Ely.*

Thus, Thomas Korab's family became early Bohemian settlers south of Cedar Rapids, where he would marry, have two children and farm eighty acres. On their journey across the Mississippi River they didn't even find a bridge—the first one at Dubuque was constructed in 1868.

Bridges and Culverts

Today, Iowa has more bridges and culverts per square mile than any state in the nation. The reason is twofold. First, the Mississippi and Missouri Rivers that form the state's east and west boundaries are fed by hundreds of tributaries. And second, because Iowa's topography is basically flat, surveyors platted the 310- by 200-mile state with a grid system of mostly straight roads every mile, east–west and north–south. Where road met water, in went a culvert or up went a bridge so that, in most cases, traveling from Point A to Point B was a straight line.

For immigrants from Bohemia, a bridge was the least of their worries. In March 1848, revolutionary action against the Habsburg Austrian Empire, of which Bohemia belonged, once again resulted in fighting on the home soil. A long history of wars and revolutions prompted many natives—who correctly predicted future fighting and bloodshed—to leave their homeland in search of peace and tranquility, land ownership and equality, opportunity and prosperity.

One man, Joseph Sosel, was packed into a wooden barrel in 1848 and smuggled out of Austria because the government had put a price on his revolutionary-minded head. A scholarly attorney, Sosel had unsuccessfully led Bohemian students in an uprising for political rights and more freedom. As the first Czech attorney to settle in the United States, according to multiple sources, Sosel eventually came to Cedar Rapids by way of Wisconsin as did so many Czech immigrants in the 1850s. They often rode in stagecoaches that followed the Military Road, a furrow dug into the wild prairie in 1839 that turned into a muddy mess every spring. Enhanced by a few bridges in the 1840s, this crooked trail meandered from Dubuque to Iowa City, the territorial capital and soon-to-be seat of state government, from 1840 to 1857. By the 1850s, the swiftest stages could complete the seventy-five-mile route in three days.

When Bohemians arrived in Iowa's wide-open territory, they came upon white settlements freshly founded by the adventurous, the industrious and, sometimes, the dishonest. One of the latter, it seems, was Osgood Shepherd, who, in 1838, became Cedar Rapids' first permanent settler of European descent. By one account, he jumped William Stone's claim and commandeered Stone's log cabin on the east bank of the Cedar River in what today is the heart of the city—First Street and First Avenue Southeast.

Shepherd, described in the 1878 history of Linn County as "a large man, shrewd and cunning, and of more than average intelligence," opened his home as a tavern. With red hair, a rugged constitution and eyes "piercing as that of a snake," he reportedly surrounded himself with outlaws. The story has long been told of Shepherd's penchant for stealing horses and hiding them among thickets of trees on an island in the Cedar River, an island that decades later would, ironically, become home to the city's government as well as the courts of Linn County and its jail.

By 1850, the population of Cedar Rapids had yet to reach four hundred. Most of the early inhabitants, originally from Great Britain, Norway, Sweden,

Germany and France, had trekked west from the likes of Ohio, Indiana and Illinois or had sailed up the Mississippi River from New Orleans. Some were genuinely happy with what they found in Iowa while others simply gave up the strenuous search for nirvana when they found the new wide-open prairies satisfactory.

Gold Rush Influence

Cedar Rapids experienced a nice growth spurt when the westward movement gained momentum after James W. Marshall struck gold in 1848 at Sutter's Mill in California. Since news traveled slowly in those days, it wasn't until 1849 that Bohemians learned of the fortunes in California. Combined with the spoils of war and poor economic times, this prompted twenty-five thousand adventurous Bohemians to leave behind what little they had, including family members, in search of roads paved with gold.

Of course, by the time new European immigrants reached American shores, thousands of gold diggers on the continent had picked the mines nearly clean. While an estimated 300,000 fortune seekers reached their destination in the years to follow, thousands more realized that the weeks-long journey over huge mountains and across hundreds of unbridged waterways wouldn't be worth the effort. These people, too, abandoned their golden fantasies to follow more realistic avenues toward success.

By 1856, the population of Cedar Rapids had quadrupled to 1,600, of which 400 were Bohemians. Most of these immigrants arrived in southern Linn County and northern Johnson County as they veered off the Military Road. Soon, some of them began the short migration to Cedar Rapids, where they settled along the east side of the Cedar River, downstream several blocks from the site of Osgood Shepherd's log house. Shepherd, it seems, moved to Wisconsin in 1841 and was killed there in a railroad accident. But it was this year, 1856, that Cedar Rapids revised its seven-year-old charter and officially became a city in many historians' eyes. And it was here, along today's Seventh Avenue, that the first bridge in Cedar Rapids to cross the Cedar River was constructed in 1857.

Prior to 1857, travelers and merchants who wished to cross the river did so in the winter when it was frozen, waited for the river level to subside in the spring and the fall or took a ferry, explained Luther A. Brewer and Barthinius L. Wick in their 1911 book *History of Linn County Iowa: From Its*

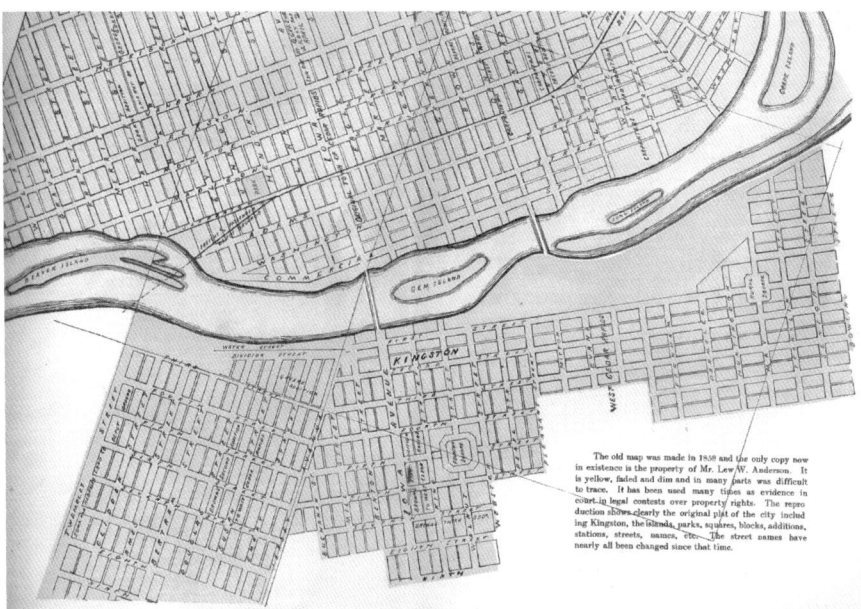

An artist's copy of an 1859 map of Cedar Rapids shows the street names originally given when the city was platted. At right, Crocker Street on the east side of the river would become Fourteenth Avenue Southeast in the New Bohemia district. It was later connected by a bridge over the Cedar River to May Street (today's Sixteenth Avenue Southwest) that runs through the "Rural Square" that would become part of Czech Village. *Courtesy of the Cedar Rapids Gazette.*

Earliest Settlement to the Present Time. They explained that use of the river had been popular since 1839, when keel boats plied their trade, and that it reached a new level when the first steamboat, *The Maid of Iowa*, brought a few settlers to Cedar Rapids in June 1846. Steamboats in a variety of shapes and sizes, including *The Uncle Tobey* with a two-hundred-ton cargo in 1853, traveled the Cedar River through the 1850s.

David W. King, one of the area's most industrious entrepreneurs and founder of a village named Kingston on the west bank of the Cedar River across from Cedar Rapids, operated the semblance of a toll bridge. He charged customers to cross the river along his trail "when the boulder in the river near the Watrous mill was visible." In 1848, King secured official rights to operate a ferry for the next ten years with the "exclusive privilege for the space of one mile on either side."

As King prospered, city leaders began talk in 1853 of erecting a bridge that would be free for everyone. While early efforts at bridging the river may have been noble, Mother Nature had other ideas.

First, in the winter of 1856–57, three prominent Cedar Rapids businessmen received state legislative approval to form a bridge building board, raised $20,000 and completed the bridge at Seventh Avenue. That spring, however, they watched it wash away in a flood. The real tragedy was the death of two sisters with the surname of Black who were carried away with the bridge.

Second, a floating bridge completed in the fall of 1857 across the Cedar River at First Avenue fell victim to a rapidly flowing ice gorge the following spring.

For a while, the chore of crossing the river reverted back to the ferry man, until the winter of 1859–60, when a group of businessmen whose last names soon became synonymous with success in Cedar Rapids—among them Greene, Earle, Steadman, Higley and Daniels—erected a toll bridge. Tolls ranged from a quarter for a wagon pulled by a double team of horses to a nickel per head for driven cattle and a penny for each pedestrian.

In the meantime, "Little Bohemia" grew downriver, and Czech attorney Joseph Sosel became a neighborhood leader. He arrived in 1858 with Jacob Polak, who settled about ten miles southeast of Cedar Rapids. Since Sosel could speak English, he became a trusted adviser to the Bohemian immigrants for business and legal dealings with Cedar Rapids residents of other nationalities. It was also said that while Sosel remained true to his homeland, he insisted that his countrymen observe the laws and customs of their new country.

Praise for Bohemians

"These people have always made good citizens," wrote Brewer and Wick in their 1911 history when they called Bohemians the most important foreign element in Linn County.

> *They possess the desirable faculty of adapting themselves readily to new environments. Without destroying their own vigorous vitality, they grasp quickly the best there is in our thought and mode of life. They have borne nobly their share of the burdens incident to the establishment of new centers of civilization and of progress. They have acted their part in our civic life. They have adapted themselves to and have adopted our institutions. They have helped and are helping to make the county and the city centers of growth and prosperity.*

One man, Anton Sulek, summed up Bohemian sentiments to a "T" when, in Hoosier Grove in Johnson County near the Linn County border on an elevated spot, he christened his land "Hradek"—"Little Castle."

Whether these early immigrants settled in the country or in the city, one of the first tasks was to build their own "dream castles." Early houses were generally built out of logs with an ample supply of lumber, although an occasional sod home appeared on the prairie. While roofs might be thatched, they were usually made of four-foot-long wooden shingles held in place by logs laid on top of them. Since furniture was scarce at first, immigrants often hewed their own. Beds were bundles of straw piled on the floor with a featherbed, often transported from the old country in a large chest, lovingly spread out on top.

In this manner, "Little Bohemia" grew slowly at the southeast edge of Cedar Rapids into the 1860s and through the end of the American Civil War. Even though the Homestead Act of 1862 enabled immigrants, as long as they had never "borne arms against the U.S. Government," to homestead 160 acres for $1.25 per acre, much of the land in and around Cedar Rapids had been claimed. As a result, Bohemian immigrants bought farmland for $4.00 or $5.00 per acre and often in smaller 100-acre or 80-acre tracts that were still twice as large as any land they'd owned in the old country. The cost of property in town, as it is today, was more expensive, although it could be acquired by trading an old horse or other goods, including an occasional rifle and ammunition, for it.

While the outbreak of the American Civil War in 1861 no doubt had some Bohemians thinking they'd mistakenly made a long journey from one battleground to another (no battles were fought on Iowa soil), many of them were ready, willing and able to fight. No fewer than seventeen Bohemians from Cedar Rapids enlisted in the Union army—among them, Frank Renchin, the first to sign up despite living in Iowa only seven years.

"The United States had their quota of Bohemian patriots and it is to their credit that they did not shirk their duty, in fact, though many were not even citizens at the time of the Civil War, they performed their duty just as if America had been the land of their birth," wrote Sarka B. Hrbkova in "Bohemians Have Done Much for Cedar Rapids," published in the *Cedar Rapids Republican Semi-Centennial Magazine* June 10, 1906 edition.

Other enlistees included men with solid Czech surnames that resonate in the community today: J.F. Bednar, Joseph Wendel, Joseph Podhajsky, John Maly, Joseph Zahradnik, Wesley Horak, Frank Dolezal and Frank Peremsky.

Yes, Frank Peremsky, who immigrated to Cedar Rapids in 1856, married in 1861 and enlisted in the Sixth Iowa Cavalry of the Union army in September 1862. Born in Bohemia in January 1837, he was featured in the 1906 stories by Hrbkova as he approached his seventieth birthday. He came from Massachusetts through Wisconsin after learning "there were two or three Bohemian families in a village in Iowa in a vicinity in which the Indians were not so fierce as elsewhere."

So of course, the Sixth Iowa Cavalry was assigned to the western states to fight against Indians who were trying to take advantage of the United States being at war with itself. Though Peremsky returned with more proficient use of the English language, he would also carry for the rest of his life "an injured limb in which he received a wound in 1864 and which has disabled him at times, for active or heavy work."

The only Civil War casualty among the Bohemians was Frank Woitishek, who died of disease on July 18, 1863, in Vicksburg, Mississippi, fully two weeks after the Confederate forces surrendered to General Ulysses S. Grant in that bloody battle. His manner of death was not unusual—an estimated two of every three war deaths were due to disease.

War's end was about the time Frank and Rose Svec arrived in Iowa with their two sons. They would have three more children: John, Mary and Stephen. By the time their granddaughter Marie Melvina Svec (John's daughter) compiled the family history in 1984, they, with more than four hundred descendants through seven generations, had set a fine example of how one Czech couple could multiply.

In the 1860s, Frank Svec embarked on a varied career as he supported his growing family. He farmed, owned a tavern and cut firewood for the Northwestern Railroad. He'd ride with a crew on a flatbed car as far west as Boone to chop wood and deposit it along the railroad tracks as locomotive fuel. Before Frank died in 1899, he and Rose lived at least three places—near Shueyville south of Cedar Rapids, in Kenwood Park just north of Cedar Rapids (near today's Thirty-Second Street Northeast) and on Bowling Street Southwest, which would become a residential area of Czech Village.

Wooing Immigrants

After the Civil War, Iowa leaders took a chapter out of Wisconsin's early history book and publicized the benefits of Iowa living to prospects around the country and abroad. The result: an uptick in Bohemian immigration to Iowa and to Cedar Rapids.

Wisconsin became the first center of Czech American life in the United States in 1848 according to Karel D. Bicha's account "The Czechs in Wisconsin History." The state, through an active immigration commissioner stationed in New York City, promoted its benefits. "Low taxes, liberal residence requirements, inexpensive land, a climate of political and religious freedom, and similarities in soil and physiography attracted both the unobtrusive peasants and village artisans of southern Bohemia and the vociferous, visionary refugees of the Prague uprising of 1848," Bicha wrote.

While early Czech immigrants settled on Long Island, New York, and in Cleveland and Chicago, an area of Milwaukee became home to many Bohemians. Also, an early beneficiary of Czech immigration was the Racine, Wisconsin area, where they formed their own "neighborhood," Caledonia, in 1850. Here they paid five to ten dollars per acre for land, double what they could buy it for in Iowa.

That could be one reason a notice published in *Slavie*, a Racine Czech-language newspaper, proclaimed greater opportunities in Iowa. Indeed, Bicha noted that the migration took place until 1890 from Wisconsin to lands south and west. It also seems that pioneers in Iowa wrote home to relatives about the new life they had found. Maybe some of them read an 1868 advertisement in the *Cedar Valley Times* newspaper in Cedar Rapids about one-way steamer-railroad tickets from European ports directly to Cedar Rapids. It was aimed at residents "desiring to send for their friends in Europe or to remit money to them."

Even though Iowa had a New York City immigration agent in the early 1860s, the big recruitment push began in 1870, when the State Board of Immigration published handbooks in several languages and distributed them through agents in foreign ports. The state spent $29,500 on the three-year campaign.

While the brochure *Iowa: The Home for Immigrants, Being a Treatise on the Resources of Iowa and Giving Useful Information with Regard to the State, for the Benefit of Immigrants and Others* had a mouthful of words for a title, it provided a succinct wealth of information about the state's early history through the Louisiana Purchase in 1803 to its territorial status and eventual statehood.

"The word 'Iowa' is said to mean in the language of the Indian tribes, 'The Beautiful Land,'" the brochure read. "A band of Indians journeying toward the setting sun, reached the bank of the Great River that washes our eastern border, and looking across the broad water, beheld for the first time the green slopes of our beautiful prairies stretching away in the distance. Their exclamation was 'Iowa!'—The Beautiful Land!"

In subsequent chapters, the brochure described Iowa's geography and rivers, the fertile soil, opportunities in agriculture and horticulture, the sound educational system, the expansion of railroads and the availability of government lands that could still be claimed, mostly in northwest Iowa.

As an example of the brochure's detail, one paragraph listed the native trees: "The timbers of Iowa (1870) were white, black and burr oak, black walnut, butternut, hickory, hard and soft maple, cherry, red and white elm, ash, linn, hackberry, birch, honey locust, cottonwood, and quacking asp, plus a few sycamore and groves of red cedar, and a few isolated pines."

The *Iowa: Home for Immigrants* brochure helped boost the state's population from 1,194,000 people in 1870 to 1,625,000 a decade later; Cedar Rapids increased by more than 4,000 people from 5,940 citizens to 10,104.

T.M. Sinclair Arrives

Among the newcomers to Cedar Rapids was an Irishman not yet thirty years old by the name of Thomas McElderry Sinclair. As the son of a large meatpacking plant owner in Belfast, Ireland, he sought to establish a similar enterprise in the Midwest. He had experienced success in America by operating a branch office of his father's business, J.&T. Sinclair Co., in New York City with his cousin John. While that office flourished during the Civil War, a fire in 1866 destroyed it. After recovering financially, Thomas set out to establish his own business while his cousin remained in New York.

After the fire, a Sinclair employee, David Blakely, headed west. He opened a retail meat business in Cedar Rapids and, since he stayed in contact with T.M. Sinclair, suggested that city might be a reasonable location for a packing plant, especially since Iowa's livestock business was growing rapidly.

Upon his first visit in late 1871, T.M. Sinclair liked what he saw and bought land in northeast Cedar Rapids not far from today's Quaker Oats complex. But anxious to get started, he opened his packing plant that fall in the former Higgins Icehouse along the Cedar River near today's Fifth Avenue Southeast, between the business district and Little Bohemia.

According to an interview with Dan Anderson in "Sinclair's Celebrates Fiftieth Anniversary," by Gladys Arne in the December 3, 1921 *Cedar Rapids Evening Gazette*, Sinclair was hard at work when Anderson walked into the

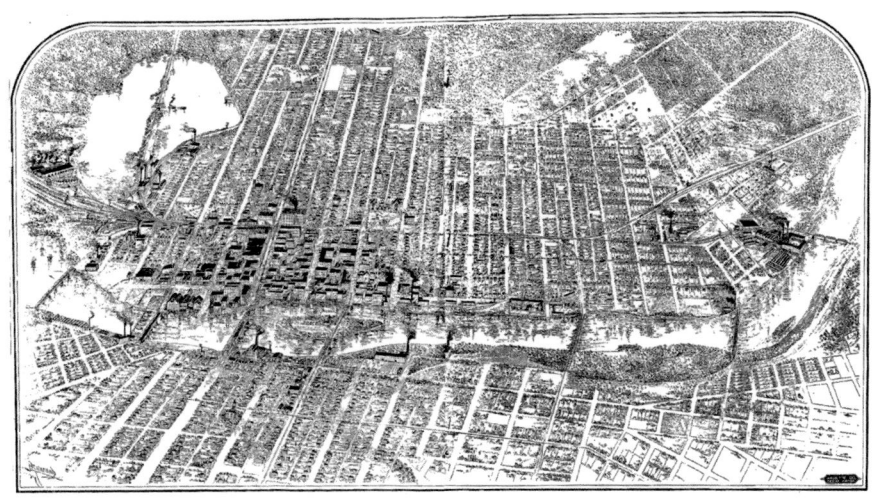

This bird's-eye view of Cedar Rapids looking northeast was printed in the *Evening Gazette* on December 23, 1887. On this map, created by a *Gazette* engraver over several months, the Third Avenue Bridge crosses May's Island at left center. The T.M. Sinclair & Company packinghouse, constructed in 1871, is at the far right. May's Park is known today as Riverside Park. *Courtesy of the* Cedar Rapids Gazette.

small building. Anderson was shocked as he came upon a man rapidly dissecting a hog.

"The man cut so fast that it scared me out," Anderson said. "I thought if they worked that fast, it was no fit place for me. The cleaver moved down, up, down. In two or three minutes, the hog was all cut. I asked a man who that fellow was cutting up the hogs so fast. He replied: 'Oh, that's T.M. Sinclair.'"

Soon enough, everyone in Cedar Rapids became familiar with the hardworking, industrious and God-fearing Sinclair. He would go on to build up T.M. Sinclair & Company to become the city's largest private employer and establish himself as a generous community benefactor, most notably to Coe College, before his untimely death in 1881 at age thirty-eight after he fell into an open elevator shaft at the packing plant.

But in 1872, after T.M. Sinclair had abandoned his icehouse packing plant for new buildings constructed at the south end of Third Street Southeast, disgruntled city leaders virtually ran him out of town on a rail.

"It must have just been a mess," speculated Mark Stoffer Hunter, research historian with the History Center in Cedar Rapids. "You can just imagine the smell."

Yes, as livestock was hauled across the river and driven along the streets of the business district, the animals obviously left behind their "calling cards" and their odors. In addition, since the packinghouse sat along the riverbank, worthless entrails of slaughtered livestock were simply tossed into the water.

City leaders raised their arms in protest. They didn't want a smelly meatpacking plant ruining their city. Sinclair was branded "a man wrapped up in his own selfish interests" according to Arne's article, and his business was labeled "a public nuisance." A court injunction prompted him to hop a switch engine steaming out of the packing plant yard, presumably to Burlington, Iowa, where he spent a few nights contemplating his future.

Fortunately, cooler heads prevailed, and T.M. Sinclair returned to Cedar Rapids as city leaders realized the value of his company. After all, the packinghouse was located on sixteen acres of land at the eastern outskirts of town. It was a dozen blocks from the business district. It also happened to be downriver and downwind from the center of town.

"He was the first 'big fish' to come along," Stoffer Hunter said with a laugh. "But a slaughterhouse? Well, that's OK. Sinclair started the smells. The City of Five Seasons (a city slogan adopted a century later); the City of Five Smells (a facetious twist on the slogan due to Cedar Rapids' industrial odors)."

Sinclair also started a new influx of Bohemian immigrants in search of better jobs and improved lives, much as packing plants in the United States would attract Mexican immigrants a century later.

Also, to Sinclair's credit, he made substantial financial contributions to the city's first water treatment plant, as well as its new sewer system and telephone service, and he brought adequate rail service to the community. Sinclair also continued to set a fine example for his workers, often putting in fourteen-hour days, establishing a Sunday school in the packing plant's box factory, becoming an elder in the Presbyterian church and moving his family into a home in the neighborhood a few blocks from the packing plant despite the odor.

In fact, Sinclair's involvement in the establishment of the Presbyterian church earned hearty words of praise from the Reverend Frank Kun, a Bohemian minister in Ely who came to the Cedar Rapids "mission" often in those days. According to the 1906 publication, "Bohemians Have Done Much for Cedar Rapids," the Reverend Kun "found the strongest encouragement in Mr. Sinclair whose kind heart and good qualities are even to this day a matter for loving remembrance to the scores of Bohemian workmen who did not look upon him as an employer to be feared but as a thoughtful, kind friend who they loved and cherished and for whom, without a doubt, many would have laid down their lives, so deep was the esteem and affection in which the wealthy owner of the packing house was held by his employees."

Most early Bohemian settlers preferred to build homes in rural areas where they cleared the land, planting potatoes where trees had been and beets where brush had been removed, to eke out a meager living. To supplement family incomes, some young women worked in stores, small industries and as maids or nannies in Cedar Rapids homes. Men would become grocers and delivery men, tanners and tailors, butchers and blacksmiths, cabinetmakers and carpenters.

Packinghouse Expands

The expansion of T.M. Sinclair & Company—where employees were summoned each morning by the ringing of a large bell that eventually hung in the belfry of Sinclair Memorial Church—changed that landscape. From meager beginnings, the packing plant grew as fast as the overall population of Cedar Rapids, from a couple dozen employees to as many as 450 in the decade that ended in 1880 when Cedar Rapids' population topped 10,000.

The packing plant went from slaughtering 15,039 hogs its first year to an amazing 113,997 hogs two years later. According to *The History of Linn County, Illustrated*, published in 1878, it became the fourth-largest packinghouse in the world, "giving the locality the appearance of a village of no mean pretensions."

The main building (the curing house)—nearly the size of a football field at 250-feet long by 132-feet wide and standing three stories tall—was surrounded by a variety of brick, stone and wooden support structures, including a cooper shop that employed fifty men. The side tracks and switches of two railroads snaked throughout the sixteen-acre grounds. By the turn of the century, T.M. Sinclair & Company would process nearly half a million hogs annually as well as 7,800 head of cattle and 1,600 sheep.

Packing plant growth at the edge of Little Bohemia undoubtedly led to the increase of the Czech population in Cedar Rapids. In fact, to attract immigrants, the packinghouse later bought property near St. Wenceslaus Church and erected nearly identical worker cottages.

According to *The History of Czechs in Cedar Rapids*, city directories in 1870 listed 128 people of Czech descent, undoubtedly heads of households, while just seven years later there were 387. Although these immigrants had a variety of occupations, the largest single group was laborers, making up 38 percent of the Czech heads of households by 1881.

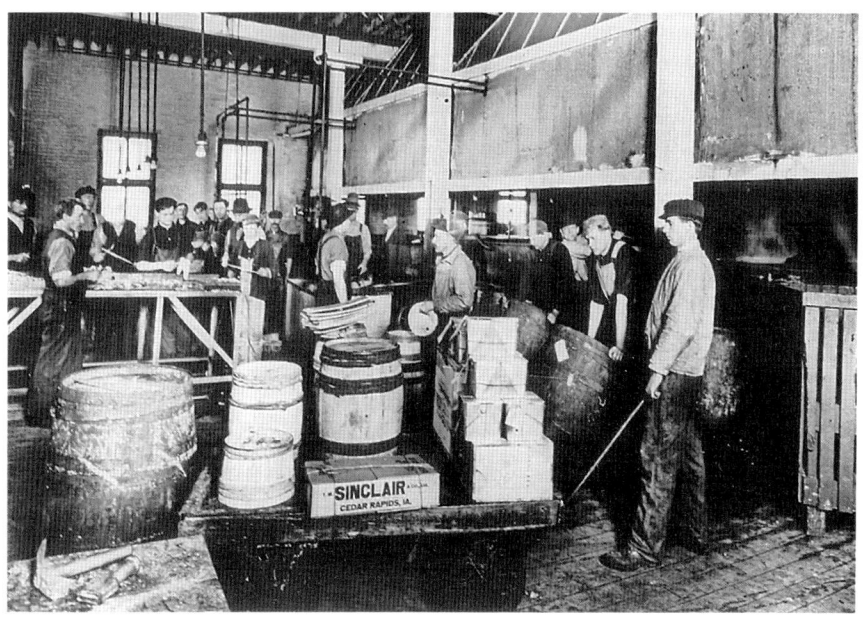

An undated photograph shows workers busy inside one of the early buildings at the T.M. Sinclair Packing House after it had relocated to the end of Third Street Southeast in Cedar Rapids. *Courtesy of the* Cedar Rapids Gazette.

In addition to the packinghouse, laborers found work at a variety of Cedar Rapids establishments. North Star Oat Meal Mills, founded in 1873, employed fifty men to process six hundred barrels of oatmeal a day. At Star Wagon Works, organized in 1866, sixty men manufactured up to 1,580 wagons a year.

If those didn't suit an immigrant's fancy, he could join thirty-five to forty-five workmen making stalk cutters, grain seeders, hay racks and sleighs at the Iowa Iron Steel Fence Co. or the twenty who made carriages, spring wagons and sleighs at the Carriage Manufactory of Soule & Miller. Other manufacturers made boilers (Cedar Rapids Steam Boiler Works), mowers and reapers (the Williams Harvester Co.), industrial soap and fancy toilet soaps (Excelsior Soap Works), furniture (G.O. Ohler), boxes (Paper Box Manufactory) and even pickles (Cedar Rapids Vinegar Works), brooms (A. Hovey) and crackers (Steam Cracker Manufactory).

Since full-blown Prohibition had yet to take effect (Iowa enacted statewide prohibition in 1916, four years before it became a national law), a couple of large breweries were going strong—the Eagle Brewery (established in 1859 by C. Magnus) could produce sixty barrels in a twelve-hour period and stored two thousand barrels in underground cellars, and the George Williams & Co. brewery (instituted in 1867) employed up to twenty men.

EARLY BOHEMIAN WAY OF LIFE

As more and more Bohemians flocked to the city for work, they brought their way of life, including their social organizations, their churches and their recreational activities.

"One of the most surprising facts in the life of Slavs in America is the degree to which they are organized in societies," wrote Emily G. Balch in *Our Slavic Fellow Citizens* as quoted in *The History of Czechs in Cedar Rapids*. Balch explained that while nothing in their European background accounted for the formation of numerous organizations, the Czechs who settled in groups where all spoke the language seemed to develop formal organizations around common interests that included a love for music, dramatics and dancing.

Since immigration was on the cusp of great expansion, 1868 stands out as a pivotal year for the integration of the Bohemian community into the whole of Cedar Rapids. For it was then that fights regularly broke out on Saturday nights at the Bohemian Dance Hall, that the "Free Thinkers" renounced the need for religion and that the first successful Czech organization, the Reading Society (Cternarsky Spokel), planted its roots.

A variety of newspaper accounts painted a bleak picture of the "first-class-rough-and-tumble-set-to" occurrences late Saturdays into early Sundays among the beer drinkers at the Bohemian Dance Hall. While the hall's exact location isn't known, one story alluded to its being outside the city limits, which most likely meant the growing business district along Third Street Southeast. By July 2, 1868, a newspaper reporter for the *Cedar Valley Times* had taken another look at the situation: "We do not wish to be understood as laying all the disgraceful occurrences in that vicinity to our Bohemian citizens; on the contrary we are informed…that all or nearly all the disturbance is caused by Americans, young men of the 'manor born,' who visit this house solely for the purpose of raising a disturbance with the Bohemians, and generally succeed in so doing, making causes for disturbing them, when if let alone to enjoy themselves in their own way, there would be no trouble."

Author Griffith wrote in her 1944 publication of *The History of Czechs in Cedar Rapids* that no accounts of disturbances appeared in newspapers by 1875 and that "reporters may have regarded the Czechs as undesirable foreigners and for that reason they may have overemphasized the disturbances at the dances."

While "Free Thinkers" didn't arouse people of opposing views to raise their fists in physical confrontation, they certainly raised the consciousness of churchgoers. Brewer and Wick, in their 1911 history, explained that "a respectable element of the Bohemian population" did not belong to a church and did not oppose religion or organized churches.

> *In the Bohemian language they are called "Svobodomyslni." This word does not mean Free Thinkers. This Bohemian word is made up of two words "Liberty" and "Mind," and it means the broadest toleration for the religious beliefs and opinions of others; and further it means that you should give the widest latitude to the religious beliefs and forms of worship of your neighbors, and that they should do the same to you; and it further means that you should honor and respect the religious views and professions of your neighbors and they should do the same by you.*

However, the Free Thinkers label stuck. As Griffith wrote, they were also known as liberals, were often negative people, felt nature was the guiding force of mankind and sometimes, like Ladimir Klacel, didn't believe in an afterlife. "There is no future…there cannot be a heaven, and there is absolutely no hell," the national figure wrote. "The heaven for which you can prepare yourself and your families is right here upon the earth."

Despite successfully convincing militant atheist Frank B. Zdrubek to relocate his newspaper, *Pokrok*, from Racine, Wisconsin, to Cedar Rapids in 1869, the Free Thinkers struggled to establish a lasting foothold. Zdrubek, who published his newspaper on Saturdays for 1,600 subscribers, making it the second-largest Czech paper in the country, left Cedar Rapids after two years for Cleveland. And even though socialist Josef Urban organized 100 laborers into the Free Thinkers in Cedar Rapids in the 1870s, group membership would be up and down into the 1930s.

The education and socialization of Bohemian immigrants got a shot in the arm when Czech leaders met at the Concert Hall in the main Cedar Rapids business district in November 1868 to form an organization, Brewer and Wick wrote. At the first meeting on November 8, Joseph Kohout's greeting explained that "an organization of some sort was absolutely necessary among the Bohemians to insure not only national strength, but social life which would have in it the idea and aim of advancement and cultural benefit."

Two meetings later, on November 22, the majority voted to form the Reading Society rather than a loan society or a dramatic club. Off to a rousing start, with the first program of orations on that December 28 making a profit of $225, the Reading Society was on its way "to encourage reading, to promote lectures, and to present dramatic performances 'for universal education and entertainment.'" It immediately purchased books from Prague and would spend $200 to $400 annually on Czech-language books for a library that would swell to 2,500 volumes by 1911.

The Reading Society's success prompted plans for a new building. It spent $1,000 for property along First Street Southeast at Fifth Avenue and another $3,000 to build Brown Hall, a one-story frame structure forty-two feet wide and one hundred feet long that included a twenty-foot-deep stage. Dedicated on June 6, 1870, the Reading Society building was off and running with regular performances, community dances and public programs.

In fact, the Reading Society spawned several auxiliaries, among them a gymnastics club that was the forerunner of the Sokol Society. That group's progress stalled for a while with the drowning death of its first leader, Joseph Sommer, but soon picked up.

On July 6, 1870, exactly a month after the building's dedication, the Reading Society celebrated Jan Hus day. Hus, a revered Czech priest who reformed the Christian movement, was burned at the stake July 6, 1415, for heresy against doctrines of the Catholic Church. The Reading Society ceremony included a girl carrying the society's flag made of silk with three wide stripes of red, white and blue and, in the center, a two-headed lion that was the symbol of Bohemia with the inscription, Cternarsky Spolek (Reading Society).

For two decades, the Reading Society became the central entertainment attraction for Bohemian citizens in Cedar Rapids. "The records tell that numerous farm wagons bringing in visitors to see the performances, followed one another in a continuous stream over the bridges in the city," wrote Hrbkova in the 1906 account.

Iron Bridges

By 1876, Cedar Rapids had three iron bridges crossing the Cedar River. None, however, was that 1860 toll bridge, the city's first successful bridge.

History repeated itself in March 1871. A cold and severe winter followed by warm temperatures and heavy rains elevated the river level. The subsequent ice floe not only wiped out the toll bridge but also wreaked havoc along the riverbank. Bourne Saw Mill was a total loss, all other mills suffered heavy damage and communication between Cedar Rapids and Kingston was cut off.

Fortunately, the boat *Aurora*, used to transport goods from Cedar Rapids to Vinton, went back into service, hauling up to eight teams of horses on each trip across the river. Simultaneously, Keech & Company stretched a horse-powered cable across the river to pull its ferry boat between Cedar Rapids and Kingston.

Officials knew ferry boats were but a temporary fix. The Linn County supervisors had been asked to provide a "free" bridge by farmers who hauled produce across the river from as far away as Benton County, and the City of Cedar Rapids had heard from residents asking for a bridge because they wanted to buy real estate in Kingston and rightfully predicted the merger of the two communities.

Two bridge-building petitions had been submitted to the city council. One, signed by S.C. Bever, an early banker, and more than fifty citizens wanted the bridge to replace the toll bridge at First Avenue. It asked the city to issue $6,000 in bonds and promised to raise the remaining cost from private interests. The other, signed by John F. Ely and one hundred citizens, asked for a bridge at Park Avenue (today's Third Avenue) to cross the center of May's Island toward Kingston. It wanted the issuance of $12,000 in bonds and guaranteed to raise anything the city and county didn't pay. Each faction, of course, looked out for its best interests.

In the end, Mayor Thomas Z. Cook and the council set an election where voters approved the second option 483 "for" to 83 "against," and Linn County agreed to chip in a third of the $42,000 cost of the bridge with two caveats: it had to be a "first-class" bridge, and no county money could be spent until the rest of the funds had been raised. Business leaders and citizens quickly committed the rest of the money, and in record time, less than two months after the toll bridge had gone out, bids were let. In ninety days, on August 15, 1871, according to the contract, the bridge opened on time.

With that success came a clamoring for more. In 1874, the city electorate approved issuing another $12,000 in bonds for bridges at Burton Street (later B Avenue Northwest) and James Street (where today's Bridge of Lions now spans the Cedar River).

The Burton Street Bridge opened in the summer of 1875 at a cost of $32,000: $6,000 from city bonds, $8,000 from the county supervisors and the rest subscribed by city leaders N.B. Brown, George Greene, William Greene and the Higley estate.

The James Street Bridge, completed a year later, cost $27,000: $6,000 from city bonds, $11,500 from Linn County and $9,500 from private concerns, mostly from T.M. Sinclair & Company, which benefited from this nearby bridge for its transportation needs as well as to haul livestock across the river outside of Cedar Rapids' central business district.

The History of Linn County, Illustrated, published in 1878, gushed about the progress:

> *It will thus be seen that Cedar Rapids has a magnificent system of communication giving free transit across the river. Three splendid iron bridges clear waters of the Cedar within the city limits, the extreme upper and lower being about a mile apart. No other city in Iowa can compare with her respect...These structures are all good and substantial and for years, our citizens evidently concluded that in this matter was the cheapest and their liberality is commendable in the highest degree.*

2
2008

THE GREAT FLOOD

When officials closed the bridges across the Cedar River in downtown Cedar Rapids on June 11, 2008, due to the high water level, everybody knew this wasn't going to be any ordinary flood.

Cedar Rapids—and its Czech Village and New Bohemia neighborhoods—had weathered floods before. The one on people's minds had occurred fifteen years earlier when the river crested at more than nineteen feet. It had hit nearly twenty feet in the floods of 1961 and 1929.

That Wednesday in 2008, the river continued to inch past the 12.0-foot flood stage it had reached a week earlier. Heavy snowfall, a quick melt in the spring and what seemed like constant rain in early June prompted predictions of an all-time high crest of 24.7 feet and, by day's end, an amazing 28.0 feet. Sandbagging of buildings in the one-hundred-year flood plain commenced. Soon, residents in those areas as well as people living in the generally "safe" five-hundred-year flood plain were mandatorily evacuated. The Red Cross set up an emergency shelter. The worst was yet to come.

That Thursday, June 12, the 793-foot CRANDIC railroad bridge built in 1903 to serve the T.M. Sinclair & Company packinghouse washed out under the water's constant pressure despite being secured with heavy railroad cars on its bed. More than eight thousand people were evacuated. The National Guard arrived. The lights went out in the city's core areas.

By Friday, June 13, the only luck seemed to be bad. Clouds had dumped six more inches of rain on Cedar Rapids, another ten thousand people were evacuated and the U.S. Coast Guard arrived. More than one thousand volunteers in a heroic effort made and stacked ten thousand sandbags to save the city's last operating treated-water well, yet citizens were asked to forgo showers, doing laundry and even flushing toilets if possible to conserve water for drinking.

At 10:15 a.m. that Friday morning, the river crested at 31.1 feet, almost 20.0 feet above flood stage. Water flowed over the bridges at First, Second and Third Avenues, making them nearly invisible from the air. The Bridge of Lions connecting New Bohemia to Czech Village was almost the same. The nearby bridges at Twelfth Avenue and Eighth Avenue appeared to be dams. Only the elevated I-380 bridge at the northwest end of the main business district remained open.

"I believe they knew what was going to happen, but they wanted to avoid panic," said Jon Jelinek, a business owner and resident of the New Bohemia area who said he had very little warning about potential flood damage. "It went from them thinking it would be six inches deep to being eleven feet, six inches." Jelinek lost not only $300,000 in sports memorabilia and collectibles but also his home, not being allowed to return for days.

"There's a lot of people worse off from me. But I lost my future," Mike Ferguson, owner of Polehna's Meat Market in Czech Village told

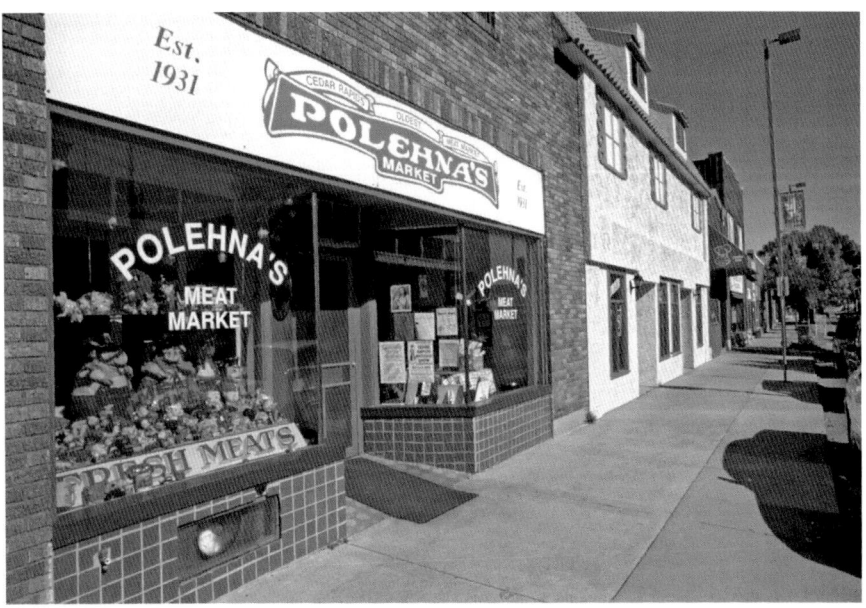

Polehna's Meat Market, a family-operated business on Sixteenth Avenue in Czech Village, had been in business more than seventy years when this picture was taken in 2003. *Courtesy of the* Cedar Rapids Gazette.

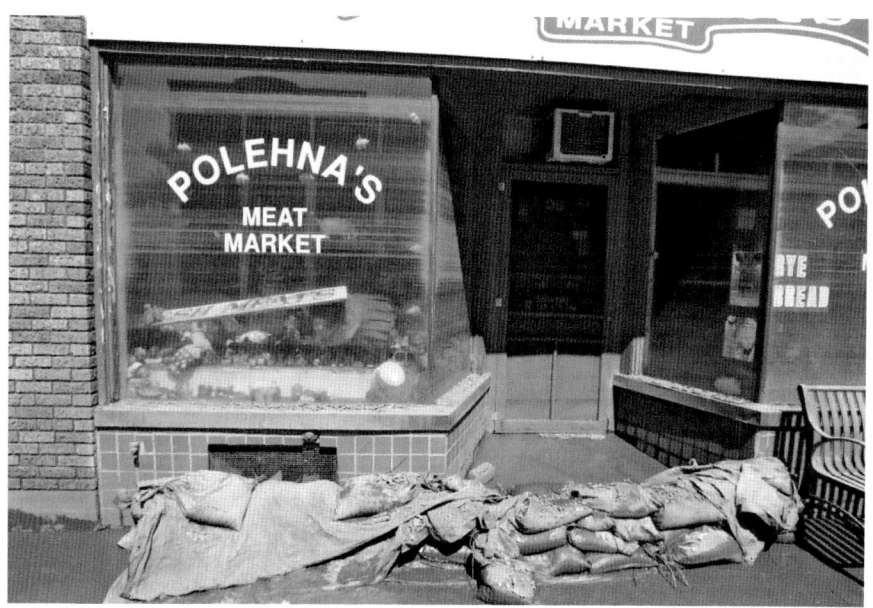

Polehna's Meat Market in Czech Village—water lines clearly visible across its front windows three days after the June 13, 2008 flood—never reopened after being in business for seventy-five years. *Courtesy of the* Cedar Rapids Gazette.

the *Gazette* newspaper. Polehna's, which had served customers since 1931, never reopened.

"I heard the reports that the flood was coming, that we could get a pretty good amount of water," said Baron Stark, who had opened Deda and Babi's Antiques & Collectibles in Czech Village less than a year earlier in one of the newer buildings on ground higher than most in the village. While Stark thought it would be safe, he notified his fifty vendors and consignees to remove their goods, which most of them did. "We got most everything out except the display cases," he said. "We worked night and day. I was exhausted."

"It won't be the same ever again…but hey, I'm not the only one, right?" said Jeff Melsha, manager of his family's Little Bohemia tavern—nicknamed "Little Bo"—on the opposite side of the river in New Bohemia. The tavern had served customers, many of them on packinghouse lunch breaks, since Prohibition ended.

On Saturday, June 14, Cedar Rapids was declared a federal disaster area. As the river level fell to 24.3 feet the next day, strike team members who used boats to evaluate flooded areas had to duck their heads beneath an I-380 overpass that was normally high enough for semi-trucks. Residents held

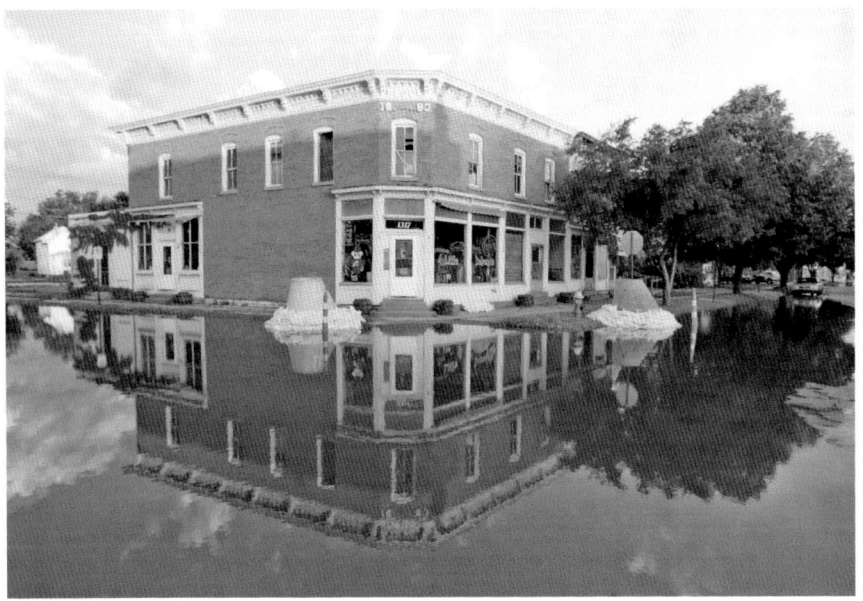

Little Bohemia, a landmark tavern/restaurant operating since the end of Prohibition in an 1883 building at the intersection of Third Street Southeast and Fourteenth Avenue Southeast in the New Bohemia district, is surrounded by water on June 11, 2008, two days before epic flooding destroyed the interior. *Courtesy of the* Cedar Rapids Gazette.

at bay, not being allowed to check out their own homes for safety reasons, became very upset.

"It's a terrible mess, and we need to be there cleaning it up," shouted an emotional Vince Fiala to police as his daughter, Diane Stanek, in tears as she clutched his arm, stood by him at the roadblock on Bowling Street Southeast that prevented residents from returning to Czech Village. His picture in the *Gazette* became the symbol of frustration.

Another iconic image became the orange-tiled roof of the National Czech & Slovak Museum & Library as it seemed to float on the water, the building itself filled with ten feet of water in the heart of Czech Village.

Museum staff and volunteers, who had begun moving collections to higher ground on Monday, could only sit and wait as the floodwaters receded. Gail Naughton, president and CEO, expected water inside but expressed hope everything would be fine. She said the Pergo floor was fairly indestructible.

"We can't get depressed," Naughton said in an interview after surveying damage. "We have to focus on the future."

Across the river, Mel Andringa, co-founder of Legion Arts, which occupied much of the former CSPS Hall, a three-story New Bohemia neighborhood

CZECH VILLAGE & NEW BOHEMIA

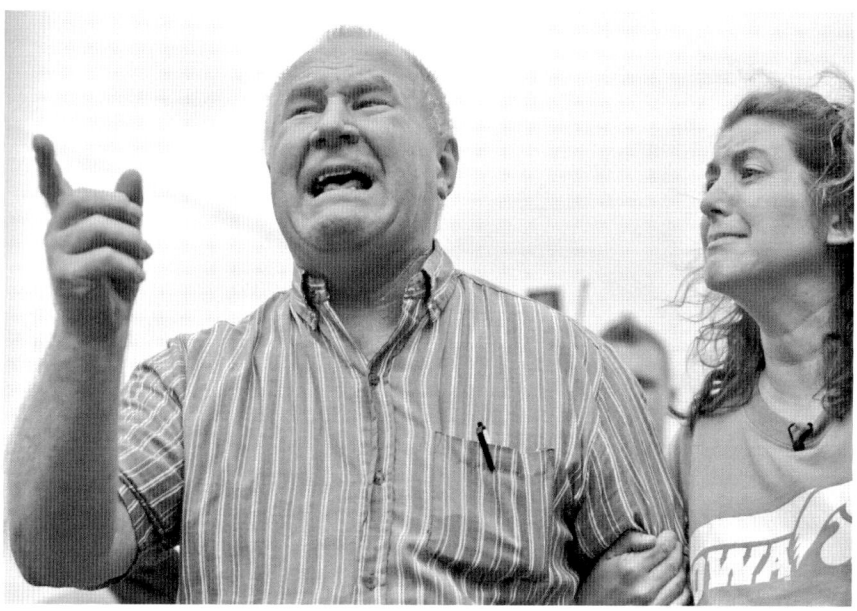

Vince Fiala expresses his frustrations to a police officer about not having access to his flooded home outside a checkpoint on Bowling Street and Twenty-first Avenue on June 15, 2008, as his daughter, Diane Stanek, clutches his arm. *Courtesy of the* Cedar Rapids Gazette.

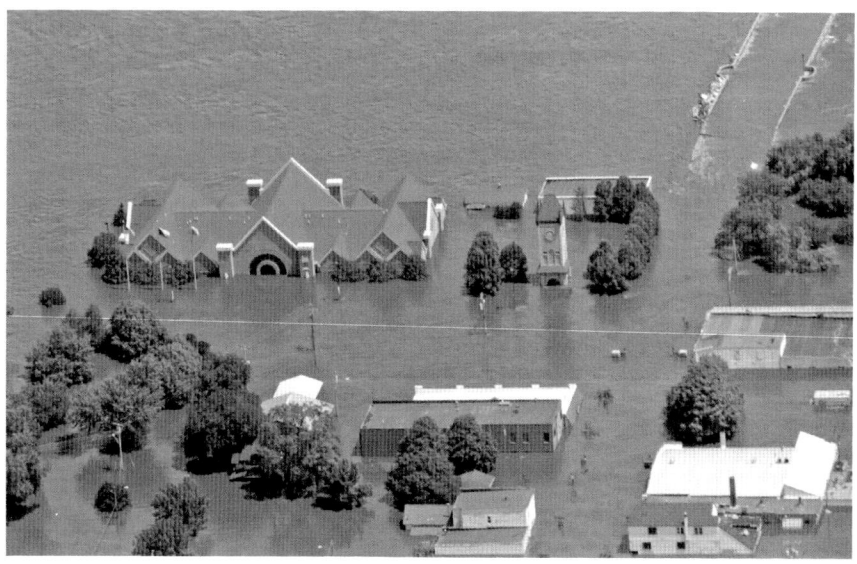

Floodwaters continued to rise on June 13, 2008, around the National Czech & Slovak Museum & Library, eventually reaching a historic 31.2 feet above flood stage and filling the museum with about ten feet of water. *Courtesy of the* Cedar Rapids Gazette.

fixture of art and entertainment since it was built in 1891 at Third Street and Eleventh Avenue Southeast, wasn't overly worried.

"The warning was, we could expect a foot, maybe a foot and a half in the buildings in the neighborhood," said Andringa, a longtime creative painter and artist. "We got ten and a half feet. All of my materials from working the previous forty years were water damaged or lost. It was devastating to us all."

A couple blocks away and farther from the river, the story was the same at the J.G. Cherry Building, a huge three-story manufacturing and warehouse facility constructed in 1919. The movement to locate artists into loft studios begun in the mid-1980s and a full building renovation in 1999 had paid off. On June 1, it reached 100 percent occupancy with small businesses, start-ups and artists filling its 104,000 square feet of floor space. A celebration was planned. Nobody seemed too worried about the rising river.

"The day it flooded, we didn't have any notice until the day water started coming in," said Lijun Chadima, president of Thorland Co., owner of the Cherry Building. They expected water on the main level to be knee deep at most, even though the building sits in the one-hundred-year flood plain. Water filled the first floor nearly to its ceiling.

Fortunately, Friends of the Library, which occupied the basement, benefited from hardworking volunteers and the generosity of tenants upstairs to move donated books to the second and third levels.

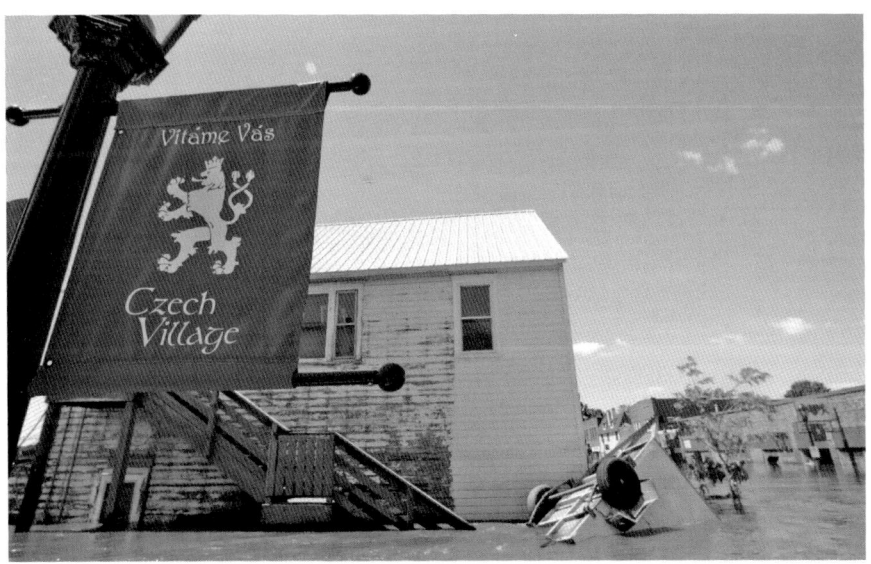

Water rushes through the streets of Czech Village the day after the river crested in Cedar Rapids on June 13, 2008. *Courtesy of the* Cedar Rapids Gazette.

Czech Village & New Bohemia

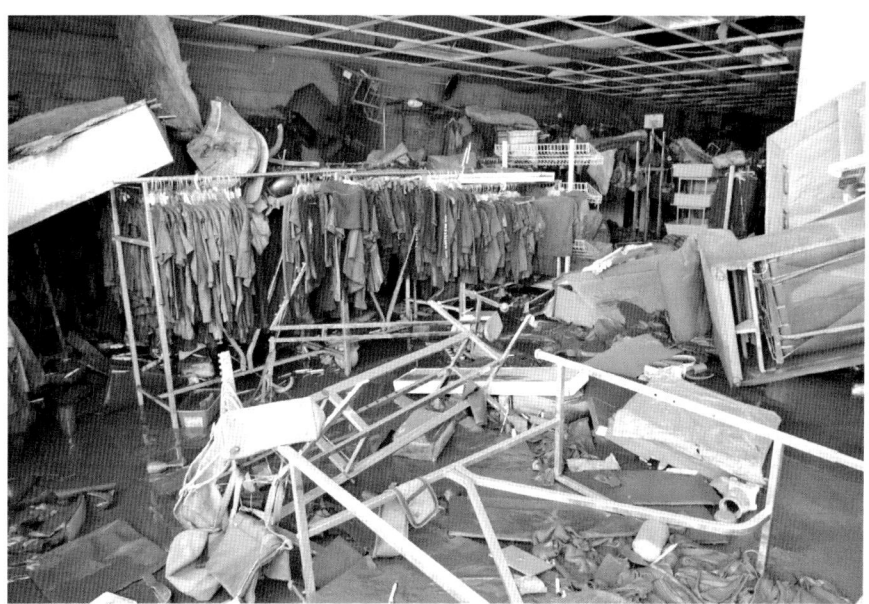

Floodwater-stained clothes and other damaged items fill the Czech Village Salvation Army in Czech Village on June 16, 2008. *Courtesy of the* Cedar Rapids Gazette.

Unfortunately, the main Cedar Rapids Public Library along First Street Southeast near Fifth Avenue, not far from T.M. Sinclair's first packinghouse, took on water like a sinking ship.

In subsequent days and weeks, the flood's toll to all of Cedar Rapids was tallied. The flood affected ten square miles, or about 1,300 city blocks, in a city with 120,000 people. An estimated 5,400 homes, 1,050 businesses and 310 public buildings were destroyed or damaged. The dollar value of damage exceeded $1.3 billion and didn't include the cost of cleanup, the unrealized dollars from lost sales and productivity and the anguish of human heartache.

For Czech Village and New Bohemia, the flood of 2008 washed away in one week what had evolved into a community over 150 years. It tested the faith of worshippers at St. Wenceslaus Catholic Church, which was filled with water. It shuttered businesses that had been in operation for up to a century. And it wiped out hundreds of homes of Czech immigrants and those loyal generations that had followed.

On June 18, 2008, a week after the downtown bridges closed, they reopened. It would take another three days for the river level to drop below its twelve-foot flood stage. But there was no time to waste. The healing and rebuilding had to begin.

3

THE EARLY 1900s

THE NEXT GENERATIONS

When Vaclav Drahozal sent for his wife and four children from the old country in 1910, Cedar Rapids had become a changed place. The population mushroomed to more than thirty-two thousand people with nearly a fourth of them from Bohemia and surrounding areas.

Vaclav, as did his countrymen, probably arrived by way of a steam-driven passenger train to Union Station, a massive two-block-long structure built along the Fourth Street tracks in 1897 that hosted nearly one hundred trains a day. If Vaclav left the station on a Cedar Rapids and Marion railway trolley car, he'd see that they not only ran on electricity but also that electric lights illuminated the avenues and boulevards. He'd learn that friends could easily ring up friends on a telephone. Plumbing and indoor bathrooms had replaced many an odorous vine-covered outhouse.

Cedar Rapids, to its residents and to people who hardly knew it, had become "the Parlor City."

Yet, for Vaclav, life in the United States was undoubtedly anything but evenings relaxing in the parlor. He lived with a brother-in-law, Jacob Burian, who was married with three children. Jacob labored at the T.M. Sinclair & Company packinghouse, which is probably how Vaclav got his job there as a lard renderer.

"It sounds like a smelly job," said Vaclav's grandson Bob Drahozal, eighty, who retired from a career in the accounting and early computer programming department at Collins Radio in Cedar Rapids. "The

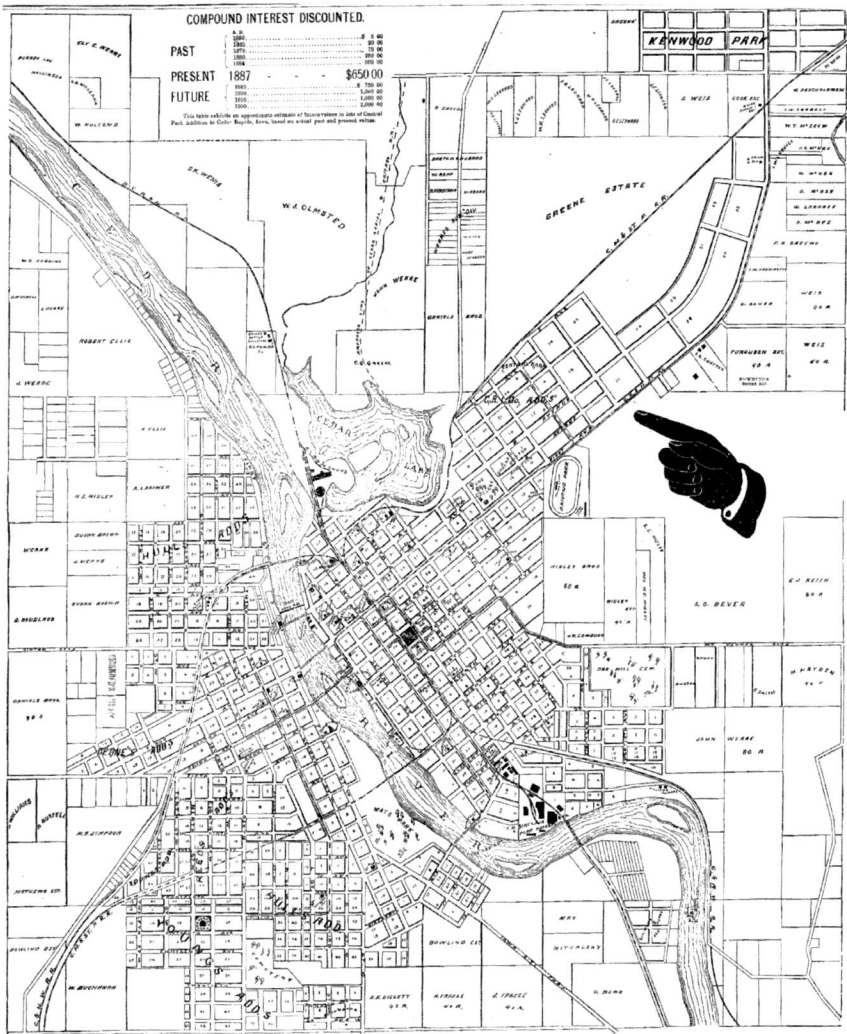

An artist's rendering shows an 1887 plat of Cedar Rapids. In 1884, just three years earlier, downtown street designations in the city were changed from names to numbers and letters, with "West" added to all streets on the west side of the river. May's Park, seen at middle lower on the map is today Riverside Park. *Courtesy of the* Cedar Rapids Gazette.

story is that they came over to the United States to keep the kids out of the war."

Living in Bohemia, southeast of Prague in the Austro-Hungarian Empire, Vaclav knew his country was in turmoil. He had an inkling that World War I could break out—which it did in 1914.

U.S. naturalization papers made it official in 1919; members of the Vaclav Drahozel family who immigrated to the United States in 1910 were all U.S. citizens. *Photo by Robert F. Drahozel.*

A baptismal record shows that Vaclav was born in Houstovlice, Bohemia, in 1868. He married Marie Tucek on September 25, 1893, there and came alone to Cedar Rapids in 1909. A year later, Marie (Mary) crossed the ocean in the *George Washington*, a twin-stacked steamer that cruised at eighteen knots per hour, with their children—Wencil, thirteen; Josef, eleven; Rudolf, nine; and Frans (later known as Frank, Bob's father), age four. They arrived in New York City on October 9, 1910.

Eventually settling a block from Vaclav's temporary home, not far from St. Wenceslaus Catholic Church, the family became naturalized citizens on June 9, 1919. The document included the youngest son—Charles, six—even though he was born in Cedar Rapids. "They were very loyal to the United States," Bob explained.

Patriotic Bohemians

That would have described most Bohemian citizens in Cedar Rapids. While they would never forget the motherland, they quickly adopted their new home, as indicated by their July 4 parades held as early as 1877, when the Bohemian Brass Band led a procession that included one hundred little girls in white dresses wearing red and blue ribbons. The following year was even more elaborate with young women carrying a "bouquet-decorated" standard. Soon, the Bohemians integrated themselves into the city's Independence Day parade. By 1889 it had sixty-five industrial floats with nine of them advertising Czech firms—one with tinners fashioning tin cups that were handed out to the crowd and another with thirteen tailors hard at work.

"It is a source of genuine pleasure and an assurance of safety in the future to see our foreign-born citizens celebrate the anniversary of American Independence," wrote a reporter in the July 11, 1878 *Cedar Rapids Times*.

By 1904, Czech immigrants were learning about citizenship and how to speak and write the English language at their own Czech School, thanks to requests by students and the diligent efforts of teacher Sara Hrbek. The Czech School had opened in 1901 and was the first building in the United States dedicated as a Czech school. It came about when the Damska Matice

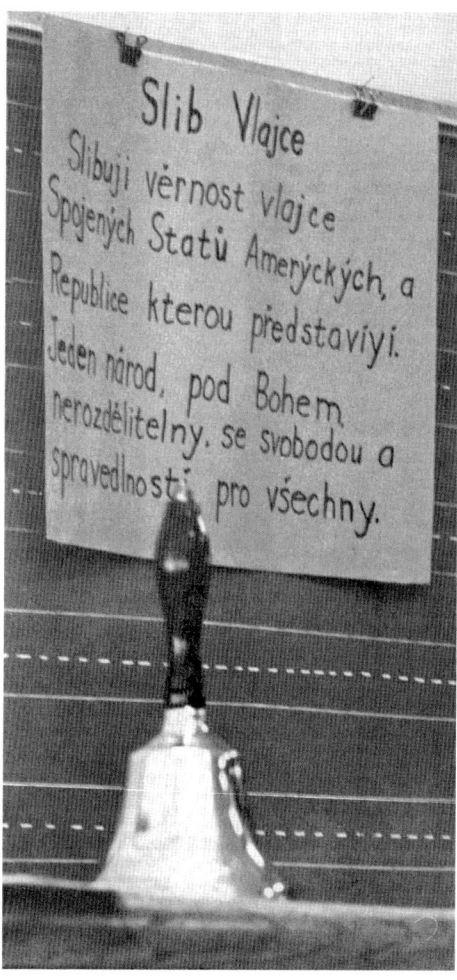

The Pledge of Allegiance written in Czech was posted over a chalkboard during class at the Czech School held in the summer of 1981 at Hayes Elementary School. *Photo courtesy of the Cedar Rapids Gazette.*

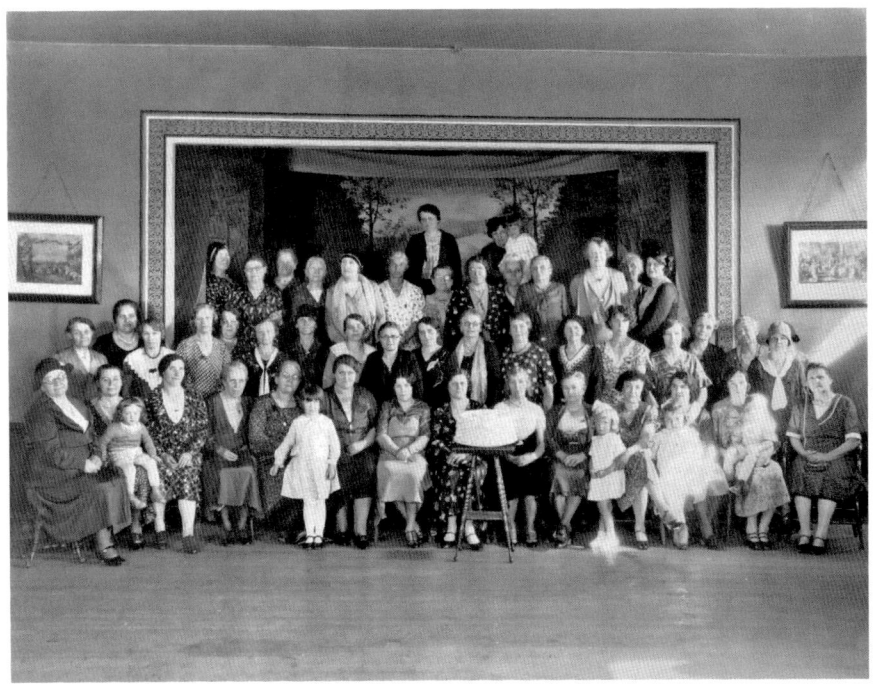

The Damska Matice Skolska, or Czech Ladies Educational Society, met on the second floor of the old Czech School on Second Street Southeast in the 1930s, figures Tom Polehna of Cedar Rapids, who discovered this old Czech photo among the possessions of his late father and grandfather. *Courtesy of the* Cedar Rapids Gazette.

Skolska was founded by Czech women in 1892 with that sole purpose. They held bazaars and programs to raise money for the building and supported the school for decades.

While Vaclav wouldn't have had Hrbek as a teacher, he might have attended classes taught by John C. Stepan, a Bohemian immigrant who studied eight languages and taught evening citizenship classes to Bohemians in Cedar Rapids for thirty-six years. Stepan also taught classes at the packinghouse beginning in 1917.

"Our Bohemian people all seem to be doing splendidly and to be recognized everywhere as good American citizens, which is very gratifying," University of Prague philosophy professor Thomas Masaryk told a *Cedar Rapids Evening Gazette* reporter on July 15, 1902, before a pair of lectures at the CSPS Hall that, oddly enough, were given in Czech.

"I advise them to learn the English language as quickly as possible after coming here and to become full-fledged American citizens," added the

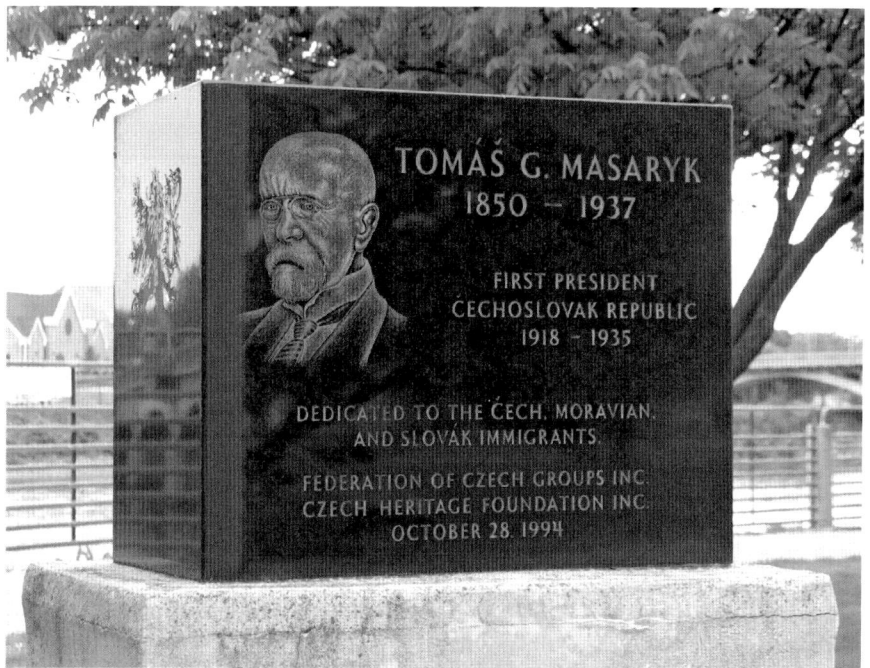

Masaryk Park along the Cedar River in New Bohemia is dedicated to Thomas G. Masaryk, the first president of the Czech Republic. He visited Cedar Rapids several times, including in 1907, when he talked to children at the Czech School. *Photo by Dave Rasdal.*

politician, who later pushed for the independence of Czechoslovakia. "Yet we like to see them preserve the best that there is of their Bohemian customs and to remember with thankfulness the patriots who are so many and conspicuous in our national history. Bohemia is a wonderful little country and we love it dearly."

Masaryk would return to Cedar Rapids five years later to talk about the ideals of progressive Bohemian youth and to, again, discuss the immigration of Bohemians to the midwestern United States. A popular figure in Cedar Rapids at this time, he obviously became more popular at the conclusion of World War I, when he was elected the first president of Czechoslovakia.

When Sarka B. Hrbkova published "Bohemians Have Done Much for Cedar Rapids" in the June 10, 1906 Semi-Centennial Magazine Edition of the *Cedar Rapids Republican*, it was estimated that 500,000 Bohemians resided in the United States and that 7,000 lived in Cedar Rapids with the numbers "constantly being increased by new arrivals from Bohemia."

"Cedar Rapids has the largest Bohemian population in the state," Hrbkova continued, "Iowa City coming next, Chelsea, Clutier, Tama, Oxford Junction, Protovin, Belle Plaine, Riverside, etc. following with a goodly sprinkling of Bohemian inhabitants or those of Bohemian parentage."

Who Are These People?

In response to those 1906 articles, Dr. John Rudis-Jicinsky wrote the essay "Bohemians in Linn County, Iowa" to clarify not only who these people were but also what they were about. He was a Cedar Rapids resident who would soon be in charge of an American Red Cross unit sent to Serbia during World War I.

"Some call us 'Bohemians,' meaning gypsies; others 'Czechs,' according to the German version; still others name us properly Bohemians, of Slavonic race, forming the bulk of our people, but such are not very many," he wrote. "Very often they honor with that name those who do not deserve it and vice versa call every artist of a light and very elastic life and different characteristic also Bohemian."

Of course, he's alluding to Bohemians being the butts of jokes. But if that's your nationality, it's nothing to laugh at.

> *The Bohemians came from Bohemia, formerly one of the kingdoms of Europe, now forming a part of the Austro-Hungarian monarchy. The mineral wealth of Bohemia is extensive, the soil generally fertile and in manufactures the land holds a very high place among continental countries. In population there are Bohemians and Germans with many Jews. The vast majority of the population belongs to the Roman Catholic Church. Protestants and others are Free-Thinkers. The educational establishments include the two universities in the Capitol Prague, with many Latin schools, technical schools, business colleges, colleges of agriculture, manufacture, textile industry, many high schools, beside the thousands [of] schools and private national Bohemian schools of the Ustredni Matrice supported by the Bohemian people only.*

Obviously well-educated, Dr. Rudis-Jicinsky discussed the early settlement of Cedar Rapids and the formation of the "Little Bohemian" community with its quickly expanding social organizations. It was, as Hrbkova wrote,

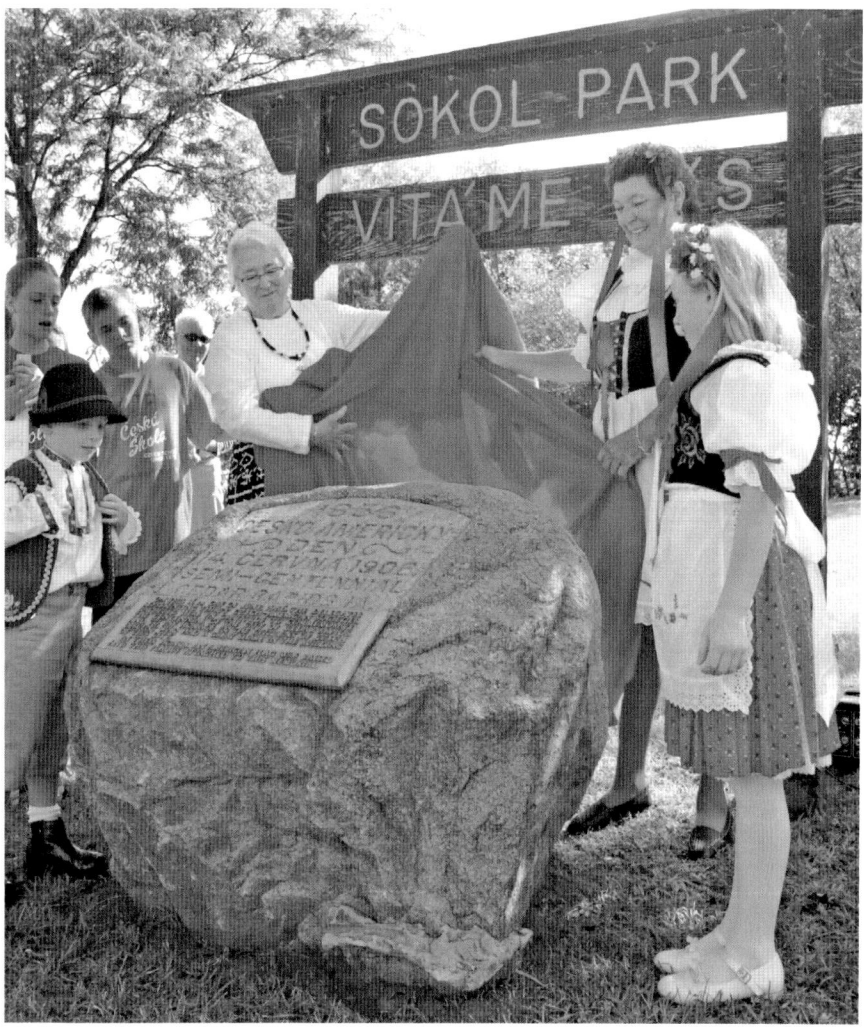

From left: Thomas Nejdl (in black hat), five; Mayor Kay Halloran; Angela Nejdl; and Emily Nejdl, seven, unveil the boulder for a rededication at Sokol Park in Czech Village on July 15, 2006. The boulder had been dedicated one hundred years earlier and rededicated in 1956, when Angela Nejdl, then seven, helped. *Courtesy of the* Cedar Rapids Gazette.

"wherever there is a handful of Bohemians who think alike about music, literature, education, religion or what not—they at once band together and form an association for the pursuit of the common object."

The weeklong semi-centennial celebration that began on June 10, 1906, included a program at the City Auditorium in downtown Cedar Rapids with flowery speeches, music by a two-hundred-voice chorus, dedication of the city's new Second Avenue Bridge and the placement of large boulders in both Washington Park (later known as Greene Square Park) in downtown Cedar Rapids and Riverside Park. Since that Thursday was "Bohemian-American" day, it began with a fifty-gun salute and a parade with four hundred farmers on horseback accompanied by dancers in Bohemian and Moravian costumes.

Cedar Rapids exploded into the twentieth century with the growth and addition of such employers as Quaker Oats, Star Wagon Works, Whiting's Foundry and Douglas Starch Works. The Czech culture matured with the formation of organizations and the dedication of new buildings.

Bridges, not only the esoteric one to the old country's ways but also the physical bridges across the Cedar River, allowed Czech immigrants to live and work where they wanted. The addition of a First Avenue bridge in 1884 and a Second Avenue bridge in 1905, the city's first reinforced concrete bridge at a cost of more than $100,000, meant Cedar Rapids had five bridges spanning the water. And just as important for Bohemian immigrants was the 1910 replacement of the bridge from Fourteenth Avenue Southeast in Little Bohemia to the multicultural business district on Sixteenth Avenue Southwest that would become Czech Village. This grand bridge—40 feet wide, 2,600 feet long—opened to traffic that January. This bridge, combined with the redesignation of the earliest Bohemian settlement near Fifth Avenue Southeast and downtown into a warehousing and manufacturing district, pushed Little Bohemia development south along Third Street Southeast and east across Fourth Street Southeast, which had become a railroad corridor.

The flat topography of this area (not annexed into the corporate limits of Cedar Rapids until 1884) made expansion relatively easy. The mostly frame-construction houses and cottages, with a few brick ones sprinkled in, were located on narrow but deep lots that provided plenty of room for backyard gardens. These one-story and one-and-a-half-story homes, often with a narrow gable end facing the street, would be decorated with fish-scale, square-cut or diamond-cut shingles; have modestly ornate posts on the porches; and might even feature a stained-glass window.

The influx of Bohemians in the neighborhoods on both sides of the river showed up at the public schools. On the east side, Monroe School, built as the Third Ward School in 1873 and renamed two years later, had 85 percent Bohemian students by the late 1890s. On the west side, Van Buren School, built in 1884 and expanded by 1900, had 60 percent of its eight hundred students come from Bohemian families by 1906.

Strike Up the Bands

Music, understood for centuries as the language to bridge cultures, had become central to the Bohemian community by the 1870s. Even though an old German saying put down Czech musicians, Hrbkova wrote, they continued to play in an effort to make the rest of the world appreciate their brand of music.

"Among the common people of Bohemia, music songs and dancing accompany all festivities. It matters not what walk of life there is sure to be in every family some member who can play on some instrument or other. Hence, it is not to be wondered at that musical organizations among the Bohemian people are much more common than among their more fortunately situated brothers of other nationalities."

The Light Guard Band, with just eleven members, probably made its first appearance at the dedication of the Reading Society Hall in 1870. The Czech-speaking band gained popularity after Frank Dvorak became its manager and Vaclav Charipar its leader because they could speak English.

Frank Kouba's arrival in 1872 brought with it the formation of the Bohemian Brass Band, also known at times as Kouba's National Band and the National Cornet Band & Orchestra. Under Kouba's leadership the band secured uniforms and earned a reputation across Iowa for its excellence. Soon it provided music in surrounding towns for parties, plays, fairs, picnics, parades and even election rallies.

Other bands followed, among them Jansa's Band, organized in 1900 by a musician who had played in the military band in Bohemia. He reportedly directed his band of ten young men, all under the age of twenty-one, with military precision, often saying, "Boys, the beginnings of pieces are important. Do your work willingly, be polite to your instructor, and see that no discord comes between you."

The first Czech orchestra grew out of the demand for parlor music—yes, in "the Parlor City"—when violinist Vaclav Koubat gathered seven highly skilled musicians for his orchestra. Soon, the group was performing as far away as one hundred miles. A second orchestra was formed by Frank Pirkl, a well-educated musician who gave violin, guitar, piano and vocal lessons, and a third followed under the direction of Josef Tlapa.

The Choral Club, the first auxiliary of the Reading Society, assembled ten vocalists for area performances and soon had eighty members. It became so popular that by 1872 it was affiliated with the Tahlee Society and built its own hall in New Bohemia. Orchestra leaders Pirkl and Tlapa also organized vocal groups.

History in the Heartland

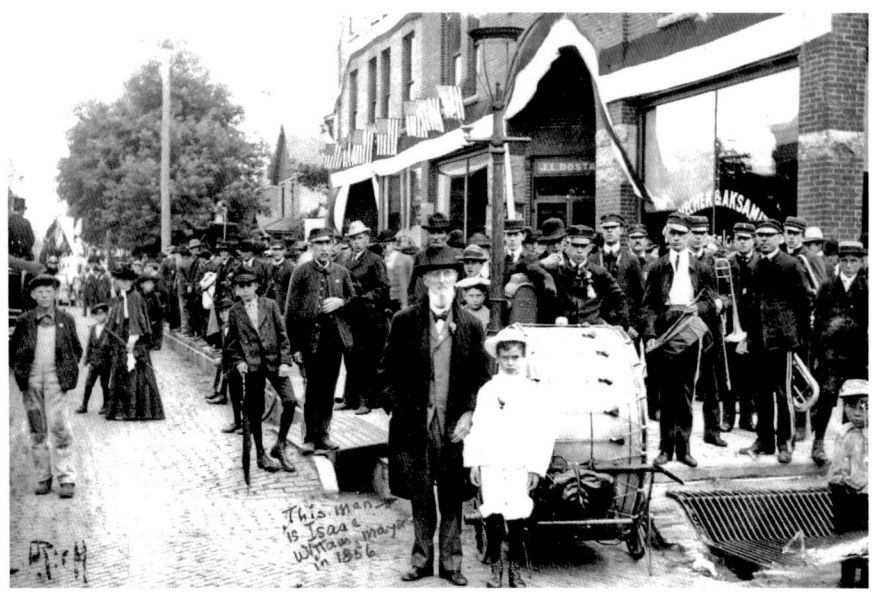

A crowd gathers for a parade outside the CSPS Hall in Cedar Rapids in this June 14, 1906 photograph. *Courtesy of the Carl & Mary Koehler History Center.*

In fact, Tlapa directed the Hlahol Society singing group, formed in 1905 with nineteen men and expanded a year later when he allowed women to join. Tlapa and an assistant wrote out the vocal music parts so it wasn't necessary to buy music books, thus saving money that, combined with donations, allowed him to buy a group piano.

Of all the organizations the Bohemian people in Cedar Rapids founded in the late nineteenth century, three would stand out and endure for at least a century, if not in actuality, at least in spirit: the Sokols, the CSPS and the ZCBJ, which all have their names on landmark buildings.

The Sokols, known for gymnastics, was spawned by its formation in 1862 in Bohemia, where *sokol* means "falcon." It grew in Cedar Rapids after two organizations merged in 1888. The first, the Jednota Tyrs, emerged from the Reading Society in 1873. The second, the Cedar Rapids Sokols, formed in 1876. According to Bohemian founder Dr. Miroslav Tyrs, "Sokol does not mean physical training only—Sokol's aim is to educate our people to the highest physical efficiency, to nobleness, and to morality…When we address a Sokol the response will come from a man in the truest sense of the word—a man physically, mentally and morally—a Patriot who is ever ready to respond to the call of his country, ever ready to draw the sword in defense of Democracy, Liberty, and Humanity."

The Jednota Tyrs organization grew from twenty-nine members to seventy. It purchased gymnastics drilling apparatuses that it installed at the Reading Society Hall. By 1878, members decided against wearing the gray suit, red shirt and small black cap with a falcon feather adopted by the Sokol organization in Bohemia for a navy blue suit with a broad-brimmed blue hat in tribute to "the boys in blue" who had fought for the Union army in the American Civil War.

The Cedar Rapids Sokols increased from eleven members to fifty in its first year. It met twice a week in Thalee Hall, the building constructed by the Choral Society.

The Sokols in Cedar Rapids became known by outsiders not only for their physical prowess but also for a masquerade ball, or Sibrinky, held the Monday before Ash Wednesday. Originated in Bohemia, the wearing of masks at the elaborate festival gave attendees the chance to make new friends without preconceived notions. After early balls, the merrymakers could often be seen parading through the streets of Cedar Rapids.

Following the merger, the Cedar Rapids Sokols welcomed women into their ranks who would form a drill team that appeared at the national tournament in Chicago in 1896. The organization was also known for rather strict rules for attendance and collecting a dime per member per week as an insurance program for members who might fall ill.

As the Sokol organization grew, it purchased a house in Little Bohemia and converted it into a gymnasium. When it outgrew that, an adjacent lot was purchased for construction of a new Sokol Hall that included a seventy-five-foot-square gymnasium with a twenty-three-foot-tall ceiling and a gallery for spectators. The building, opened in 1901, included showers and a gym equipped with dumbbells, Indian clubs, wands and other physical apparatuses. Chairman of the building committee was none other than Dr. John Rudis-Jicinsky, an editor of *Sokol Americky*, the national Sokol magazine published in Cedar Rapids.

But an expansion by the Chicago, Rock Island and Pacific Railway Company included acquisition of this hall in 1907, forcing the Sokol organization to relocate. It built another Sokol Hall at 417 Third Street Southeast in 1908 that opened the following January. Although the building was taller than before with three stories, the gymnasium was smaller at fifty-eight feet by forty-six feet. But it was as well furnished as ever with gymnastics equipment and a second-floor parlor and trophy room.

At this time, the local Sokols found success on the national and international levels. In 1907, Rudolf Novak, Wesley Melsha and William

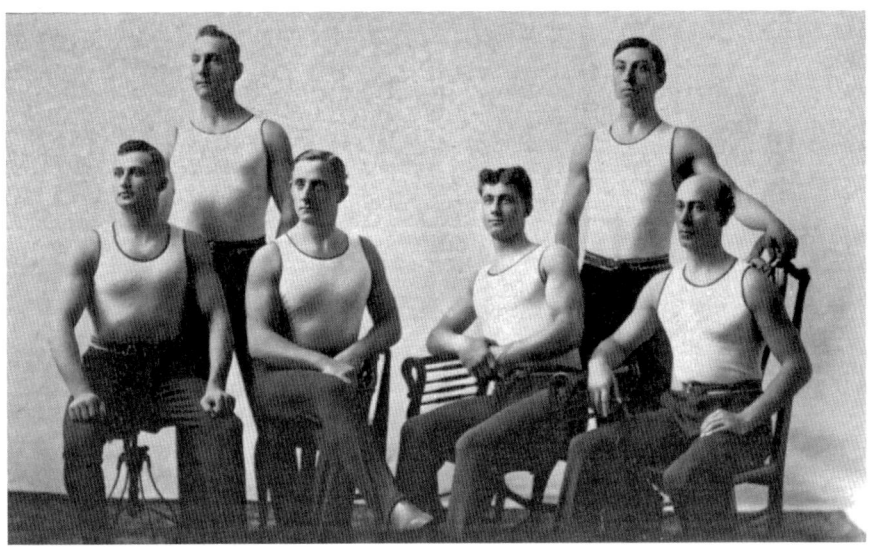

The award-winning Sokol team of 1912 from Cedar Rapids included, *from left*, Rudolf Novak, Vilem Hruska, Franta Filip, Vaclav Melsa, Emil Kohout and Boleslav Hasek. Novak was a United States representative to the Olympic Games in Paris, France, in 1912. Photo circa 1910. *Courtesy of the Czech Heritage Foundation.*

Hruska won honors in the All-Sokol Slets in Prague, according to Mary Helen Armstrong's 1950 Cornell College (Mount Vernon, Iowa) thesis, "The Cechs in Cedar Rapids." In 1909, the men's and women's Cedar Rapids Sokol teams won the Amateur Athletic Union championship in the United States. In 1912, Rudolf Novak was a United States representative to the Olympic Games in Paris, France. And in 1915, Cedar Rapids became the central district headquarters for Iowa, Illinois, Minnesota, Wisconsin and Missouri.

CSPS Makes Its Mark

A few blocks away, also on the west side of Third Street Southeast at Eleventh Avenue, stands the brick three-story CSPS Hall, the result of the 1879 formation of the fraternal organization Cesko-Slovanska Podporujici Spolku, or Czech Slavonian Benevolent Association, as a branch of the national organization in St. Louis. Founders named the new Cedar Rapids branch Prokop Velky Lodge in honor of Procopius the Great, who brought

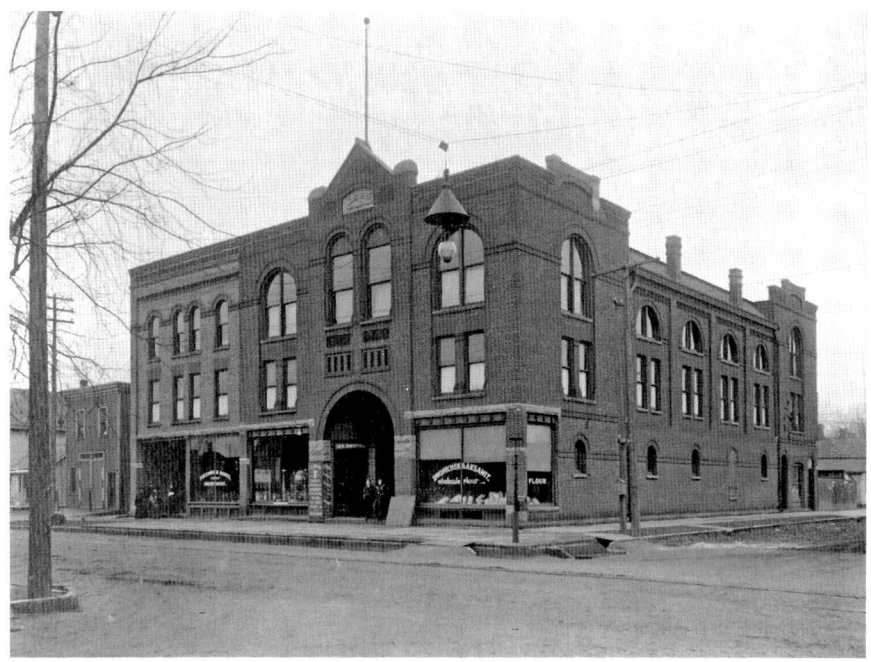

The CSPS Hall on Third Street Southeast was a central fixture in the New Bohemian area when this picture was taken in 1907. The flour shop on the main floor was under Czech ownership. *Courtesy of the National Czech & Slovak Museum & Library.*

Bohemia to the peak of its military glory on August 14, 1431, when it defeated Frederick, Margrave of Brandenburg.

As sometimes happens, other Bohemian citizens decided to form their own branches of CSPS three years later. The Karel IV Number 77 was named after Charles (Karel) IV, one of Bohemia's best kings and truest patriots. The other was Mladocech (Czech Youth) Number 82 formed with younger men.

When the Prokop Velky Lodge set about erecting a new building, its members invited the other lodges to join, but they declined. So the cornerstone was laid on October 30, 1890, with Prokop Velky undertaking the full cost with donations from members and other Czech people. The $22,400 hall was dedicated seven months later with a large contingent on hand that included Horace Boies, the governor of Iowa, and the Benesh Mounted Band, the only area musical group where members rode draft horses while they performed.

The CSPS Hall had a large assembly room open to other Czech organizations as well as a stage, scenery and theatrical appliances. Just two

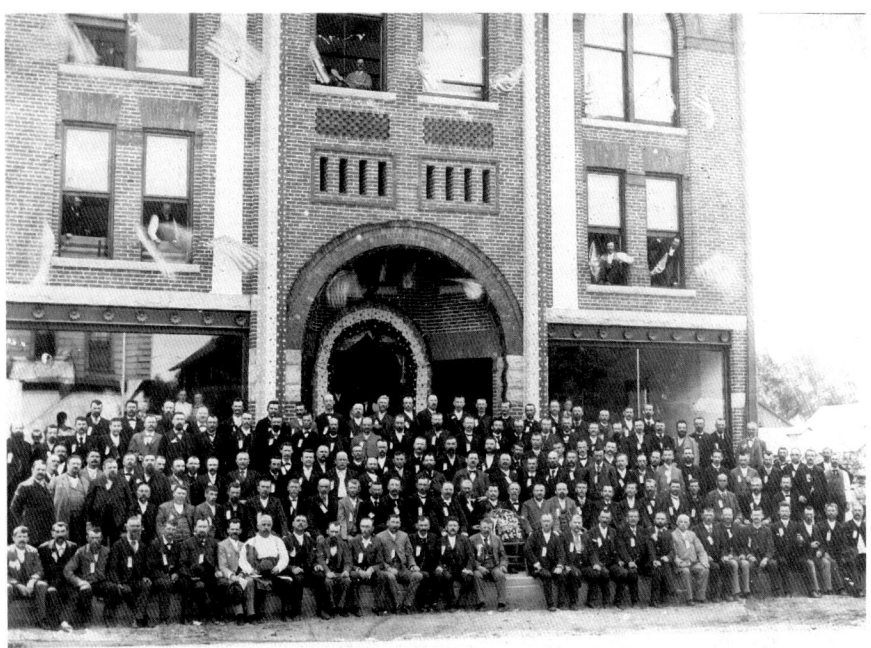

Lodge members gathered outside CSPS Hall, 1103 Third Street Southeast, at the turn of the twentieth century. *Courtesy of the* Cedar Rapids Gazette.

weeks later it hosted the tenth convention of the main CSPS lodge with 150 delegates, the largest Czech convention held in Cedar Rapids up to that time.

Additions in 1900 and 1908 to the CSPS Hall provided much-needed space that included a reception area, a reading room and a small lodge room, making the building "the most commodious in the city," according to *The History of Czechs in Cedar Rapids*.

The third community-use building in Little Bohemia along Third Street Southeast—the ZCBJ Hall—came about at CSPS when the local ZCBJ (Zapadni Cesko-Bratrska Jednota) met there to incorporate in Iowa on July 4, 1897, with the supreme office in Cedar Rapids. The national organization started that February in Omaha and by September had forty-nine chapters. It was the first Czech fraternal society for young people, to institute a juvenile department, and to establish twenty-pay-life and endowment insurance policies.

The ZCBJ Hall erected in 1908 (and expanded since) began as a three-story seventy- by fifty-foot structure with a dance hall on the second floor and office on the main level for the supreme lodge. It was immediately home to four subordinate Czech-speaking-only lodges—Prokop Velky Number 7,

Karel IV Number 13, Mladocech Number 15 and Zizkuv Dub Number 91—formed in 1897. The fourth lodge's name, which means Zizkuv's Oak, was named after a famous Czech leader who stood beneath a tree during the Hussite Wars and "swore eternal vengeance" against those who burned Jan Hus at the stake. A fifth English-speaking-only lodge wasn't formed until 1923. The ZCBJ organization, which by 1910 had more than ten thousand members in Iowa, Nebraska, North Dakota, Minnesota and Wisconsin, later became the Western Bohemian Fraternal Association and is today Western Fraternal Life Association.

While these three buildings were constructed for use by their own organizations, they followed a Reading Society precedent by allowing other groups to meet in their halls. The Reading Society building, encroached on by Cedar Rapids' expanding business district, was sold in 1891 to Faye Brothers Lumber Company. Since the Sokols had organized at the Reading Society, it let the group meet at Sokol Hall until the Czech School opened in 1901 and welcomed the Reading Society.

Other early Czech organizations included:

The Anna Naprstek Lodge Number 24, affiliated with the national Jednota Ceskych Dam (Society of Czech Women) founded in Cleveland, Ohio, in 1870, was a cultural and insurance organization. The Cedar Rapids chapter, formed in 1884 with thirty-five women, collected $2 a year in dues. After being a member for a year, a woman could collect for illness—$2 per week for six months and $1 per week the next six months. In case of death, her beneficiaries received $400. The lodge aided immigrants and ill people, decorated graves of deceased members on Memorial Day, taught hand work to girls at the Czech School and sent money to Bohemia when droughts or floods necessitated aid. Three more local lodges joined the national organization by 1900.

Jan Hus Number 51 IOOF came about in 1884 as the first Czech-speaking Odd Fellows Lodge west of the Mississippi River. Six Czech members had withdrawn from the local German branch, and five other members quickly joined.

The Praha Rebekah Lodge organized on June 23, 1888, with many of its charter members coming directly from Prague. Its activities included celebrating Czech Victory Day (October 28), Mother's Day, Christmas parties and supporting its Children's Home and the Odd Fellows Home.

Ceska Beseda, founded in 1891, was a group of thirty men who wanted to improve their knowledge of Czech national culture through music and dramatizations. It admitted women by its second meeting and later made a

$65.70 profit when it presented the opera *Kral Vondracek* (King Vondracek). While it had picnics in Frank Mitvalsky's woods and raised money for the Czech School and St. Luke's Hospital, its most popular social activity was hosting Friday night assemblies to learn and practice the beseda, the national Czech dance. Ceska Beseda disbanded in 1902 and gave its properties to the Czech School.

The Star of Progress lodge organized in 1892 as part of the national Sesterska Podporujci Jednota (SPJ), or Sisterly Benevolent Order of Lodges. This group always had dues of ten cents per month and paid beneficiaries fifty dollars when a member died. A couple of other lodges formed later.

Bohemian Savings and Loan Association came about in 1892 to help Czech people buy their own homes. The idea was hatched in 1885 when locals heard about a similar organization in Chicago. Jan V. Kouba was a leader in the later formation of Bohemian Mutual Insurance Society to insure properties against fire and lightning.

The Minerva Society, founded by fourteen Czech women in 1901, came after a call by Jennie Hasek and Anna Kurka to form a literary club. Half of each program was held in the Czech language and half in English as the women studied literature, music and history of Czech, German, Polish and American origin.

The Council of Higher Education, after a suggestion by businessman W.F. Severa in 1901 and his $2,500 seed money, awarded interest-free loans for higher education to the most capable Cedar Rapids high school graduate of Czech descent. Soon, local fraternal organizations backed the idea with more funds, and the idea grew so big the Council of Higher Education headquarters were relocated to Chicago, where the program eventually helped Czech students in thirty-two states.

Let Us Pray

While fraternal organizations were a big part of Bohemian social life, religion formed the basis for family and spiritual togetherness.

When Vaclav Drahozal welcomed his family safely to Cedar Rapids, they undoubtedly said a prayer of thanks at St. Wenceslaus Catholic Church, which had moved into its new facility five years earlier. Organized in 1874, it became the first Bohemian Catholic Church in Cedar Rapids. It grew from a desire by Czech Catholics, who had been meeting at St. Mary's Church (later Immaculate Conception), to have their own parish. Father Clement J.G. Lowery of St. Mary's had kindly invited Bohemian missionaries to speak on occasion in their native tongue. But Father Francis Chmelar, who oversaw Catholic parishes in rural areas, knew that wasn't satisfactory, so he led the formation of St. Wenceslaus.

After purchasing a lot in 1874 along Twelfth Avenue Southeast two blocks east of where the ZCBJ building would be located, the parishioners secured a loan that, combined with their collections, provided funds to erect a rock church twenty-seven feet wide and seventy-five feet long. With sixty members and growing, the parish paid off its debt by 1878, added a stand-alone bell tower with a silver bell and built a rectory for Father Chmelar adjacent to the church.

Under Father Chmelar's leadership, St. Wenceslaus began holding grade-school classes in the rectory basement. In 1881, it purchased St. John's Cemetery a couple of blocks to the south with the idea that selling burial plots could add to the church's coffers. Later, under Father Frank Kopecky, a school was built 1894 and classes taught by the Sisters of Mercy.

At the turn of the century, when Father Florian Svrdlik arrived, St. Wenceslaus members were talking about building a new church. They had grown tired of standing outside during Mass because there was no room in the sanctuary. Kicked off with $4,000 raised in a benefit fair, the parish soon had $10,000 in a building fund. Property was secured by Christmas 1903, eight priests attended the laying of the cornerstone on August 4, 1904, and the $40,000 church with a new skyscraping spire was finished in time for Christmas services. The church was dedicated by Archbishop John J. Keane on October 18, 1905.

By 1910, St. Wenceslaus had 1,200 members and 175 students in its school, contributing to the decline in enrollment at Monroe School, which closed in 1923. By 1924, church members formed nine insurance, four recreational and six religious organizations, one of the earliest being the Czech Linden club for drama in 1892.

Bohemian Protestants followed a similar course of action, branching off from existing congregations.

The Fourth Presbyterian Church (later renamed Jan Hus Memorial Presbyterian Church) was born when its congregates followed their hearts in the1860s to occasionally walk nine miles to the Reformed Church in rural Ely, which in 1858 had been founded by the Reverend Frank Kun as the first Czech Protestant church in the United States. Otherwise, they'd met in Cedar Rapids homes to sing hymns accompanied by a violin. Taken under

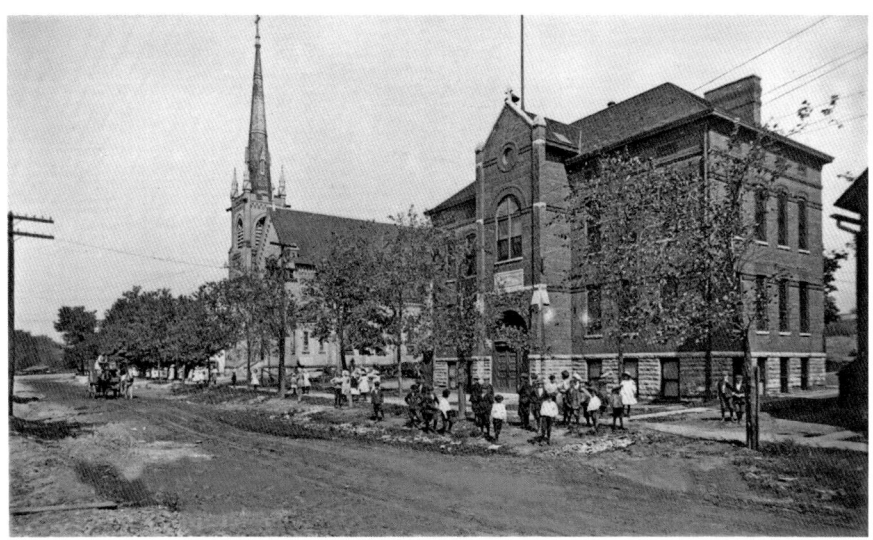

Children play in front of the St. Wenceslaus Grade School and Church (background) in the New Bohemia area about 1905. The school, the first accredited Czech Catholic school in the United States, was built in 1894, closed in 1969 and demolished in 1988. The church, built in 1904 to replace an earlier church, remains active today. *Courtesy of the* Cedar Rapids Gazette.

the wing of the First Presbyterian Church in Cedar Rapids for Sunday schools, they held services for a couple of years at T.M. Sinclair & Company, sitting on crates in the packing room.

In 1889, the congregation came up with $1,600 to buy the old First Congregational Church and move it to Ninth Avenue and Seventh Street Southeast, where they became the Fourth Presbyterian Church. The arrival of Vaclav Hlavaty in 1890 propelled the church to new heights—it retired its $735 debt and grew from 90 members to 220 by 1900 and to 257 members by 1910.

The Czech Reformed Church came about when some Ely's Reformed Church members moved to Cedar Rapids. Formally organized in 1909 with forty-two members, it temporarily met in an erected tent called Bohemian Tabernacle. A donated lot and raised funds made a new home possible a year later when the cornerstone for the $3,800 church was laid on November 6, 1910. By December, services were held in the basement, and the church was dedicated in January.

The John Hus Methodist Church, said to be the first Czech Methodist church organized in the world, emerged with assistance from St. Paul's Methodist Episcopal Church, the first church of any kind in Cedar Rapids. St. Paul's founded a mission for Czech Protestants in 1890, built Epworth

Mission two years later for the twelve members of the congregation and helped move two buildings in 1894 to Eleventh Avenue and Seventh Street Southeast, where Hus Chapel was dedicated. But since most of the Methodist church members lived west of the river, the Reverend R.N. DeCastello in 1895 proposed relocating the church near Czech Village. A vacated Second Evangelical Church building was purchased and moved to a pair of building lots at First Street and Fourteenth Avenue Southwest, where it was dedicated in 1897 with two Czech-language services and one in English.

With Czech being the predominant language for the neighborhood, a plethora of newspapers catered to the people. The first to see print, *Pokrok*, moved from Racine, Wisconsin, in 1869. Published by militant atheist Frank B. Zdrubek, it was followed in 1872 by *Slovan Americky*, a newspaper founded in Iowa City three years earlier by Jan Barta Letovsky.

The *Day* arrived in 1886, *Svit* (the Dawn) in 1896 and *Listy* (News) in 1897. After the turn of the century, *Pravda* (Truth), *Ceska Lipa* (Czech Linden), *Lidove Listy* (Paper of the People) and *Vestnik Iowsky* (Iowa Publication), a Cedar Rapids supplement to the national newspaper *Svornost*, appeared at newsstands.

Obviously, with that type of competition, some newspapers didn't last long while others moved out of town. The Czech-language newspaper with the longest shelf life began as *Humoroisticke Listy* (Humor Paper) and changed its name a couple of years later in 1900 to *Cedar Rapidske Listy*, which it would be into the 1940s, when it was acquired by a Chicago newspaper.

In the news those days, as well as dispatches from the old country, were stories about the Czech community and Cedar Rapids. New retail establishments, manufacturing facilities, banks, restaurants and hotels fueled growth in the Parlor City. The Cedar Rapids Commercial Club, modeled after one in Kansas City, organized in 1897 to entice new businesses and to promote the betterment of Cedar Rapids. The city had 31 miles of paved streets (brick, asphalt and macadam) and 102 miles of sidewalk, the vast majority made of concrete with only 2 miles of wooden boardwalk remaining. The city had twenty-eight parks, five fire stations and both sanitary and storm-water sewer systems.

The heyday for railroads in Iowa was 1910, and Cedar Rapids was right there. More than 225 railway and interurban trains arrived or departed from Cedar Rapids, which was served by four of the nation's largest railway systems—the Chicago & Northwestern and the Rock Island operated out of Union Station while the Chicago, Milwaukee & St. Paul and the Illinois Central occupied a smaller depot a couple blocks north along the Fourth Street tracks. These railroads served 1,750 stations in Iowa alone. In addition, three express companies—the American, the United States and the Wells-Fargo—maintained offices in Cedar Rapids, where about eighty thousand carloads of freight were handled annually. And the Cedar Rapids and Iowa City (CRANDIC) interurban railway had recently begun operating hourly between those two communities and Marion.

For travel in the city, the Cedar Rapids and Marion Street Railway Company, founded in 1879, began transporting passengers in steam-powered trolleys along "the Boulevard" (today's First Avenue) from Twelfth Street in Cedar Rapids to Marion and back. To get from Twelfth Street to Fourth Street, travelers hopped aboard horse-drawn cars that also followed rails. The system expanded throughout the city in the 1880s including a line directly to T.M. Sinclair & Company. An 1890 change in ownership and name—it became the Cedar Rapids and Marion City Railway Company—began the early 1890s transition to electric power on more than fifteen miles of track in Cedar Rapids and to Marion.

Big On Business

A little more than half a century after its official incorporation, Cedar Rapids had nearly one hundred manufacturing concerns employing almost 4,500 people with annual wages totaling more than $3 million. Chief among them was T.M. Sinclair & Company with 1,200 employees, and it was still growing. New to the scene was Douglas & Co., the largest independent starch works plant in the United States. It transformed corn into starch and gluten feed at its facility just north of Czech Village. And the Quaker Oats Company on the east side of the river and north of the business district had become the largest milling plant in the world, which, along with a handful of other growing mills, earned Cedar Rapids another nickname: "Cereal City."

In fact, Luther A. Brewer and Barthinius L. Wick, in their 1911 *History of Linn County*, gave a comprehensive laundry list of goods manufactured in Cedar Rapids:

> *The list is a long and mixed one. It comprehends all kinds of breakfast foods, flour, starch, gluten feed, all kinds of packing house products, woven wire fence, candy, ice cream, pumps, iron pipe, windmills, plumbers' supplies, steam heating plants, machinery of all kinds, stone and ore crushers, hot air furnaces, cornices, bank, store and office fixtures, camp and lawn furniture,*

corsets, parlor furniture, mattresses, woven wire springs, undertakers' supplies, egg cases, dairy supplies, butter, concrete fence posts, sand-lime brick, prepared plaster, ice, gasoline engines, store step-ladders, hard wood specialties, electrical supplies, gasoline storage tanks and measuring pumps, manure spreaders, overalls, women's skirts, suits and jackets, shirts, photo paper, brass goods, coffee, spices, extracts, baking powder, sash, doors and blinds, steel baskets, tanks, stoves, school books, umbrellas, vinegar, pickles, wagons, carriages, omnibusses, automobiles, patent medicines, physicians' and hospital supplies, crushed stone, cigars, etc., etc.

Only a very few businesses closed, among them the G.M. Olmstead Soap Factory operating in a variety of single- and multi-story frame buildings at the east end of the James Street (Fourteenth Avenue) Bridge into the mid-1890s. The site was perfect, not far from T.M. Sinclair & Company, which supplied fatty animal byproduct for the manufacture of soap. But the pungent odor of the process didn't mix well with the growing neighborhood, and the factory was abandoned.

Of special note, J.G. Cherry Co., founded in 1880, matured in a similar series of buildings. It employed hundreds of Bohemian laborers to manufacture an extensive line of dairy industry equipment, including milk and cream cans, butter churns, ice cream freezers and equipment for the handling and processing of milk. As manufacturing filled an old creamery building, the operation expanded into seven nearby houses by the early 1900s. When the owners decided to consolidate into one building, the 1919 J.G. Cherry Building was constructed a block east of Third Street between Tenth Avenue and Eleventh Avenue Southeast.

With all of this prosperity came growth in Little Bohemia along Third Street Southeast and around the corner on Fourteenth Avenue Southeast toward the bridge—the corridor of today's New Bohemia district. By 1910 it had come of age with a variety of retail and business establishments that included a new bank. Entrepreneurs put additions on the fronts of houses for a new venture or demolished a home or two to make way for an entirely new building.

The latter was exemplified in 1893 across Eleventh Avenue from the CSPS Hall when Peter Matyk and his son, Anton, constructed a two-story brick building for their dry goods business, "P. Matyk & Son," founded in 1880. Peter used the extra space to manufacture hosiery and mittens to sell in his store. When he retired in 1895, Anton continued to operate the business. He became a leader of the Bohemian community and served a two-year term

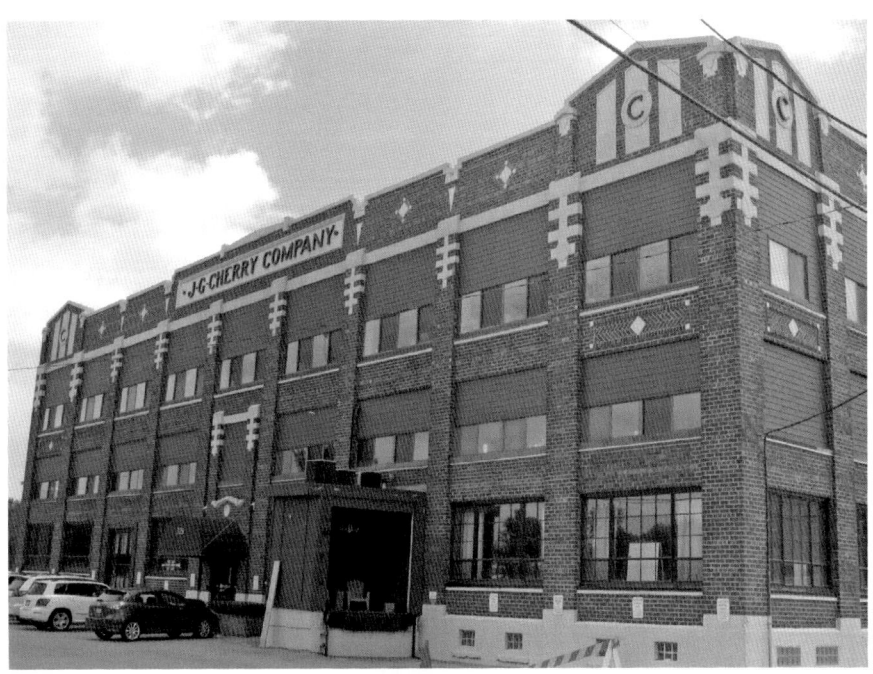

Above: The J.G. Cherry Company Building, a haven for creative talent in the New Bohemia district, was completely restored after the flood of 2008. *Photo by Dave Rasdal.*

Right: Suchy Jewelry in the New Bohemia district at the turn of the twentieth century. *Courtesy of the National Czech & Slovak Museum & Library.*

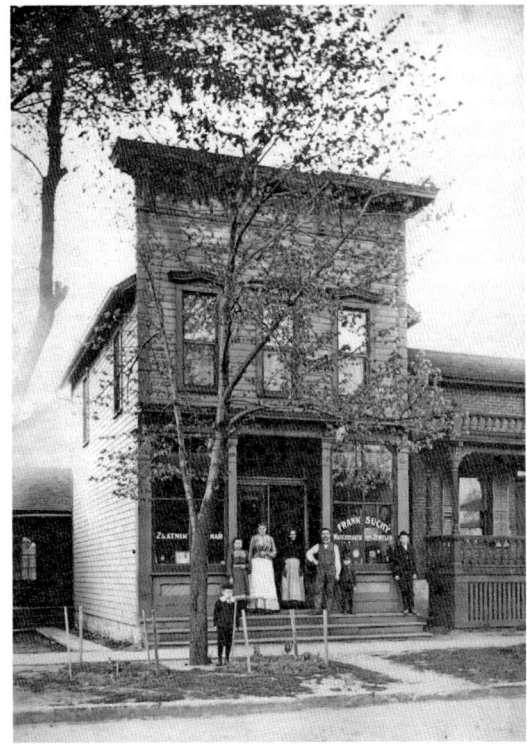

on the Cedar Rapids City Council. At the turn of the century, P. Matyk & Son was one of three dry goods business in the neighborhood.

A block to the north and across the street, Frank Suchy constructed a two-story brick building in 1907 for his jewelry and watch repair business, residing on the second floor with his wife, Theresa. They simply built 1006 Third Street Southeast next to their smaller, former location at 1010 Third Street.

In 1906, a block to the south of the Matyk building, cater-corner across Twelfth Avenue Southeast from the ZCJB building at 1127 Third Street Southeast, a group of business and civic leaders built Iowa State Savings Bank, which they'd founded earlier that year. It started with $50,000 in capital and attracted frugal Bohemian families to not only save money but also to take out loans to build new homes. Not only did the bank help attract patrons to neighboring businesses, it became so successful that a 1910 addition doubled its size.

A couple blocks farther south, the longtime grocery and dry goods business in the Lesinger Block, built in 1883 at Third Street and Fourteenth Avenue, changed hands. It was 1907 when Louis Pazdernik opened his saloon here in what later became the Little Bohemia tavern.

Two-story buildings, both brick and wood frame, became very popular with cost-conscious owners because of their efficiency. The business would be located on the main level, and the owning/operating family would live upstairs or have additional apartments to rent to area workers.

The Wencil Martinek and Sons hardware store, built about 1890 at 129 and 131 Fourteenth Avenue Southeast, had space upstairs for owners Wencil Martinek and his son, Wencil Jr., to live as well as rooms to rent out. Wencil Jr., a tinsmith, did much of the sheet metal work on the building to keep costs in check.

Just up the street at 219 Fourteenth Avenue, Frank J. Smid and his wife, Anna, lived in a flat above their Smid Hardware Store when it opened in 1905.

And on the other side of the street, Peter Hach and his wife, Francis, nestled their family together on the second floor of the P. Hach Bottling Works, 1326 Second Street. The Hachs had torn down a smaller shoe store building at this intersection, Fourteenth Avenue and Second Street Southeast, to open their saloon and bottling works in 1901. Eventually, three sons—Edward, Peter Jr. and William—joined the business.

Crossing the River

Across the Cedar River, at the opposite end of the 1910 bridge, the commercial district started by Italian, Russian and Lebanese immigrants began to take on a Bohemian flavor. The opening of Douglas Starch Works in 1903 on the west side of the river had induced many of its Bohemian laborers to move closer to work. Louis Pochobradsky opened his grocery store on "the Avenue" in 1906 and was soon followed by other businesses, including Frank J. John's harness shop in 1908. Soon, bakeries, restaurants, butcher shops, grocery stores, pharmacies and even doctors' offices populated the area.

This combination of business growth on both sides of the river prompted proprietors to follow Cedar Rapids' lead, organizing their own promotional group in 1907. The South End Business Men's Club set as its goal boosting traffic to businesses along Third Street Southeast from Ninth Avenue to Fourteenth Avenue and across the Cedar River

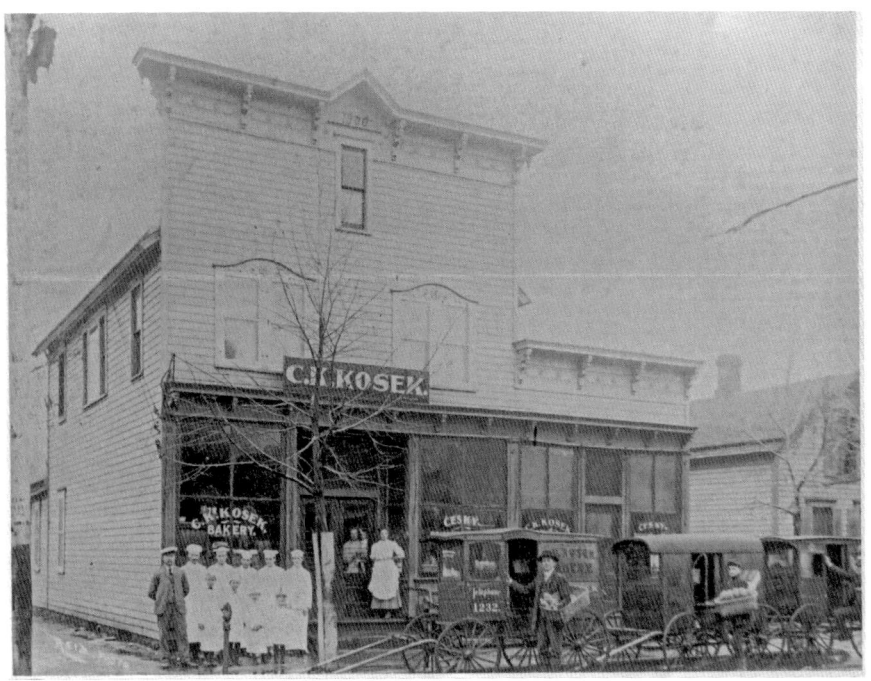

The entire staff and deliverymen assembled in front of the C.K. Kosek Bakery (today's Sykora Bakery) at 73 Sixteenth Avenue Southwest in Czech Village in 1906. *Courtesy of the Czech Heritage Foundation.*

Bridge down Sixteenth Avenue Southwest. The club had sixty members by 1912.

Yes, there was no question that Little Bohemia was booming. In their 1911 *History of Linn County*, authors Luther A. Brewer and Barthinius L. Wick praised the Bohemian people: "When we consider that less than two generations ago their ancestors came here with bare hands and not knowing the English language and unacquainted with the customs and without any particular advantages, except those of honesty and willingness to work, it is remarkable that such strides forward have been made by this nationality in the realms of labor, business, and the professions."

Beyond that, the authors added, "We are proud of the fact that our city has won the beautiful title of 'Parlor City,' but more proud should we be of the fact that in all the Bohemian communities and large centers of Bohemian population from New York to California, Cedar Rapids is known as 'The Bohemian Athens of America.'"

That latest moniker came about in 1906, when Bohemians dedicated a large boulder to their heritage in Sokol Park (acquired by the city in 1916 and renamed Riverside Park), which had become popular among young people for its bathing beaches along the Cedar River. A speaker coined the "Bohemian Athens of America" for Cedar Rapids.

Undoubtedly, it was the best of times for the area in no small part due to the earlier construction and continued expansion of the T.M. Sinclair & Company packinghouse. The sixteen-acre site was a sprawling collection of brick, stone and frame buildings connected by catwalks as well as elevators and storage tanks. The Chicago, Rock Island and Pacific Railroad with multiple spur lines was central to its operation, hauling in livestock (hogs, sheep and cattle) and fuel (wood and coal) and taking away processed meat and tanned hides. There was even an on-site railroad repair shop.

The packinghouse, innovative in many ways, became just the second plant in the United States to harvest ice from a river and store it for use in the summer, thus refrigerating processed meat during warm weather.

Harvesting ice from the Cedar River became big business before the turn of the century, in particular for a couple sons of Thomas and Anna Chadima who were in their thirties when they immigrated from Chrudim, East Bohemia, to Cedar Rapids with one son, Frank, in 1866. About thirteen years later, they traded their Cedar Rapids property for an eighty-acre farm near Center Point and moved there with their growing family that would number eight children. While Frank would work at the packinghouse, the third- and fourth-born, Joseph and Thomas, would start Chadima Brothers Ice Company.

Joseph, nine when the family moved to the farm, completed only the sixth grade according to the family history written in 1986 by his great-granddaughter Kitty Chadima. At fourteen, Joseph became a hired hand, and by eighteen, he'd had enough of hard fieldwork, moving to Cedar Rapids for a job at Faye Brothers Lumber Yard. Soon, he became a foreman, a job he held for five years.

While at the lumberyard, Joseph married Katherine Horak, also a second-generation Bohemian, and they started their family while living in an apartment above the lumberyard.

About the turn of the century, Joseph's restless bones got the best of him. He bought a team of mules and a wagon to peddle ice in the city. Apparently he liked the ice business—maybe because it was cool in summer—and convinced his brother Thomas to join him in 1901. They formed Chadima Brothers Ice Company outside the Bohemian area on the west side of the river across from Quaker Oats, for the best-quality ice in town formed there above the dam.

The ice harvest usually began in February, once measurement of the ice thickness confirmed a "good crop." Workers laid out "a field" on the ice bed, scored it into large-sized cakes and broke it up with spud bars and, later, electric saws. The cakes would be moved into storage along elevated chutes, where they would be coated with either new-mown timothy hay (the last crop of the fall) or sawdust as insulation to keep summertime melting at a minimum.

"Grandpa took pride in the fact that he never lost a mule or horse during harvest," Bob Chadima told his daughter, Kitty, during her research. "If one fell through the ice into the river, he would drag it out, give it a quart of whisky, run it up to Ellis Park and back, and then wipe it down and put it in the barn. I'm not sure that's what the vet would have recommended, but it worked."

Joseph knew what he was doing. By 1911, the Chadmia brothers—two younger brothers, Bill and John, had joined the company, too—put up fifteen thousand tons of ice while competing with at least five other ice-harvesting firms. By 1921, Joseph would acquire them all and a year later incorporate under the name of the one that had ice-making equipment, Hubbard Ice and Coal.

Celebrating Christmas

As a close family, the Chadimas had celebrated holidays together ever since arriving from the old country. Kitty, a freelance writer when she researched

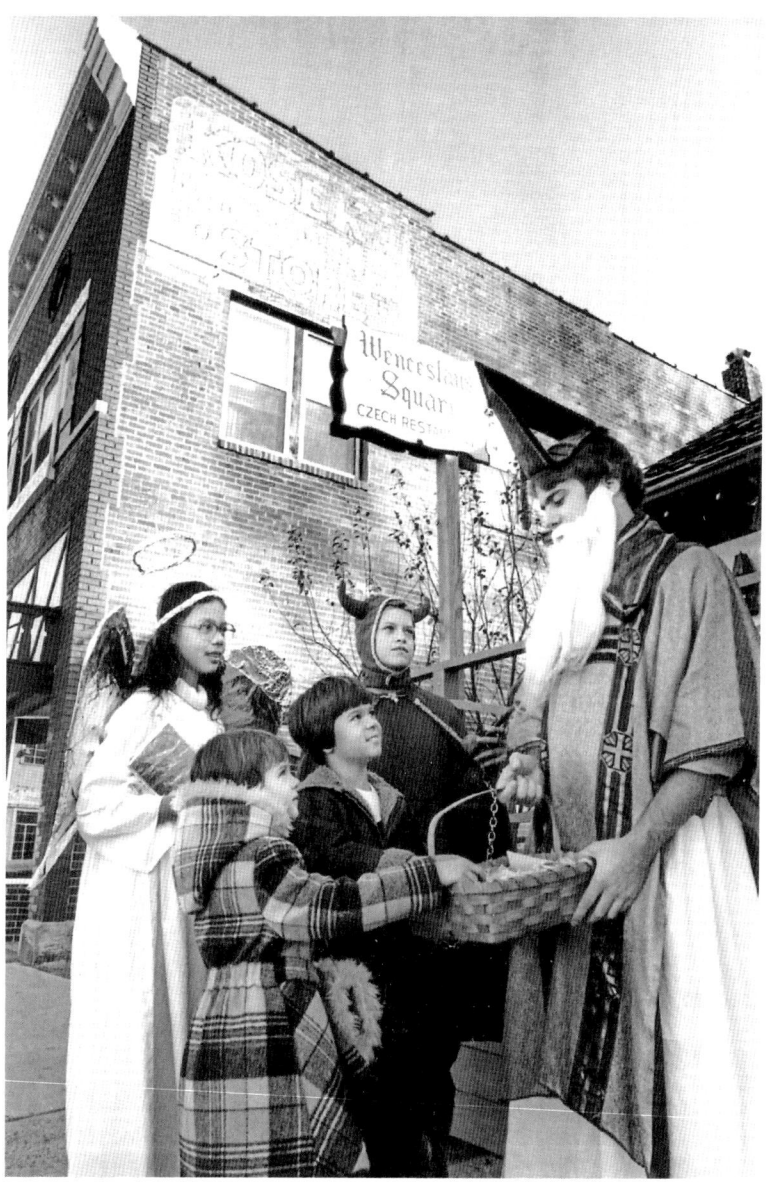

Observing a beloved Yule custom in Cedar Rapids' Czech Village, Svaty Mikulas (the Czechs' Saint Nicholas) took to the streets on November 24, 1979, asking children if they'd been good or bad and if they were saying their prayers. Accompanied by an angel (Chris-Ann Hikiji) and the devil (Lynne Marie Nejdl), Svaty Mikulas (Dave Stastny) gave treats to Brian and Lisa Bartunek, who apparently had been good. All were from Cedar Rapids. According to the custom, the angel records the children's responses, and on Christmas Eve, Svaty Mikulas gives good children candy, nuts and fruit and the bad children old potatoes. *Courtesy of the* Cedar Rapids Gazette.

her family, wrote a piece about old-fashioned Bohemian Christmases for the December 27, 1985 *Gazette*.

While the Czech holiday begins with St. Mikulas (Nicholas) Day on December 6 and continues through January 6 to honor the three kings, the highlight is the food. Bowls of apples and hazelnuts were often placed throughout the house, and families served a beverage similar to wassail. The real feast was reserved for Christmas and Christmas Eve.

"Czech immigrants then were more likely to think of a Christmas goose with dumplings and sauerkraut for dinner on Christmas Day, rather than turkey and cranberries," Kitty Chadima wrote.

> *There must have been a lot more fat geese running around in those days, or else a lot more geese hunters.*
>
> *On Christmas Eve, they had the traditional Czech fish, carp, which could be prepared several ways. Many people say carp is just awful because it's a scavenger fish when you get it from the Cedar River. But in Europe, where they still raise carp in fish farms, it's considered clean and good. The carp was served with potatoes and lentil, dumpling or cabbage soup, and some always had pearl barley, mushrooms and parsley with the meal as well. For dessert it was cookies, apple strudel, kolaches, houska (braided Christmas bread with nuts, raisins and candied fruit) and babovka (kolache dough with poppy seed filling).*

Czech immigrants in the late 1800s, Kitty wrote,

> *decorated in all hand-made ornaments and lit candles in candleholders, until, of course, they realized how dangerous that was and substituted electric lights. These traditional ornaments were made of hand-blown glass from northwest Czechoslovakia.*
>
> *Other ornaments were intricately carved dough figures, such as the traditional Czech bird, and hedgehogs, wreaths, candles, mermaids and almost any other imaginable shape. Also popular then were straw, cloth, gingerbread and sometimes chocolate ornaments, as well as chains of straw or glass beads.*

Kitty continued, "The early immigrants from Czechoslovakia also made their own creches of paper, cloth, carved wood or ceramic figures, sometimes by using little cutouts of the holy family and mounting them."

After all, the season was not only a time to feast and rejoice, but a time to pray and give thanks for what had been and for what could be.

4
1918

THE GREAT WAR—"FREE AT LAST"

"Big Celebration of Independence of Slav Peoples" proclaimed the November 6, 1918 headline above an announcement that Czech and Slovak people would gather on November 10 at Hus Memorial Presbyterian Church. That story, in the *Cedar Rapids Evening Gazette*, referenced, of course, the formation of Czechoslovakia.

"The American citizens of Bohemian descent have every reason to rejoice that at last after centuries of struggles and suffering the land of their forefathers will be free and the Czech people allowed to proceed freely in their process of evolution which heretofore has been hampered in every way," the story said. It explained the Czechs' five-hundred-year quest since John Hus proclaimed their freedom, the defeat at the Battle of White Mountain near Prague in 1620 and the centuries of oppression since.

Every Cedar Rapids citizen was invited to participate in appreciation for "their brethren of Bohemian descent that not only do they value them for their commercial, industrial and political efficiency but that from now on they will try to become better acquainted with the Slav soul than they have been heretofore, thus bringing about a better, clearer understanding of our mutual ideals."

The afternoon program began in English and was followed by addresses in Czech. Passing a collection plate raised eighty dollars for relief in Czechoslovakia. Bohemians in attendance decided that the Reverend Dr. Edward R. Burkhalter of the First Presbyterian Church should affectionately be called "uncle" for his unwavering support.

The first hint of freedom came on September 3, 1918, when U.S. secretary of state Robert Lansing announced that the United States would recognize the government of Czechoslovakia "in accordance with the rules and practices of civilized nations." The journey had begun on June 28, 1914, with the shot heard around the world when Yugoslav nationalist Gavrilo Princip assassinated Archduke Franz Ferdinand, heir to the Austria-Hungary throne. Europe was thrown in a tizzy, new nations declared their independence from the Austro-Hungarian Empire, a Russian Revolution broke out in 1917 and, throughout the war, more than seventy million military personnel would be involved.

By the end of fighting in November 1918 (the last being the United States' armistice signed with Germany that took effect with a ceasefire at 11:00 a.m. on November 11 and became the impetus for Veterans Day), the powerful and widespread Austro-Hungarian Empire was dissolved—as had been the German, Russian and Ottoman empires. In 1919, the winners—major among them Great Britain, France, the United States and Italy—imposed their wills with a series of treaties. The United Nations for world peace and cooperation was born. And so were many new nations, among them—formed generally along ethnic lines—Austria, Hungary, Yugoslavia and, of course, Czechoslovakia.

"The name in itself is confusing," wrote Charles F. Horne in "The Odyssey of the Czecho-Slovaks—The Wandering War of the Army Without a Country" published in 1920 in *Great Events of the Great War* (National Alumni Press).

"The Czechs are the Bohemians or North Slavs, commonly known as the Czecho-Slavs, to distinguish them from the Jugo-Slavs or South-Slavs of the Balkan States," Horne wrote. "There exist, however, contiguous to the Czechs, a people of another branch of the Slavic race, known as Slovaks; and their home, a northern district of Hungary, they have named Slovakia. As these people have united with the Czechs to form the new independent republic, its authorities have decided that both the land and the people should be called, not Czecho-Slavic as they were at first, but Czecho-Slovak."

Welcome, Czechoslovakia

So, after the borders were outlined and Prague designated its capital, Czechoslovakia became the homeland of this faction of Cedar Rapids citizens. They were Czechs from Czechoslovakia.

While the fight for freedom had been long in Europe, it was a cause enthusiastically taken up in Cedar Rapids.

The Bohemian Relief Society organized in October 1914 to raise money for orphans and widows in Bohemia. Before it got off the ground, $600 was pledged to the effort. In the next few months, hundreds of dollars more poured in from lodges, the proceeds of plays and concerts and from individuals. On February 26, 1915, the Bohemian Relief Society aligned with the Bohemian National Alliance that worked through local organizations to support the liberation of Bohemia. Cedar Rapids became the Iowa headquarters.

While the local Bohemians raised $2,700 for the freedom movement, merchants throughout Cedar Rapids contributed another $10,000. It truly appeared that the Czech people had been accepted by the entire community.

The Bohemian National Alliance organized annual fall bazaars in every United States community with a Czech population throughout the war. While bazaars held at the CSPS Hall in Cedar Rapids successfully raised $1,000 or more each year, it went over the top in 1917 with $10,800. Nationwide, that amount was exceeded only by funds raised at Chicago and New York City bazaars.

It was April 1915 when our good Dr. John Rudis-Jicinsky knew he was going to Serbia and that he'd need local support. Each Friday afternoon, a group of women known as the Vcelky (Bees) held sewing bees at the Czech School to make clothes for war orphans and Czech prisoners. This had been added to their regular war effort sewing bees on Wednesday afternoons at the American Red Cross. Among their contributions were 248 pairs of muslin underwear for Czech soldiers, as well as towels, bandages, handkerchiefs, stockings and new leather for shoes. In the last couple of years, the group had sent twenty-six large chests of clothing to the Czech Red Cross in Prague.

At the Jan Hus Methodist Church, two "Ladies Aid" organizations, one meeting in Czech and the other meeting in English, were formed during the war. Women of the neighborhood and church met at the parsonage several times weekly to refurbish used clothing for the Red Cross in Belgium.

Cedar Rapids and its Czech population sent soldiers to fight, too. The Linn County honor roll listed 474 Czechs or men of Czech descent out of the 2,541 men who fought in Europe. In addition, after being recruited around the July 4 holiday in 1918, another 14 Czechs in Cedar Rapids, unable for one reason or another to enlist in the U.S. Army, volunteered to become Czech Legionnaires.

That July 4, 1918 celebration was huge—a mile-long parade included numerous Czech groups, among them five hundred Czech schoolchildren. An assembly at Riverside Park had Czech people pledging their allegiance and support to the United States. This, obviously, occurred because the United States had entered the war the previous year. And, just maybe, these people sensed an impending victory.

If nothing else, 1918 brought stepped-up efforts in the already noble effort to support fighting soldiers. Planning for the fall bazaar began in September and went into November after a flu epidemic postponed it.

"Each Sunday during the months of September and October 1918, from twenty to forty cars of workers, known as the Flying Squadrons, solicited goods and money in Cedar Rapids and the surrounding area," explained *The History of Czechs in Cedar Rapids*. "Contributions included such things as a wagonload of corn, live pigs, geese, chickens, cows, rabbits, vegetables, a bicycle, a colt, two forty-acre tracts of land, and a piece of real estate in Cedar Rapids. Perishables were sold at once and other products were stored until the week of the bazaar."

That seven-day bazaar was the best ever. News of the liberation of Bohemia and surrounding area "added new zest to the occasion." Bands and orchestras played daily. Goods (potatoes, livestock, even rabbits) were raffled off. Chances on the real estate were sold for $1. A huge Thanksgiving Day feast featuring Czech jitrnice, a highly seasoned liver sausage, highlighted festivities. The bazaar netted an amazing $30,200, or nearly three times the record produced the year before.

While the war effort solidified the purpose of many organizations, the opposite occurred with the Sokols. Until 1917, the Sokols remained strong with members participating in local and area Slets—calisthenics, exercise on the apparatus, track events, high jumps and broad jumps, the shot put and discus throw for young men, exercises on the balance beam for women and mass exercise for all of the participants, according to *The History of Czechs in Cedar Rapids*. The group was also immensely popular for its social activities—the masquerade ball in 1916 drew one thousand attendees, and eighty couples or more would regularly perform the beseda dance at the Majovy Venecek (May Wreath) dance on the first of May.

Male participation in the Sokols waned after the war, however, because many of them were off fighting or had done so and needed to tend to other business upon their return. Boys, it seemed, showed more interest in competitive sports.

But enthusiastic support for Czechoslovakia continued after the war with the Komensky Society at Coe College in Cedar Rapids raising money to establish a camp for children threatened with tuberculosis. Dr. Anna Heyberger, who taught Czech classes at Coe, had visited Czechoslovakia during the summer and made arrangements with the Czech Red Cross to create the camp. The Komensky Society raised $5,800 during spring recitals and through donations. By early fall, "Coe Camp" opened near Tabor, Czechoslovakia.

Neighborhood Grows

On the homefront, development and growth in Little Bohemia and on the Avenue continued as the country underwent two major societal changes in 1920—national Prohibition solidified Iowa's own prohibition law enacted four years earlier, and the states ratified the Nineteenth Amendment to the Constitution, granting women the right to vote.

The South End Business Men's Club of 1907 reorganized in 1912 as the South Side Commercial Club and in 1917 erected its own clubhouse at 1213 Second Street Southeast in Little Bohemia. In addition to promoting that area and Czech Village, it became a strong advocate of better roads to expand the customer base. New businesses in existing space included a pharmacy, two shoe stores, a furniture store, a print shop and several restaurants.

In front of the ZCBJ Hall, a unique form of advertising had appeared in 1912. Colorful tiled mosaics—forty-three in all—built into the sidewalk promoted a variety of Bohemian businesses on both sides of the river and helped cover the cost of the concrete walkway.

Iowa State Savings Bank continued its rapid growth to the extent that officials built a new bank across Twelfth Avenue Southeast rather than expanding again. It purchased and demolished the Frank and Katherine Nemecek home to put up its two-story Classic Revival building with terracotta elements and huge columns in front designed by a New York City architectural firm. The building opened at 1201 Third Street Southeast in 1917, just eleven years after the bank was organized.

The bank's former location at 1127 Third Street Southeast became the Globe Grocery & Market owned by Otto and Leo Lzicar. The store would soon use the slogan "The Best Foods for Less" and expand into the adjacent one-story brick building erected in 1911 that was first occupied by John Krejci's grocery store.

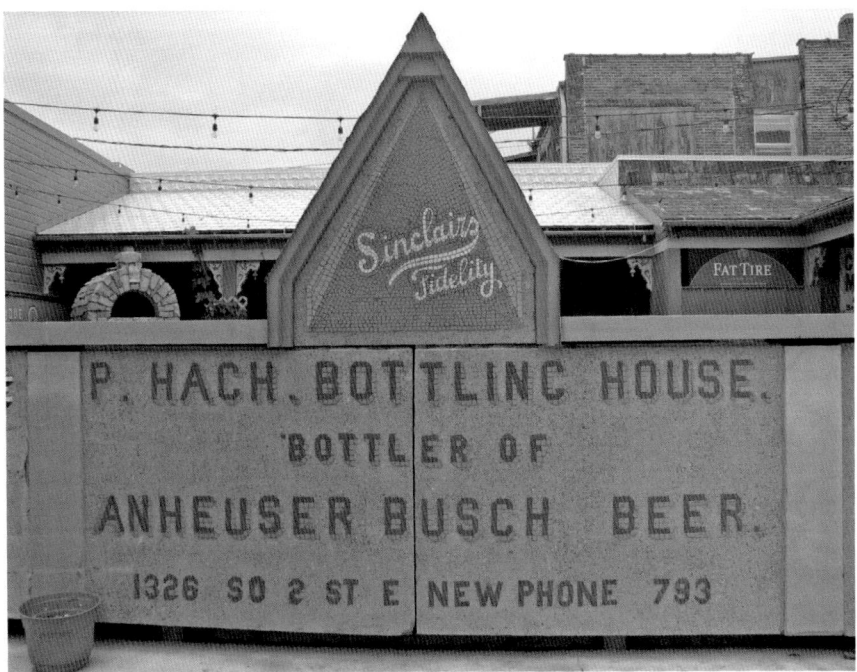

Historic sidewalk tiles advertising Sinclair Fidelity meats and P. Hach Bottling House that were recovered from in front of the ZCBJ Hall in 2012 now decorate the exterior wall of the beer garden at Parlor City Pub & Eatery. *Photo by Dave Rasdal.*

Next door, at 1121 Third Street Southeast, the district's only female merchants, Anna Jacobs and Anna Kurik, operated Jacobs and Kurik Drygoods store in the two-story Jacobs Building constructed in 1914. At one time, they leased space to another Anna—Anna Lesinger, an undertaker.

That other former grocery store, down the street at Fourteenth Avenue Southeast that had become a tavern in 1907, changed its ways by 1916. Owner Louis Pazdernik served soft drinks rather than alcohol and emphasized the sale of prepared meals to stave off the ill effects of Prohibition.

The same occurred down Fourteenth Avenue toward the bridge when Peter Hach converted his beer bottle works to soft drinks and added a bowling alley to keep customers happy.

New competitive entertainment included the Ideal Theater at 213 Fourteenth Avenue Southeast, one of three theaters to open in Little Bohemia. The others were the nearby Praha Theater at 227 Fourteenth Avenue Southeast and the Standard Theater around the corner at 1124 Third Street Southeast across from Globe Grocery. Only the Ideal Theater would be operating by 1917, when Cedar Rapids had eleven other theaters in its business district, and even then, its life would be cut short. The building was empty by 1920, soon to be converted into a box factory.

The Ideal Theater, owned by Frank J. Smid, who had his hardware store across the alley, had opened to much fanfare on July 4, 1914. It was equipped with a mirror screen, a Power's Cameragraph projector, eight ventilators to ensure pure air at all times and seated up to five hundred people. Smid, apparently, was an enthusiastic entrepreneur, for he had recently opened his hardware store in what had been Pugh & Kucera, a livery and an undertaking business built in 1899.

On January 1, 1915, the Ideal advertised in the *Gazette* the showing of "the greatest Bohemian motion play ever produced. PRODANA NEVESTA. Played 100 nights in the National Theater Prague Bohemia. Shown for the first time west of New York." Of course, this was a silent picture accompanied by a newsreel of war action. Admission was a dime or a nickel, depending on time of day and age.

Construction seemed to be the norm along Fourteenth Avenue Southeast, for three new buildings appeared at the turn of the century in the vicinity of the old Olmstead Soap Factory. First, Krejci Blacksmith shop opened in a small frame building at 119 Fourteenth Avenue Southeast, followed by a feed and flour store in the Karban Building at 123–25 Fourteenth Avenue Southeast that would soon close in favor of an early automobile repair shop and the Martinek Hardware store at 131 Fourteenth Avenue Southeast.

Hose Station No. 4, a two-story brick structure south of the CSPS Hall on Third Avenue Southeast, went up in 1916 to replace an 1899 wood-frame building that had given the Bohemian-American Hose Company a new home, allowing it to move from its quarters at the rear of the CSPS Hall. The firefighting unit, formed in 1882 as a volunteer group, had located its equipment and horses there in 1891. But by 1916, the Cedar Rapids Fire Department bypassed the twenty-nine-member volunteer group of mostly Bohemians by housing professional firefighters at the new station—two crews of three men each, a captain and two firemen.

Across the Cedar River, development was booming in the wake of the 1903 opening of the Douglas Starch Works north of Riverside Park. It promised plenty of job opportunities, which swayed many Bohemian workers to move nearby, thus increasing the population and business opportunities on the west side. During the war, the plant processed twenty thousand bushels of corn every day into cornstarch.

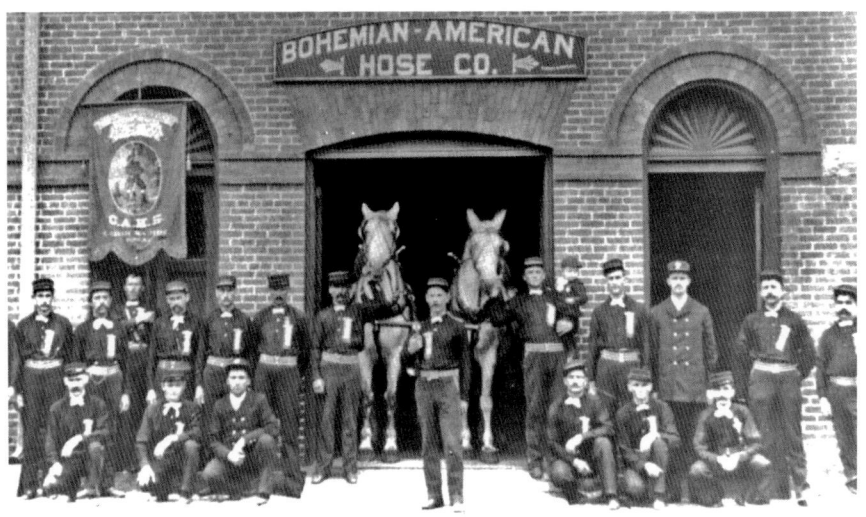

Firefighters from the Bohemian-American Hose Company pose in 1895 in front of the doors to their station at the rear of the CSPS Hall in the New Bohemia district. *Courtesy of the CSPS/Legion Arts.*

Combined with the new bridge in 1910, this manufacturing and employment development prompted businessmen to sell their wares along the Avenue. Stores included a meat market, grocery stores, a drugstore with a soda fountain, a shoe store, a bank and a bakery. Dentists, doctors and other professionals practiced on the second floor of these buildings, or the upper rooms were occupied by owners and renters. In a few years, the area became the second-largest retail district in Cedar Rapids after the central downtown area.

Earliest among the dominant structures was the 1880s Lzicar Building at 62 Sixteenth Avenue Southeast that was moved in the early 1900s to the rear of its lot to make room for a larger two-story building with two business entrances. The old building had housed John Viktor's shoe store until 1913, when he moved into the two-story brick Viktor and Prochaska Building across the avenue at 87 Sixteenth Avenue Southeast.

In 1903, Charles Kosek bought a brewery/saloon at 73 Sixteenth Avenue Southeast and opened C.K. Kosek bakery. The two-story Italianate building adjoining a one-story structure, built before the turn of the century, would become Sykora Bakery in 1927 when one of Charles's bakers, Joseph Sykora, purchased it.

The Skvor and Tichy Druggist building at Sixteenth Avenue Southwest and C Street was erected in 1898 by Czech pharmacists Charles Tichy and

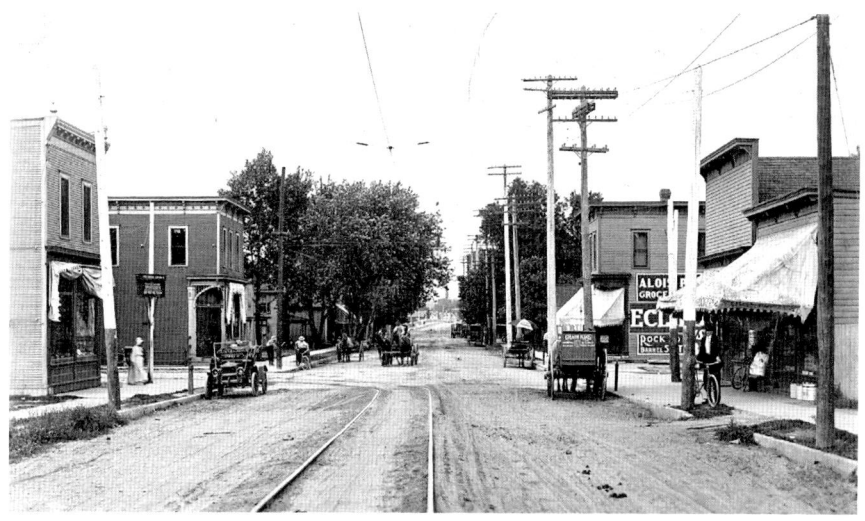

Trolley tracks run down Sixteenth Avenue Southwest, the heart of Czech Village in Cedar Rapids, in 1910. *Courtesy of the National Czech & Slovak Museum & Library.*

John Skvor. By 1917, Skvor had been replaced by Charles Zastera, who in 1922 took sole ownership and changed the name to Zastera Pharmacy.

In the early 1900s, both the Klinger Building at 96–98 Sixteenth Avenue Southwest and the Krejci Clothing Company Building at 92 Sixteenth Avenue Southwest opened. John Kucera, who lived on B Street Southwest with his wife, Mary, and their daughter, Anna, operated his hardware and sheet metal business at 56 Sixteenth Avenue, the future site of Novak Heating and Air Conditioning. In 1907, a streetcar line installed down the center of Sixteenth Avenue looped around the neighborhood to help businesses cater to west-side residents.

In 1914, Pochobradsky, the grocer, decided to bring banking to the west-side neighborhood. He opened Citizens Savings Bank in a two-story brick building with a diagonal entrance that faced both Sixteenth Avenue Southwest and C Street Southwest with an advertised $50,000 in capital. Pochobradsky, who lived adjacent to the bank at 1607 C Street Southwest, foresaw success at issuing mortgages because, to Bohemians, the importance of home ownership was a guiding principal—"God, motherhood and homeownership." His one-and-a-half-story American folk house later served as a rental unit and the first Czech museum.

A modern brick automobile garage with a large plate glass window affording pedestrians a view of brand-new Studebakers was put up by the Kadlec Brothers in 1919 at the opposite end of the Avenue near the bridge.

While houses of worship had been established on the west side in the form of the John Hus Methodist Church, the Czech Reformed Church and the Reformed Bohemian Church, the Catholic faith began its presence in 1914 when St. Ludmila Catholic Church and School were founded as a mission of St. Wenceslaus Catholic Church. That's when five Notre Dame Nuns from Bohemia arrived in Cedar Rapids, moved into an old house and started a school with sixty students.

Immediately, the nuns were saying Mass, and the congregation became so large that attendees were forced to stand outside. Even though a tent protected them from inclement weather, talk began about building a larger church. The Reverend Florian Svrdlik of St. Wenceslaus and businessman John Viktor, who in 1906 had paid $2,800 for land off Wilson Avenue near J Street Southwest, donated that five acres to the cause. The first Mass in a new chapel/school was said on February 13, 1916. Two years later, Father Thomas Ballon of Bohemia arrived to serve as pastor without any pay except for his lodging.

Explosion Rocks Bohemian Area

While prayer houses were instrumental in the personal lives of the Bohemian people, they truly became a blessing on May 22, 1919. For at 6:30 p.m. that night, the Douglas Starch Works blew up. The explosion sent flames high into the air, broke windows of all sizes throughout downtown Cedar Rapids as well as in Little Bohemia and along the Avenue. The ceiling at the Jan Hus Methodist Church sanctuary collapsed, and all the church windows were blown out.

By the time the *Evening Gazette* hit the streets the next afternoon, headlines proclaimed 11 people dead and another 35 missing out of 109 workers on the job. Fortunately, the newspaper said, the much larger day shift had gone home an hour earlier.

The newspaper said the explosion had been heard ten miles away, rained debris down on both sides of the Cedar River and ignited a fire that burned into the next morning. The paper listed the names of those known dead, those in hospitals and those missing.

"One of the sad phases is the number of employees' homes wrecked or partially wrecked," wrote the editor in his front-page column. "A double hardship is imposed on families thus deprived of residence and employment.

In numerous cases one entire wall of the home would be blown in, while in others the roof was destroyed by the falling chimney and debris from the factory. Great chunks of cement, metal and brick wall were hurled for many feet and splintered timbers were picked up three and four blocks away."

The Cedar Rapids Chamber of Commerce established two committees, one to work with the Red Cross to assist families affected by the explosion and the other to help Douglas Starch Works with its recovery. The newspaper estimated damage at more than $3 million, even though company officials wouldn't comment.

At the time, nobody knew how bad the explosion had really been. They had no idea it would go down in history as the most horrific single-incident tragedy in Cedar Rapids.

5
1930s

THE GREAT DEPRESSION

By the time fires were extinguished and rubble cleared from the Douglas Starch Works, forty-eight funerals had been held. The May 22, 1919 explosion had become news the world over. And in a way, it signaled more bad times in the Parlor City, for a decade later Cedar Rapids would experience its worst flood and, along with the rest of the country, be plunged into the Great Depression while Iowa's only native-son president, Herbert Hoover, sat in the White House.

Inquiries and trials more than a year later never determined the cause of the starch works explosion, even though officials speculated that a combination of starch dust and gas in the enclosed factory had ignited it. One survivor blamed a cigarette because workers continued to smoke inside despite pleas not to. Others pointed to acid used in the starch-making process.

Whatever the cause, the catastrophe brought up memories of recent disasters—the February 1903 fire at the Clifton Hotel in Cedar Rapids' central business district that claimed a dozen lives and the March 7, 1905 fire at the American Cereal Company, later Quaker Oats, that killed two men and caused $1.5 million in damage. But those events didn't directly affect the Bohemian area of the city as did the starch works explosion.

"South side business houses suffered wide damage from broken windows," the *Evening Gazette* reported. "Not a single store front with large windows escaped on either side of the river. The Citizens Savings Bank on the west side and the Iowa State on the east side suffered the heaviest loss in that section of the city. All of the lower floor huge windows on the north side of the Iowa State were blown in. Riverside Park was strewn with wreckage carried there by the force of the explosion."

One man, blown into the air, was rescued from the Cedar River. A salesman from Chicago staying in a hotel had his nose sliced off by flying glass when his room's window imploded. Water lines were ruptured, cutting off service and hampering firefighting. Two firemen were injured.

Daily the newspaper updated lists of the dead, injured and missing. Many lived in the vicinity of the plant. Some were extracted from piles of rubble where only their feet remained exposed.

"All the bodies removed from the ruins were blackened and charred," the *Gazette* said. "In practically every case a hand had been thrown up and literally baked in that position. It was as if the men had thrown up a hand in less than the winking of an eyelash to ward off a vague something."

As families of victims mourned, city leaders, workers and volunteers made repairs and planned for the future. They met in committees, donated money, replaced broken glass windows, fixed damaged roofs and comforted survivors. A monument dedicated to those who died in the explosion was placed in Linwood Cemetery in southwest Cedar Rapids. This was not a time to give up.

The Clifton Hotel, demolished after its fire, had been replaced along First Avenue Southeast by the Allison Hotel. The American Cereal Mill, leveled in its fire, had been rebuilt despite offers to move elsewhere.

Citizens hoped the same could be said for Douglas Starch Works. The process took longer than the others, but seven months later, after other investors had pulled out, George Douglas sold what remained to Penick & Ford, a Louisiana sugar cane processor. Construction on the new $8 million plant began in 1920, and it was up and running the next year. Despite early financial difficulties, Penick & Ford would have a $1 million payroll by the 1930s as cornstarch became a staple in many of our foods.

Optimistic Czechs

Otherwise, optimism followed the Great War. Activity in Little Bohemia and along the Avenue in the 1920s showed that Cedar Rapids' Czech citizens were eager.

The South Side Commercial Club realized its dream when a nationwide "Good Roads Movement" dovetailed with its cause. Improved local roads and development of more efficient road-building equipment brought additional traffic to its commercial districts.

When the first bridge connecting Fourteenth Avenue Southeast to Sixteenth Avenue Southwest was built in 1875, it established a wagon route through the south end of Cedar Rapids. The 1910 reinforced concrete bridge that replaced it promptly increased traffic, including motor vehicles, so that by 1915 the Third Street Southeast corridor, the bridge and Sixteenth Avenue Southeast were designated part of the national "Red Ball Route." This meant travelers following the six-hundred-mile Red Ball from St. Louis, Missouri, to St. Paul, Minnesota, would come through the Czech area. With the national numbering system implemented in 1926, the Red Ball became Highway 218.

Coincidentally, young Cedar Rapids entrepreneur Howard Hall had a vision. In 1918, he bought controlling interest in a Little Bohemia foundry established in 1880 and expanded by J.T. Carmody in 1889. It produced iron and steel beams, boilers, pulleys and architectural ironwork. In 1922, Hall gave it a new name—Iowa Steel and Iron Works—and in 1923 established his Iowa Manufacturing Company on the other side of Cedar Rapids to build portable rock-crushing equipment used in road construction. As Iowa Steel provided gray iron castings and steel to Iowa Manufacturing, both companies grew by leaps and bounds. Soon, the Iowa Steel and Iron Works foundry, steel fabrication and steel storage facilities would occupy a three-block-long area north of the Sinclair packinghouse.

Across the railroad tracks, the St. Wenceslaus Catholic Church built and dedicated its $45,000 high school with a large assembly hall and gymnasium. Until 1926, high school students met in the elementary building. (As the first accredited Czech high school in the United States, it remained active for decades with sixty-seven students enrolled in 1950, when they were still studying the Czech language.)

Nearby, the ZCBJ was going great guns as a fraternal organization and life insurance provider. Youth clubs formed in 1913, and the successful (and unanimous) resistance in 1917 to relocating national headquarters to Omaha solidified the organization's place in Cedar Rapids. So did the decision in 1927 to open up membership to English-speaking members with the decline of Czech speakers and the 1929 absorption of the Czechoslovakian Workmen's Benevolent Association of St. Paul, Minnesota, immediately adding more than one thousand members.

About this time, business expansion had slowed in Little Bohemia, giving way to the increased development on the other side of the Cedar River along Sixteenth Avenue. By 1929, at least half a dozen new brick-front commercial buildings had been raised along the Avenue—the Barta Building at 65 Sixteenth Avenue, the Novotny Tavern at 69 Sixteenth Avenue, the Gatto Building at 72–74 Sixteenth Avenue, Harold Fine Foods Store at 76 Sixteenth Avenue, the Modern Bakery Building at 86 Sixteenth Avenue and the People's Grocery and Market Building at 88 Sixteenth Avenue.

Kolaches for Everyone

With this prosperity, why not celebrate? At least that's what John N. Kucera, operator of a hardware/sheet metal business on Sixteenth Avenue, thought when he concocted the first Kolach Festival in 1924. Area women baked the

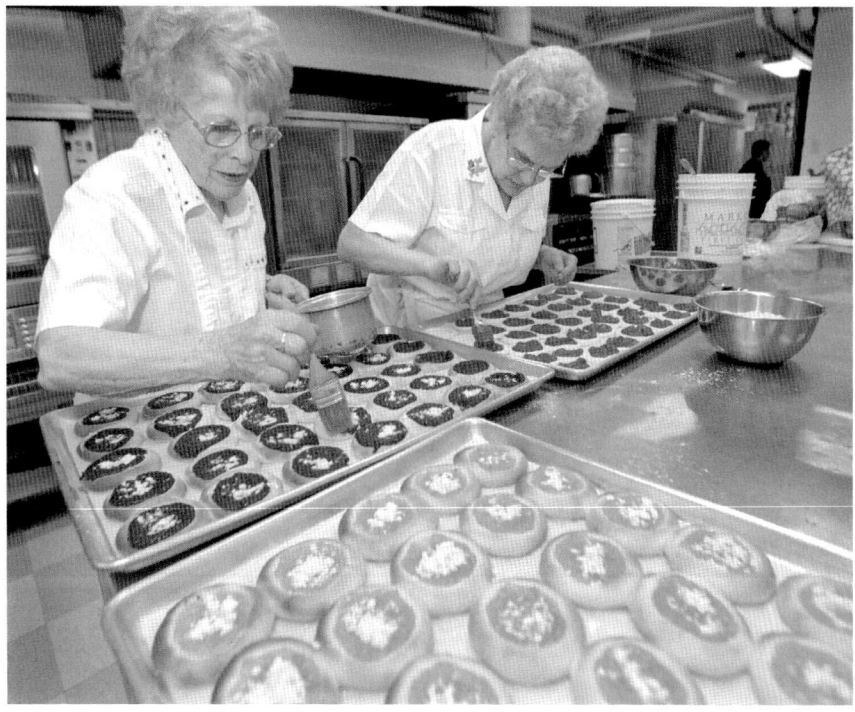

Czech kolaches in a variety of flavors receive finishing touches from Irma Kelly (left) of St. Ludmila Catholic Church and Lydia Elias of St. Wenceslaus Catholic Church in preparation for the Taste of Czech event in May 2002. At the conclusion of that event, volunteers planned to bake forty thousand kolaches for the annual Kolache Festival in June. *Courtesy of the* Cedar Rapids Gazette.

delicious pastries in their own ovens with a variety of fillings and donated the kolaches to the cause. Free kolaches for everyone! When word got out, the Avenue was full of customers. In gratitude to the women, the following year they earned twenty cents per dozen kolaches (later, up to thirty-five cents), and customers paid a few cents for each one they ate.

Adding to festivities a few years later, grocer Peter Anthony used his connections to convince the Ringling Bros. and Barnum & Bailey Circus to parade down the Avenue. The elephants and circus wagons attracted great street crowds as they made their way down Third Street, Fourteenth Avenue, the bridge and Sixteenth Avenue to the circus grounds at Ninth Avenue and Sixth Street Southwest.

The Kolach Festival became such a success that Kosek Bakery and Pechacek Bakery supplied the tasty pastries until 1929, when the flood and the Great Depression temporarily ended the festival. Luckily for kolach lovers, the rapidly growing St. Ludmila Parish had revived the festival by 1931.

That church began new growth with the 1922 appointment of the Reverend Francis Hruby, an assistant at St. Wenceslaus, as its first regular priest. The first chapel, in the 1916 school building, had become too small. Combined with the move of the Notre Dame Nuns to Omaha in 1925 and the purchase of their home and additional land, a new $27,000 church was erected in 1926. A stained-glass window was added in 1932. The St. Ludmila Parish also opened Frolic Field, a project of the Frolic Club, for recreation by 1935, which became home to the Kolach Festival. With paid admission to the grounds for the bazaar, patrons received a free kolach.

But it was March 1929 that people would remember. Floodwaters reached an unheard-of twenty feet high, or seven feet above the record, during the March 17–19 flood. Water inundated Little Bohemia from Ninth Avenue Southeast to the packing plant and up to the Fourth Street tracks, as well as the west side along the river.

The flood forced hundreds of people from their homes and prompted the shutdown of operations at the packinghouse, the starch works and the cereal mills. It caused telephone and electrical outrages, stopped some trains from running (especially the local streetcar lines) and delayed construction projects because sand and rock were unavailable to make concrete.

A story in the *Cedar Rapids Tribune* on March 22, 1929, said the record flooding brought back memories to old-timers of 1884. "A record has been established which probably will endure as long as that set 45 years ago." Even though bridges were rebuilt at higher elevations and various streets had been raised in the ensuing 45 years, the story said water covered a far greater

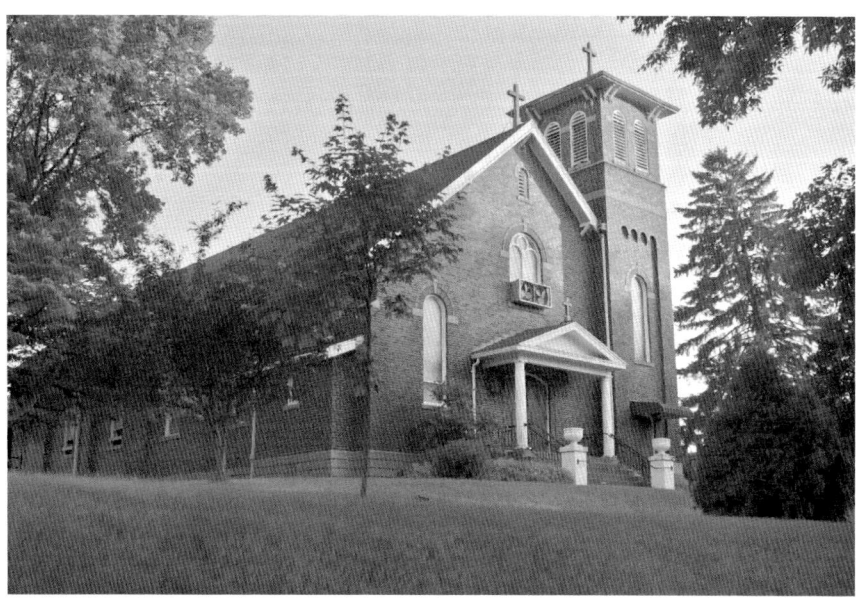

Final services were held at St. Ludmila Catholic Church, 215 Twenty-first Avenue Southwest, on June 25, 2000, before it was demolished for a new church that opened a couple years later. *Courtesy of the* Cedar Rapids Gazette.

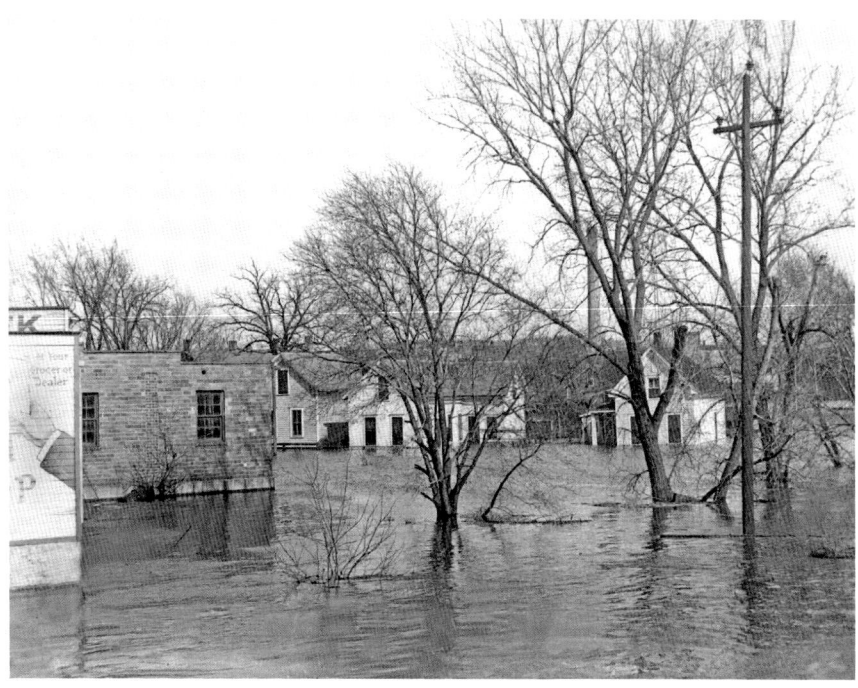

area than even before. "It was the record flood of history to date. Nature had her fling and mere man as usual was helpless when its fury was aroused."

The newspaper praised efforts by city commissioners, the Red Cross and the Salvation Army, which set up two relief stations. It also noted that something needed to be done to prevent future disasters.

In a column note titled "The Ways of Nature and the Folly of Man," H.G. Stewart, editor and publisher of the *Tribune*, wrote what obviously had to be on residents' minds: "Viewing the destruction wrought by this week's flood, people's thoughts naturally have turned to schemes for guarding against another such disaster in the future. The truth is that thinking along that line is largely futile—there is little that can be done to keep the Cedar from overflowing and, in overflowing, doing great damage."

Flood of 1929 Suggestions

Stewart suggested that storm sewers and sanitary sewers be fitted with flood gates to keep high river water from back-flowing into the streets. He said strategically placed dikes could keep that damage to a minimum. And he added an obvious prediction: "What the water did once it may do again. A super-flood might inundate every inch of Cedar Rapids that lies as low as the Fourth Street tracks. In fact a two-day's rain over the watershed of the Cedar last week probably would have caused that calamity."

As cleanup progressed through the summer (it was mostly mucking out basements and scrubbing down the floors and walls of damaged homes and businesses) Cedar Rapids citizens pretty much went about their business—that is, until the stock market crash in October.

The decade had begun on such a promising note for Cedar Rapids banks, especially those in Little Bohemia and Sixteenth Avenue, because of an improved economy on the heels of manufacturing growth. On the east side of the river, the Bohemian Savings and Loan Association, established in 1892 and located on the main level of Sokol Hall, thrived on home mortgage

Opposite, bottom: The historic flood of 1929, as shown on March 18 of that year, not only put these New Bohemia houses under water but also flooded the hog yards of the Sinclair packinghouse (the smokestack is visible through the trees), forcing it to temporarily shut down. *Courtesy of the* Cedar Rapids Gazette.

loans while Iowa State Savings Bank did just fine in its new building. Across the river, United State Bank, established from the fledgling Citizens Savings Bank in 1922 when additional investors from the Bohemian business community came aboard, had gained a strong foothold.

But the bottom fell out on Black Thursday—October 24, 1929. Heavy trading before the opening bell and an immediate 11 percent plunge in the Dow Jones Average portended of a truly dark future. After all, the stock market had increased tenfold in value during the past nine years and saw a 20 percent increase three months earlier in 1929. Even President Hoover made a public announcement to reassure investors and the American public that the nation's economy was strong. But when Black Tuesday—October 29, 1929—followed, investors and, especially risky speculators, realized good times don't last forever. They traded sixteen million shares of stock, mostly to sell, a record that stood for forty years.

In Cedar Rapids, the poor farm economy (agriculture had basically been ignored during the boom times) exacerbated financial woes. As thousands of banks were forced to close, the Iowa legislature enacted the State Bank Stabilization Act in January 1933, allowing financially troubled state-chartered banks to put themselves under protective supervision of the State Department of Banks. In Cedar Rapids, four banks did this, including Iowa State Bank. After closing for a week in March for the National Bank Holiday, the bank reopened. Still, trouble persisted, and it soon closed for good.

South Side business owners, however, wanted their local bank. They paid former investors forty-five cents on the dollar, reorganized the bank and on November 5, 1934, reopened as First Trust and Savings Bank.

Still, the Great Depression had arrived. A shortage of money meant fewer purchases, which meant fewer jobs were needed, which meant people had even less money. High unemployment, soup lines, hopping freight cars in search of better jobs and the migration west to California became lasting impressions. But it was the family hit hard that affected Cedar Rapids.

The Cedar Rapids Restoration Club, founded in 1928 with a large Czech membership, did its best to help, seining fish from the Cedar River to feed to people who couldn't afford to eat. The club, known as the Linn County Fish and Game Club by 1934, had removed fish from flooded areas in 1929. It also gave merchants along the Avenue bird seed for customers to scatter along the shoulders of roads and highways.

Iowa's farmers had come through like champs during the war, producing more and more food every year. After the war, production continued to grow as demand declined, sending prices plummeting. Farm families felt the effects of a depression years before the stock market crash made it evident to the rest of society.

While many farmers struggled to pay taxes to keep their land, at least they didn't go hungry. With large gardens, milk cows and chickens, the typical farm survived. To make ends meet, farm wives would use flour and grain sacks to create clothing. The Agricultural Stabilization Act of 1933, which began the government issues of subsidies to farmers who agreed to limit production, saved many farms.

For Mary and Frank Pisney, who owned a large farmstead off Otis Road south of Little Bohemia, produce was a saving grace. Mary Krejci had come with her parents from Bohemia to Cedar Rapids in 1869 as a two-year-old while Frank arrived in 1882 at the age of nineteen. They married in Cedar Rapids, raised their family and farmed on land Frank bought along the Cedar River bottoms. It was rough land that had to be cleared, often flooded and had been an early hangout for Indians, later replaced by gypsies and hoboes since the railroad ran through it.

Through the 1920s, the Pisney family used horse-drawn wagons to haul cucumbers and melons to market in Cedar Rapids. Their son, Adolph J. Pisney, operated a dairy. And into the 1930s, his daughter, also named Mary, delivered milk to Cedar Rapids stores, including Sebetka Brothers grocery, which employed Frank Drahozal.

Yes, that Frank, the son who was but four years old when our Bohemian immigrant Vaclav Drahozal sent for his family in 1910. Frank, now in his twenties, was up to any task needed at Sebetka Brothers, which, apparently, included following one of the brothers wife's suggestion that he "spark" that milk delivery girl, Mary Pisney. On October 24, 1933, they married and on November 11, 1934, welcomed the first of their five children, son Bob.

In 1936, Frank Drahozal opened his own grocery store a few blocks from the Sixteenth Avenue Southwest business district at Nineteenth Avenue and J Street Southwest and called it "Frank's." With a large butcher-block table in back, it hosted frequent Czech conversations. Frank used an innovative marketing ploy—since he was closed on Sunday, he'd cover his windows with ridiculously low prices Saturday evening and then erase them by Monday morning when customers arrived looking for a deal. It was a good place for young Bob to learn about hard work as he swept the floor, organized empty pop bottles and sorted potatoes.

"The part I didn't like was going to the basement," recalled Bob. "He'd buy them in one-hundred-pound bags, and we had to sort them into five-pound and ten-pound sacks. It wasn't that hard, but I didn't like the rotten potatoes. They were gushy."

Thoughts of a wagon load of potatoes could prompt Hermina Unzeitig Trejtnar to tell her daughters, Marianne and Ellen, about her birth on a farm near Little Bohemia to parents of Czech descent. On July 12, 1899, her father drove a horse-drawn wagon six miles to Cedar Rapids to sell a load of potatoes. At home, her mother fed a work crew when suddenly Hermina decided to enter the world as the youngest of five children.

Hermina's parents lived in a log cabin attached to an old schoolhouse—the log cabin was the kitchen and the schoolhouse the living quarters. She remembered the milk separator and milk cans in a kitchen corner, the steep stepladder to the attic where you could see stars at night through holes in the roof, the rough wooden floor that would give her splinters as she ran across it.

"I could only speak the Czech language when I started to school," Hermina told her daughter Marianne Klinsky during an interview of her recollections written in 1991. "In a short while I dropped Czech altogether and mother and dad couldn't get me back to using it."

She recalled construction of a barn with four horse stalls, telephones installed in 1908, mail delivery to the farm by 1914 and a new house in 1920 with a modern hand water pump in the kitchen. She reminisced about spring planting, the long tedious days of threshing oats in the summer, large family gatherings where her mother fried chickens and baked kolaches and the fall husking of corn in the field.

Czech Geese

Hermina's mother raised a dozen geese each year—a sign of a solid Czech family—for geese had more uses than providing feathers for warmth and meat for holiday feasts.

"They were as good as watchdogs as they honked loudly whenever someone other than one of our family came into the yard," she said. "Mother used their grease for cooking, and as a chest rub when we had a bad cold…We didn't like to have the grease put on our neck and chests but it did help us feel better. We also made pastry brushes out of their wing feathers."

Hermina attended Rose Dale Country School, where her last teacher was Grant Wood, the would-be famous artist, who had recently graduated from high school. Hermina herself would go to Washington High School in Cedar Rapids at age thirteen, graduate and become a teacher, too, at a couple one-room rural schools near her home.

"After World War I, the years in the twenties were good years," Hermina said. "People had work and money. Voting rights for women came about 1920. The first presidential election that I voted in was 1924. Calvin Coolidge was president. Many played the stock market. We never did."

In 1920, Hermina fell in love with Joe Trejtnar, who had emigrated from Bohemia in 1909 at the age of eighteen. Trained as a cabinetmaker, he worked for Hunting and Williams on the west side of the Cedar River, losing three fingers in the process. But he learned English, performed gymnastics with the Sokols and joined the navy during World War I to repaired wood-frame airplanes. At war's end, he put his skills to work at Klepach Construction and later, on his own, built about fifty houses in Cedar Rapids.

That fall of 1920, Hermina's mother took her to the Sokol bazaar in Little Bohemia, where they ran into Joe, the foreman of the crew building their house. After coffee, Joe and Hermina became friends. That Christmas he brought gifts to the family, including an engraved gold wristwatch for her. They married nine months later on September 3, 1921, in a simple ceremony at her parents' house.

Hermina and Joe lived with her parents while he built their house on evenings and weekends along the Lincoln Highway at Thirty-sixth Street Southeast. For entertainment they listened to the radio or attended movies.

"In 1929 the stock market collapsed and until almost 1940 a great depression followed. This meant hard times for people as jobs were lost and no work could be found in the cities. Everywhere there were long lines of people waiting in the soup lines for something to eat. The farmers experienced the worst of the depression. Corn was so cheap they couldn't even sell it, so it was used as fuel for heating. Pork sold for 5 cents a pound. Many farmers lost their farms."

Work in the city had been good to Joe, though, and in 1930 he decided they would visit his parents in Czechoslovakia. They left their daughters with his sister, Emma, boarded a Rock Island train at Union Station, sailed on the *Majestic* ship to France and arrived by train in Kostelec Nad Orlice, where Joe's parents owned a small two-room cottage with an attached lean-to for animals. They saw her relatives at Ceska Trebova and visited Parnik, the birthplace of her father, Frank Unzeitig.

Hermina's father had come to America after his father died, leaving behind a wife and six children. His mother remarried, had three more children and then "pushed" those first six children out of the house. Frank and three sisters—Agnes Tracta, Frances Pospishil and Josephine Nechville—came to Cedar Rapids.

The 1930 vacation to Czechoslovakia lasted three months. Hermina and Joe ate in castles, visited Poland, traveled near the Austrian border, bought a trunkload of souverniers (Czech dolls, handmade lace, garnets, embroidered sheets), toured Prague for a week and in England revisited places Joe had been stationed during the war. In the end, they enjoyed seeing the homeland but were glad to be home.

With new business construction in Cedar Rapids at a virtual standstill in the '30s, only the desire to travel fueled neighborhood development. After all, Henry Ford's Model T, and later his Model A, put Iowans on the road. The national designation of Highway 218 brought them to Little Bohemia, which became a haven for filling stations.

Soon after one station opened at 203 Fourteenth Avenue Southeast in 1936, the Friendly Service Station began operation at Third Street Southeast and Fourteenth Avenue, where cars naturally slowed down to make the turn. It featured several modern auto repair bays. In 1939, Park J. Fulton opened his two-bay station diagonally across the intersection at 310 Fourteenth Avenue.

When Prohibition, "the Great Experiment," was lifted in 1933, former taverns that had become restaurants serving soft drinks reverted to beer and alcohol. New taverns opened in existing empty spaces, too. Numerous taverns soon populated the business corridor of Little Bohemia and the Avenue, including one in Frank Smid's former hardware store after he'd moved into his empty Ideal Theater building. Among those returning to their old ways were the Hach brothers' tavern at Fourteenth Avenue and Second Street Southeast, later known as the South Side Tap, and the Little Bohemia at Fourteenth Avenue and Third Street Southeast, where Louis Pazdernik had opened his saloon in 1907.

Still, beer couldn't solve every problem. Times were tough for the South Side Commercial Club, forced to sell its club building on Second Street Southeast and move into a room at the CSPS Hall. And just down the street, Frank Suchy's jewelry and watch repair business closed in 1937, replaced by a secondhand clothing store.

As the 1930s neared its conclusion, the Great Depression lingered. People wondered if it would ever end, if good jobs would ever come around again, if the future held even a sliver of hope. At least the country wasn't at war.

6

1939

WORLD WAR II

For Czech citizens in Cedar Rapids who paid attention to world events, Adolf Hitler's march into Prague on March 15, 1939, came as no surprise. Still, it was a shock. Czechoslovakia, after centuries of fighting, hoping and praying for independence, had survived as a free nation for a mere twenty years.

On that day, as German troops marched through the Czech capital, the cheers of Germans and German sympathizers were interrupted by hisses and cries of "Pfui, pfui, go back home," shouted by Czech patriots who also proudly sang the Czech national anthem, according to that day's *Cedar Rapids Evening Gazette*. "The entry of Adolf Hitler's battalions," it said, "marked the end of Czech sovereignty in the shattered republic which dissolved Tuesday."

In Cedar Rapids, Jan Masaryk, son of Czechoslovakia's late first president, Thomas G. Masaryk, who died on September 14, 1937, postponed his address to the Czech Alliance from March 19 until March 26. He was to talk about "Democracy and Its Preservation" at the Memorial Coliseum, where a large crowd, including Czechs bussed in from area communities, was expected.

A United Press article said there wasn't even a whisper from officials in France and Great Britain about this latest development. Their leaders acted as if Hitler's occupation of Czechoslovakia was none of their business, as if they had no concerns about future world conflict.

Actually, though, the Munich Pact of the past September had set up Czechoslovakia as a sacrificial lamb. French premier Edouard Daladier and British prime minister Neville Chamberlain signed the pact along with Benito Mussolini, dictator of Italy, and Hitler. They figured that by giving the German Fuhrer the Sudentenland, an area where three million ethnic Germans lived, he would leave the rest of the world alone. After all, he should be happy with 66 percent of Czechoslovakia's coal and 70 percent of its iron, steel and electric power. They did it in the name of peace. Hitler promised that's all he wanted.

Of course, we know better. Slovakia had declared its independence on March 14, playing into Hitler's hand for its eventual takeover. On March 15, Czech president Emil Hacha, his back against the wall, caved in to Hitler's threats of bombing Prague if his troops weren't allowed to march freely through Bohemia and Moravia. Hitler followed his troops that evening and, the next day, sent troops into Slovakia.

The full-fledged outbreak of World War II was only a matter of time. Hitler invaded Poland that September. The war in Europe raged on for more than two years as Americans watched and waited. Then, on December 7, 1941, Japan bombed Pearl Harbor.

"Hold your American flag high so that a pussy-footing, star-gazing, willy-nilly, weak and anemic Europe can look upon democracy unassailably free," urged Jan Masaryk that March 26, 1939, to two thousand people at the Memorial Coliseum in Cedar Rapids. "My people in American can help my country by being good Americans, by helping keep the United States on the democratic pedestal. Don't preach that America must go to war. I have confidence in the leaders of the nation to make their own decision when the time comes."

Masaryk, according to the *Gazette* report, "threw up his arm in disgust with the foreign policies of Britain and France and turned to the United States as the key figure in determining the fate of democracy." He added that it was the United States' role to save democracy for the world and that Czechoslovakia got caught in the middle of a poker game in Europe, supplying the chips for both sides.

Masaryk also mourned the recent death of close family friend Dr. Rose Wistein, a Czech immigrant who became a noted physician in Cedar Rapids from 1914 until her death on February 23, 1937, at age sixty-nine. She met Thomas G. Masaryk while studying in Europe in 1909 after he heard her fiery speech about the importance of personal hygiene to the formation of an intelligent democracy. She later helped free Jan Masaryk's sister, Alice, who had been imprisoned in Austria.

Rose Wistein's life exemplified success from hard work. In 1881, in Chicago, she fulfilled a promise to her dying father to care for her invalid mother, which she did for thirty-eight years, even during stretches where Rose earned only seven dollars a week working in a factory and when she had heart surgery to survive. Still, Rose became a doctor, despite the premature death of her husband, and worked tirelessly on the homefront during World War I. She became a benefactor to hundreds of Czech immigrants through her later generosity.

Before his Cedar Rapids speech, Jan Masaryk dined at Sokol Hall with three hundred members of the Czech Alliance, a group that had formed in 1935 to bring thirty-two cultural, fraternal, religious and civic groups in Cedar Rapids together. In October 1939, it celebrated Czechoslovakia's independence (October 28, 1918) with a special program, "The Downfall and the New Birth of Czechoslovakia," indicating members' optimism that their homeland would be reborn. In 1941, it contributed $2,000 to American Friends of Czechoslovakia, an organization that assisted exiles with finding new homes in other lands.

Local War Effort

The local alliance also worked with the Czech National Alliance, founded during World War I and reorganized at the outbreak of World War II. It disseminated, especially among young people, an affection for the cultural heritage and language of the Czechs and worked for the reestablishment of freedom and independence of Czechoslovakia, according to *The History of Czechs in Cedar Rapids*.

In 1940, the annual Czech Alliance bazaar raised $5,000 for the national organization, its most successful bazaar since 1918. Also in 1940, an offshoot of the alliance, Zlata Kniha ("Gold Book"), organized to assist throughout the war.

Within a year, the local Czech Alliance had more than one thousand members in Iowa. Nationally, it raised and donated $165,000 in 1942 to the former Czech government to help refugees, soldiers and the Red Cross. It disbanded in 1945, its job done, with a concert by the Cedar Rapids Symphony Orchestra.

The Sokols, facing tough times through the 1920s, revived in 1931 when Jan J. Hrbek gave the group some property eighteen miles north of Cedar Rapids. During summers, a two-week program for youth was held at the camp's cottages, dance pavilion and picnic grounds that were open to all

CZECH VILLAGE & NEW BOHEMIA

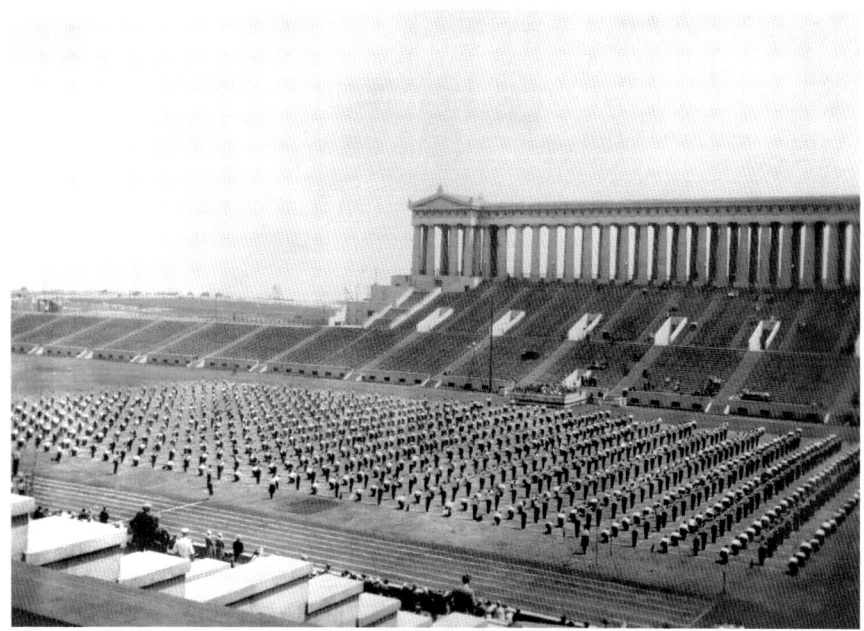

A large contingent of the Cedar Rapids Sokol community group performs a routine at Soldier Field in Chicago on June 28, 1925. *Courtesy of the* Cedar Rapids Gazette.

members the rest of the year. In 1936, Junior Falcons was organized for young men ages twelve to eighteen to develop and foster the ideals of the national group.

Throughout the 1930s, Cedar Rapids was represented at gymnastics Slets all around the Midwest. Women in the group were particularly active, sending representatives to Prague in 1932 when Rose Paidar was selected and in 1938 when several members participated and also placed memorial wreaths at the tombs of Thomas G. Masaryk and Renata Tyrs, the wife of Sokol co-founder Miroslav Tyrs, an advocate for participation by women.

While sympathetic to the activity in the homeland, it wasn't until after Pearl Harbor that eighty members of the Cedar Rapids Sokols organized a first-aid and home-nursing unit. In March 1942, it registered sixty-one Czech men for the Czech Home Guard with World War I veteran Rudolf Novak installed as commander.

The Cedar Rapids Czech Home Guard, reported to be the only such group in the United States, trained for service in the war, first at the CSPS Hall and later at Hayes Elementary School grounds. It sent twenty-five men to the armed forces, the others remaining behind to help with civil defense and to serve as a volunteer unit for the Cedar Rapids Police Department.

A total of 375 Czech men from the local area served in the United States armed forces during the war, with 45 losing their lives, said Frank Mekota, a longtime Cedar Rapids resident and participant in various organizations, during an interview with Mary Helen Armstrong for her thesis, "The Cechs in Cedar Rapids."

To honor seventeen members (sixteen men and one woman) who went off to war, Sokolice Renata Tyrsova, the women's Sokol unit, made a special service flag with seventeen stars, wrote Martha Griffith in *The History of Czechs in Cedar Rapids*.

The Czech Home Guard first appeared in uniform for Memorial Day services in 1942 at the Bohemian National Cemetery in Cedar Rapids. On June 27, it presented colors at the western division Slet at ZCBJ Park six miles south of Cedar Rapids while everyone in attendance recited an oath of allegiance to the United States.

The final event of this two-day Slet featured six little girls holding a Czech flag and a Lidice sign draped in mourning for the recent martyrs of Lidice, Czechoslovakia. According to *The History of Czechs in Cedar Rapids*, "The audience bowed their heads as the Karla Masaryk Chorus, attired in Czech costumes, sang the Czech national anthem."

Less than three weeks earlier, on June 10, 1942, all 173 men over the age of fifteen in the village of Lidice, in the Nazi Protectorate of Bohemia and Moravia, had been executed. The village's 184 women and 88 children were deported to concentration camps. Hitler ordered the village destroyed in retaliation for the earlier assassination of Reinhard Heydrich, a Reich Protector.

The performance at the Slet was particularly moving to Czech people with close ties to the old country, for their assimilation into American society in Cedar Rapids had relegated many of their former activities to memory. Most associations and organizations had switched from using the Czech language to English, the Czech bands of yore no longer played and fewer Czech performances of any kind were given. "Instead," Griffith wrote, "the Czech people find satisfaction in concerts presented by others, in their folksongs sung over the radio, and in the music of their country enjoyed in informal groups."

The Fisher Concertina Orchestra, founded in 1930 by Frank Fisher and his son, Joe, was one music group that hung on until the war started. The father-son duo played barn dances in the 1920s with Joe up front squeezing and pushing the buttons on his large custom-made concertina, attracting attention wherever he went. The orchestra, which played polkas, waltzes, two-step and modern music, even appeared at the 1933 Century of Progress World's Fair in Chicago and one year, traveling by bus, performed every single night (364 in all) with only Christmas Eve off. But as you might expect, an orchestra this popular also recorded music on the Victor and Decca labels and gave live shows on several radio stations.

On the Radio

The first area Czech radio program, featuring the instrumental music of Ben Jansa and his band, was broadcast in 1932 on WMT radio in Cedar Rapids. The program continued for six years with a variety of Czech musicians, semi-weekly concerts by George Cervenka's orchestra, vocal numbers by Alice Spevacek and stories by Jaroslava Holubova. In 1940, Sunday morning broadcasts were sponsored by the Czech Alliance. They featured a vocal quartet—Helen Sykora, Helen Melsha, Mildred Mahring and Henrietta Kubic—the Czech school chorus and recorded music. Announcements and some advertisements were given in Czech.

In the 1942 *The History of Czechs in Cedar Rapids*, author Griffith lamented other changes, too. "Certain customs and traditions brought by the Czech people from the 'old country' are disappearing; others have become a part of the cultural pattern of the community," she wrote.

> *The dracky or feather-stripping party, the Sibrinky and beseda dances, and the ZCBJ pout (modeled after an old-world pilgrimage to cities with cathedrals accompanied by puppet shows and eating heart-shaped cookies) are still a part of the social life of the Czech people. The dracky is now, however, enjoyed only by older women; the Sibrinky fails to serve its original purpose because few of the dancers now wear masks; the beseda dance has been revived as a novelty; and the pout is now chiefly a children's party. The Karla Masaryk Chorus attracts attention by donning Czech costumes.*
>
> *A phase of the national life of the Czech people, however, which has always been evident in Cedar Rapids, is their food. Kolaches and other Czech pastries are sold in all the bakeries and food shops of the city. People who attend bazaars are either served jitrnice or the favorite meal of the Czech people which consists of roast goose, dumplings, sauerkraut, and kolaches.*

Griffith praised the Czech people for their skill and industry, their contributions to the civic development of Cedar Rapids and the stability they had given to the community with their conscientious ownership of property and the formation of insurance organizations. She said they voluntarily became American citizens, often teaching one another the principles of the U.S. Constitution and the customs of other nationalities in Cedar Rapids.

While it would be difficult to select outstanding Czechs in the city, Griffith pointed to three men who received the rare Bily Lef (the White Lion) insignia from Czechoslovakia presented to Czech Americans who performed distinguished civic service: Frank Filip, the Linn County chairman for Liberty Loan drives and a principal for the Czech Alliance; W.F. Severa, a major financial supporter of the Czech school and the Council for Higher Education; and Charles B. Svoboda, an insurance agent and a strong proponent of music and the arts who served as secretary of the Czech National Alliance during World War I.

As important as anything, Griffith said, were the upbringings these people had in their native land or the solid, upstanding, good-neighbor, hardworking lessons they acquired in their new country that included the Czech maxim "Bez prace nejsou kolace," which, translated literally, means "Without work there are no kolaches."

As an example, Louis Zika served as Cedar Rapids Commissioner of Public Improvements from 1910 to 1926 and from 1928 until his death on April 13, 1934. He followed in the footsteps of Frank Witousek, the first Czech alderman elected to the city council in 1877, and Frank Kouba, the second one, first elected in 1883. In all, a dozen Czech people had served on the city council. Others who worked for the city with long tenures included Vaclav Vane, auditor for thirty-two years; Anton Tlusty, health officer for twenty-six years and assistant health officer for twelve years; Vaclav Janda, sidewalk inspector for fourteen years and streets commission for sixteen years; and Frank Barta, sewer inspector for forty-three years. William Stepanek, one-time mayor, and Ernest Kosek were among those who would serve in the Iowa legislature.

During World War II, the ZCBJ, then known as the Western Bohemian Fraternal Association, contributed mightily to the war effort with a pair of successful fund drives to buy equipment for Allied fighting forces. Members also mailed special Christmas care packages overseas to servicemen and women that included playing cards, a pocket knife, hard candy, razors and soap.

The ZCBJ Drill Team, organized in 1931, worked with the Red Cross during the war, serving meals to servicemen and women as they passed through Cedar Rapids on trains at Union Station. It financed the effort by holding bingo and card parties, rummage sales and accepting donations. When rationing came about, some team members even dug into their own personal meat rations to feed the soldiers. The drill team had gone by train to Chicago in 1939 to participate in a tableau titled *Zvitezime* (meaning "We will win over") at the outset of the Nazi occupation of Czechoslovakia.

In June 1942, the Western Bohemian Fraternal Association announced that it had achieved a 10 percent payroll deduction bond drive for firms with ten to twenty-five employees, jump-starting its campaign to raise enough money to buy ten ambulances for war service. This announcement meant that six ambulances could be purchased immediately. At the time, the organization had two thousand members in Cedar Rapids and forty-five thousand nationwide.

By September 1943, the ambulance fund had grown to $18,700, allowing the association to purchase a dozen ambulances. Each ambulance had a special plate: "Donated to the U.S. army by the Western Bohemian Fraternal Association, headquarters, Cedar Rapids, Iowa." One ambulance was displayed in the city to inspire donations. It was presented to the army in a special ceremony on September 12.

Simultaneously, the Western Bohemian Fraternal Association announced plans to raise funds to buy a bomber from Iowa. It succeeded, using $195,000 to purchase a B-25 Mitchell bomber emblazed with the words "Spirit of Iowa Czechs." Nebraska members purchased a second bomber.

Cedar Rapids and Linn County had separate campaigns to raise money for a dozen bombers with an overall goal to collect $3.6 million. Also by early 1943, the Western Bohemian Fraternal Association had purchased more than $1 million in war bonds and added to that throughout the war. Dozens, if not hundreds, of other Cedar Rapids businesses had employees contribute to the 10 percent payroll deduction plan, one of the largest being Iowa Manufacturing with more than five hundred employees.

Also some Czech men belonged to various service clubs—the Kiwanis, Rotary and Lions—which raised $25,000 to help destitute Czechoslovakian widows and orphans.

By now, much of the Little Bohemia and Sixteenth Avenue news appeared in a regular *Gazette* column, "South Side News."

Female seamstresses, known as the Vcelky during World War I, picked up their needles and thread and yarn again. This group of 135 women made surgical dressings, sweaters, socks, mittens and pillow slipcovers for the Czech and American Red Cross. Monetary contributions, raised

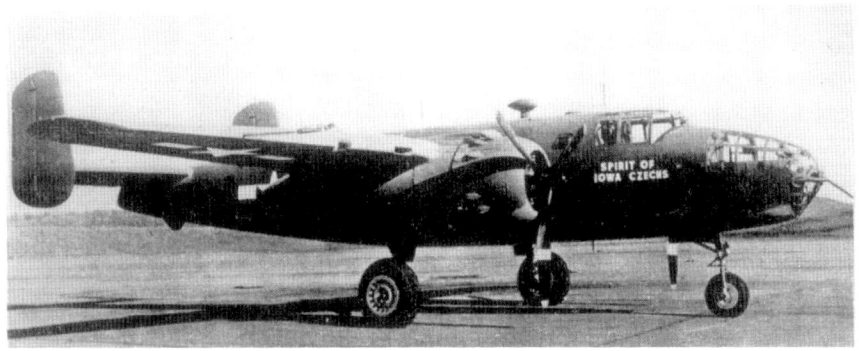

The Western Bohemian Fraternal Association of Cedar Rapids raised $195,000 in Iowa in 1943 to buy this B-25 Mitchell bomber. A second bomber was purchased by Nebraska members. The words on the bomber say "Spirit of Iowa Czechs." *Courtesy of the* Cedar Rapids Gazette.

voluntarily rather than by solicitation, came from the ZCBJ, the CSPS, the Sokols, the Bohemian National Alliance and the churches. As an example, the Jan Hus Memorial Presbyterian Church donated food, clothing and $2,450 to the national Presbyterian Church's war restoration fund sent to Bohemia and Moravia.

The Karla Masaryk Chorus, formed in 1937 by Cedar Rapids–area Czech housewives and named in honor of Thomas Masaryk's wife, became a staple of bond drives while performing in native costumes. Even though many of the women had to learn to read music and correctly pronounce Czech words, the chorus appeared with national stars at the Iowa Theater and made recordings broadcast in Europe by Voice of America.

In Europe, on August 29, 1944, the Czechoslovak underground emerged from hiding in an attempt to seize Slovakian soil in what became known as the Slovak Uprising. This happened to coincide with the final days of the liberation of Paris from the Nazis. While underground resistance to Germany helped in Paris, the Slovak uprising was premature. The Slovaks had anticipated assistance from the Soviet Union, but it never came and Hitler's troops quashed the uprising that October.

Still, Slovak troops continued fighting through the end of the war. Their efforts strengthened the Slovak national consciousness against the inhumane ways of Hitler and the Third Reich. Their gallant efforts gave hope to Czechs and Slovaks everywhere that, one day, Czechoslovakia would live again.

7
1960s

THE MALL, ANOTHER FLOOD AND OTHER THINGS

Postwar Cedar Rapids became a boomtown for baby boomers. Returning GIs needed jobs and housing. New brides needed places to spend their money and educate their children. The kids would need recreational opportunities and even more homes, stores and schools.

Developers more than happily obliged. New housing sprouted up seemingly overnight with several major residential developments–Cherry Hills in the far northwest quadrant, Lincolnway Village in the far southwest, Vernon Village in the southeast and, into the 1960s, Bowman Woods in the northeast quadrant.

That meant new shopping centers—not the grocery store, neighborhood service station and coin-operated laundry, but real shopping centers that permanently changed the retail landscape. First, in 1956, Town and Country Shopping Center opened with an underground bowling alley in the 3600 block of First Avenue Southeast as Iowa's first suburban shopping center. Four years later and a little farther north, Lindale Plaza welcomed shoppers to its thirty stores and five thousand free parking spaces. Its highly publicized grand opening on September 15, 1960, caused consternation for not only retailers in downtown Cedar Rapids but also those in Czech Village, the city's second-largest retail area at war's end.

With the surrenders of Italy, Germany and then Japan in 1945, life on the city's South Side would never be the same.

For one reason, a lot of lives had been lost. Soon after the war, the Federation of Czech Groups established a Soldiers' Field at the Czech

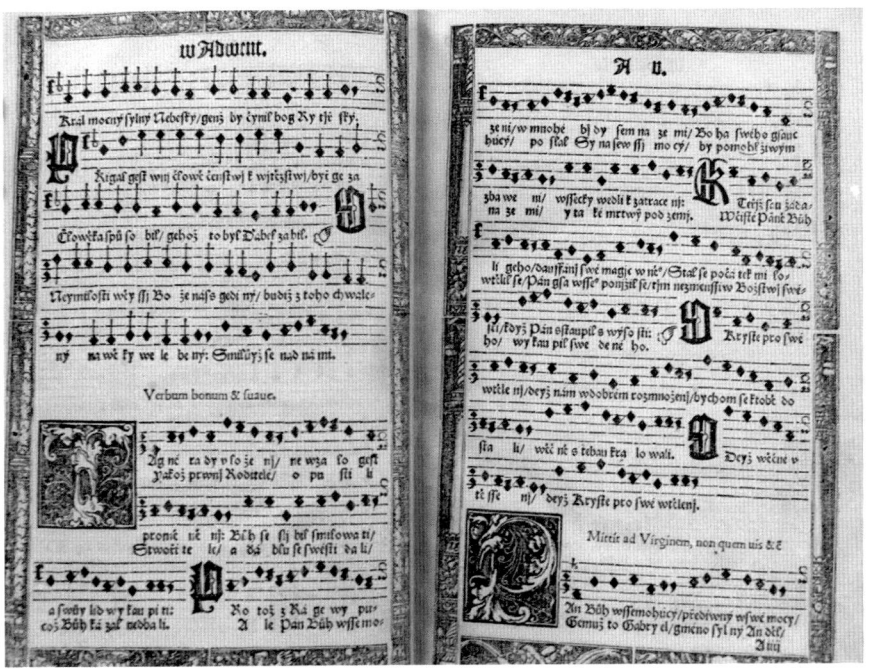

A Czech hymnal from 1561 was donated to the National Czech & Slovak Museum & Library by Robert and Marge Stone of Marion. *Courtesy of the* Cedar Rapids Gazette.

National Cemetery where a monument, a tall gray column of granite, rests on a base inscribed with the names of fallen soldiers with Czech ancestry. A parade, with a marching band and songs by the Karla Masaryk Chorus, commemorated each Czech Memorial Day on the first Sunday in June.

For another reason, Czechoslovakia no longer existed as a democracy. President Eduard Benes hoped the Soviet Union would allow the country to choose its own government, that it could again become a bridge between eastern and western Europe. Alas, that wasn't to be. In 1948, the Czechoslovak Republic became a communist state.

Once again, foreigners ruled a Czech homeland that had made significant contributions to world civilization—the first hymn book in a native tongue was in Czech, and the Bible was translated into Czech before it was translated into English, wrote Helen Armstrong in her 1950 thesis.

In 1948, a contingent of Sokol competitors from Cedar Rapids won prizes at the All-Sokol Slets in Prague, but communist rule meant no more competition.

By decade's end, the immigration of Czech people to Cedar Rapids dried up. Even though A.L. Killian, head of the large central-district department

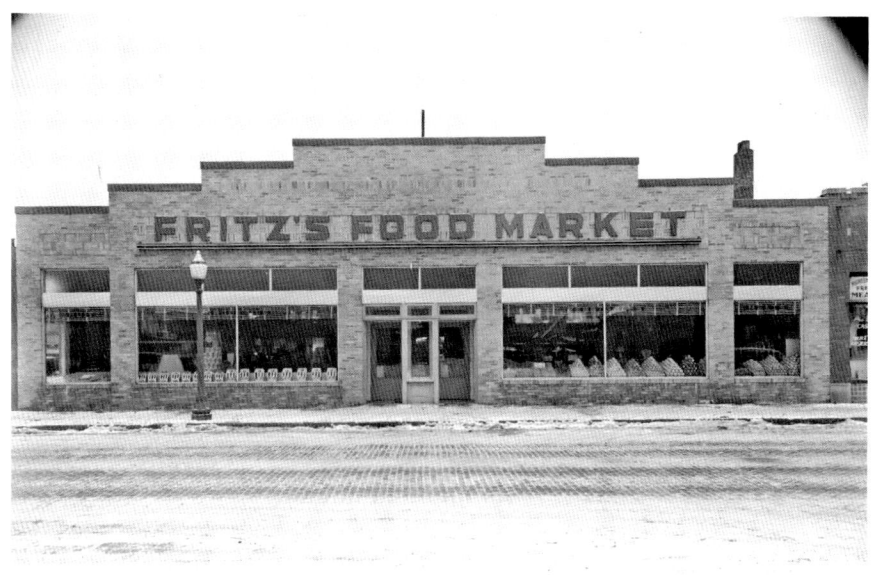

Fritz's Food Market opened in 1938 in Czech Village. It later became a Me Too grocery store and is the Lion Bridge Brewing Company today. *Courtesy of the National Czech & Slovak Museum & Library.*

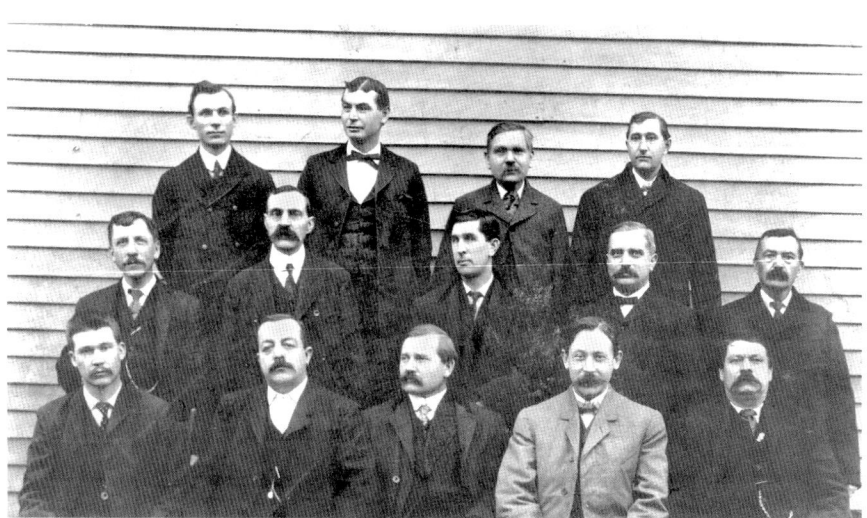

The Industrial Club of 16th Avenue West in the early 1900s. *Courtesy of the National Czech & Slovak Museum & Library.*

store bearing his name, tried to bring Czechs to Cedar Rapids by promising them work and homes, only about thirty-five new Czech citizens moved to town in the 1940s.

The South Side survived, but the war had slowed development. Sure, the seven-thousand-square-foot Fritz's Food Market building opened in 1938 on Sixteenth Avenue Southwest and the Sirowy & Novak Service Station opened at the end of the war at 1318 Third Street Southeast across from the Little Bohemia tavern. But mostly, it was business as usual.

The Sixteenth Avenue Commercial Club, incorporated in 1939, grew out of the Industrial Club of 16th Avenue West. "The purposes of the new corporation are to be of educational, civic, business and social character, that is, the promotion of education, civic, business and social welfare of the members and the advancement of the community in which it is located," wrote Chuck Jungman, former vice-president, in his 2005 recollections of the business district in the 1930s and 1940s.

He recalled businesses that were or had been along the Avenue, from Vic Holets Potato Chip factory to Muzik Cigar Manufacturer, the Big Barn Livery Stable and Barta Saddle & Leather. There were several taverns and barbershops, a pharmacy, at least two groceries and an egg buying station. Other stores sold hardware, shoes, motorcycles, boat motors, dry goods, radios and processed meat. One place reportedly fronted bootlegging during Prohibition while another housed prostitutes. That was simply the way of the world in those days when law enforcement might look the other way from backroom slot machines, illegal card games and pull tabs and bootlegged hooch. Horse-head iron hitching posts lined the Avenue.

The club met monthly in a rented second-floor office until dues (about five dollars per year) didn't cover expenses, and it had to meet wherever it could for free. About that time, Jungman recalled, differences of opinions led to friction between members and a reduction in membership. Still, the group sponsored Boy Scouts, held events and played cards after meetings. At one time, he wrote, it had "a cracker-jack" pinochle team that competed around eastern Iowa.

In the '40s, Cedar Rapids' population increased by 10,000 people, but that was nothing. It would increase by 20,000 in the '50s and by another 18,500 in the '60s to become a metropolitan area of 110,642 people by 1970.

With Cedar Rapids businesses hopping, young guys like Bob Drahozal had no problem finding odd jobs. The grandson of immigrant Vaclav Drahozal could no longer work for his father since Frank had closed the grocery store in 1947 and become a traveling salesman for Polehna's Meats. So after he

Czech Village & New Bohemia

graduated from St. Wenceslaus High School in 1952 while attending Loras College in Dubuque, Bob spent summers working in Cedar Rapids. In 1953, he operated a tractor to load ice into railroad cars at the packinghouse, then known as Wilson Foods, and watched burly high school football players load sides of beef. The next two summers, he ran an overhead crane at Iowa Steel and Iron Works, moving steel into the welding shop.

The Roundhouse

Bob loved to wander the neighborhood, especially on the other side of the river, where he'd visit the farmers' market that began in the 1920s. By 1962, it was held in a new iron-framed structure known as the Roundhouse, just north of the Avenue.

"I'd go over there and buy gladiolus," Bob said. "We loved the Roundhouse. I think a lot of people were sad to see it go [after the flood in 2008]."

In 1956, Cedar Rapids commemorated its centennial with a four-day celebration sponsored by thirty Czech lodges, clubs, churches and other

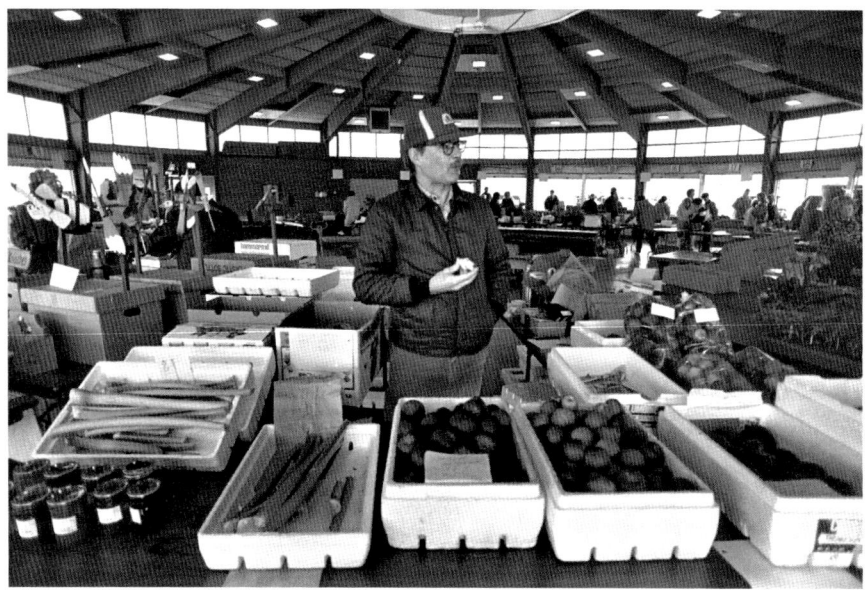

Merle Williams of Williams Orchards in Cedar Rapids samples some of his own goods on sale on May 5, 1990, during the opening of the City Market at the Riverside Roundhouse. *Courtesy of the* Cedar Rapids Gazette.

HISTORY IN THE HEARTLAND

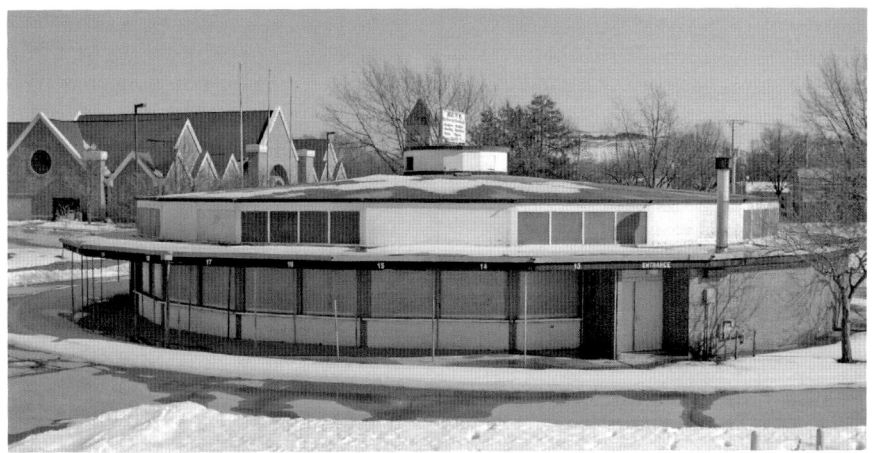

The Roundhouse in Czech Village as it looked in 2010, when plans called for it be renovated into a year-round building. It has since been torn down, although a group of people is working to resurrect it. *Courtesy of the* Cedar Rapids Gazette.

Czech organizations. A Saturday parade began in downtown Cedar Rapids and wound its way past Riverside Park for the dedication of a commemorative centennial plaque and a flag raising. "The Star Spangled Banner" was performed by the Lyra Singing Society of Chicago before the parade, which was broadcast live on KCRG-TV and proceeded up the Avenue and across the bridge through Little Bohemia.

The commemorative plaque, attached to a boulder placed in the park fifty years earlier by Czech American groups, read: "On this 16th day of June, 1956, the delegates representing 30 Czech-American societies gathered here in gratitude to commemorate the Centennial of the city of Cedar Rapids and pay homage to the citizens of Czech descent who had a great share in the building of this city. In their honor, an American flag was raised and this plaque attached to this memorial."

The celebration included a street fair, gymnastics and athletic demonstrations by the Sokols from Chicago, St. Louis and Omaha; Czech music concerts by the Cedar Rapids Symphony Orchestra and the Cedar Rapids Municipal Band; dancing at both the CSPS and ZCBJ halls; and a Sunday Mass at St. Wenceslaus Catholic Church. There was also a special stamp cancelation mark by the post office.

"Starting from the empty prairies, today Cedar Rapids is one of the greatest cities on the face of this earth," said Iowa senator Bourke B. Hickenlooper at the closing ceremonies. "Much of the credit for that greatness is due to the Czech population."

Among longtime Czechs was Vaclav Jakoubek, seventy-one, who retired that week after fifty-five years as a baker. He closed his South-Side Bakery at 1110 Third Street Southeast, where he'd been known citywide for kneading dough by hand and baking his rollicki, babouvka and kolaches in the only brick oven still operating in Cedar Rapids. Jakoubek had come to Iowa from Czechoslovakia as a lad of fifteen. He worked for other bakers until he opened a couple of bakeries on his own. In 1914, he settled into the South-Side Bakery, which included family living quarters.

Since 1929, Jakoubek's shop and his neighbors in Little Bohemia had been safe from disaster, but then the spring of 1961 arrived. The permanent levee system in Cedar Rapids, constructed after the 1929 flood, could reportedly withstand nineteen-foot crests. But with water levels predicted to reach twenty-one feet, city officials declared a flood emergency on March 30. Hundreds of volunteers, including children younger than ten out on Easter break, built a temporary levee in north Cedar Rapids. Residents near the river were advised to move belongings up onto tables or, if possible, up to the second floor or attic. They should prepare to evacuate.

That afternoon, officials closed the bridges across the Cedar River to all but emergency personnel. But those emergency vehicles couldn't get through when regular traffic created a bottleneck at every bridge—B Avenue East/F Avenue West, First Avenue, Second Avenue, Third Avenue, Fourth Avenue, Eighth Avenue and Fourteenth Avenue/Sixteenth Avenue from Little Bohemia to the west side.

While the temporary dikes—including one made of snow fence, sandbags and a coating of clay south of the packinghouse—held, water pooled a foot to eighteen inches deep along Twelfth Avenue Southeast and Third Street Southeast from the ZCBJ Hall to the Little Bohemia tavern. Most of the water came up through sewer system catch basins even though they were surrounded by sandbags.

"Everything is saturated," warned public improvements commissioner Woody Stolba. "If anything breaks now and we don't get it quick we're in trouble."

As the old CRANDIC railroad bridge struggled to stay intact, Stolba said he wouldn't hesitate to blow it up if water rose high enough to turn it into a dam.

Flood of 1961 Peaks

The flood of 1961 peaked at 19.66 feet after noon on Friday, March 31, just short of the 1929 record. The river level held steady for twelve hours before it began dropping rapidly. Water had barely slopped over the permanent dikes.

The Red Cross, which set up temporary shelters, estimated that 4,800 people evacuated 1,200 homes, many of them in the neighborhood surrounding the Sixteenth Avenue business district and an area farther south known as Stumptown. Iowa Electric had cut power to these areas because of the flood threat but promised to restore electricity as the floodwaters receded.

By early April, work began on a permanent levee on the east side of the river from the Sixteenth Avenue Bridge upriver to better protect Little Bohemia from future floods. The army corps of engineers studied aerial photos to see what could be done to prevent similar flooding. At city hall, officials evaluated flood response and future needs. And citizens who had taken sandbags home for use in their children's sandboxes were advised to sterilize the flood-contaminated sand with a solution of a half-cup of bleach to two gallons of water.

That Christmas, 1961, Santa Claus arrived at Lindale Plaza via helicopter. It was just another indication that the Czech business districts needed to come up with innovative ways to stay afloat.

In the next decade, the Sixteenth Avenue Commercial Club approached the City of Cedar Rapids and the chamber of commerce for assistance, financially and for publicity. While some Czech businessmen were willing to invest in a group effort, others were reluctant. Jungman said they could not come up with a consensus "master plan."

In 1972, though, a small group of merchants willing to invest in the future of "Czech Town" began working with the city council. On October 15, 1975, the city officially designated the Sixteenth Avenue Southwest business district "Czech Village."

Early developments included approval from the city in 1976 to close B Avenue Southwest and to use an existing home as a Czech museum. That was followed in 1977 with construction of a bandstand for musicians to play Czech music during village celebrations. Other plans would take shape by the 1980s.

In the meantime, the city of Cedar Rapids reinvented itself. Urban renewal in the main business district saw old, dilapidated buildings torn down for wide-open green space along the river or the construction of new buildings. The city had long abandoned any tie-in with the Parlor City theme and adopted a new slogan—"the City of Five Seasons"—where the "fifth season" was the time to enjoy the other four.

In early 1979, the city opened its $7 million, 8,500-seat Five Seasons Center indoor entertainment venue with an eight-hundred-car parking ramp and the privately owned 284-room Stouffer's Five Seasons Hotel rising sixteen stories above the arena.

In June, the city and the Iowa Department of Transportation opened the Five-in-One Bridge. It replaced the old F Avenue/B Avenue Bridge and dam, adding the divided lanes of I-380 on an elevated level to extend that interstate from I-80 near Iowa City into downtown Cedar Rapids.

And in October, Westdale Mall opened on the city's far southwest side with about 90 of its 121 stores ready for business. The two-level $50 million enclosed mall altered the retail landscape once again, for it prompted Lindale Plaza to enclose its courtyard to become Lindale Mall.

In Czech Village, the Christmas season took on its traditional flavor. Lights blazed in storefront windows as shoppers wrapped up in heavy coats found their way along the open sidewalks whether it snowed or not. Svaty Mikulas, the Czech Saint Nick, made his rounds accompanied by an angel and a devil, asking children if they had behaved all year. To those who had, he gave candy, nuts and fruit; to those who hadn't, he gave a raw potato.

8
1980s

THE PACKINGHOUSE PACKS IT IN

The good times rolled in Czech Village in the 1980s despite double-digit inflation, a farm crisis in Iowa and trouble for the Bohemian neighborhood's largest employers.

In early 1977, Penick & Ford—the former Douglas Starch Works that quickly rebuilt after the explosion of 1919—"mothballed" its corn syrup operation due to rapidly falling prices. A changing market with fructose produced by other companies as a substitute for more expensive sugar as a sweetener had a lot to do with it.

The "line" closure idled 600 of the plant's 750 workers. The plant had closed before—in 1947, a strike of 600 AFL workers and 950 CIO workers halted production at both Penick & Ford and Quaker Oats. But in 1977, laid-off workers wondered if it would ever become a large production facility again. In fact, the main office building was sold to Linn County government in 1979 for its administrative offices.

In 1979, Iowa Manufacturing, the old Carmody Foundry, began the process of closing for good. Despite boom times after the war—it had moved some production to the J.G. Cherry Building after that company relocated to new facilities in southwest Cedar Rapids—orders were off. Steel manufacturing ceased in 1979, steel fabrication stopped in 1982 and foundry activity halted by 1996.

Into the 1980s, Wilson Foods, successor to T.M. Sinclair & Company, faced its own adversities, not the least of which was a long and contentious worker strike in 1983.

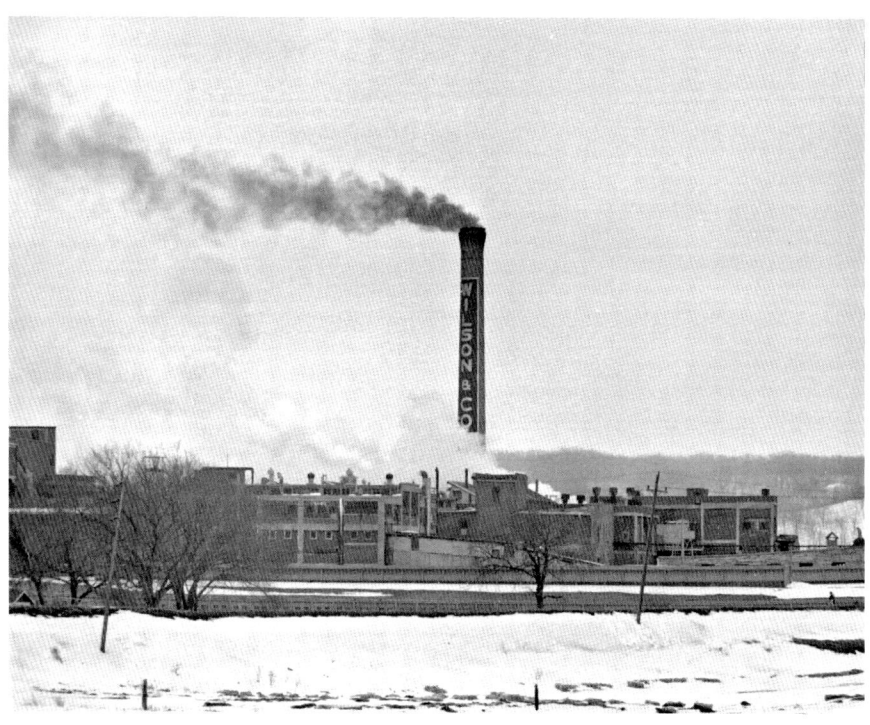

Smoke pours from a smokestack at Wilson Foods, formerly Sinclair Packing, in 1981. *Courtesy of the* Cedar Rapids Gazette.

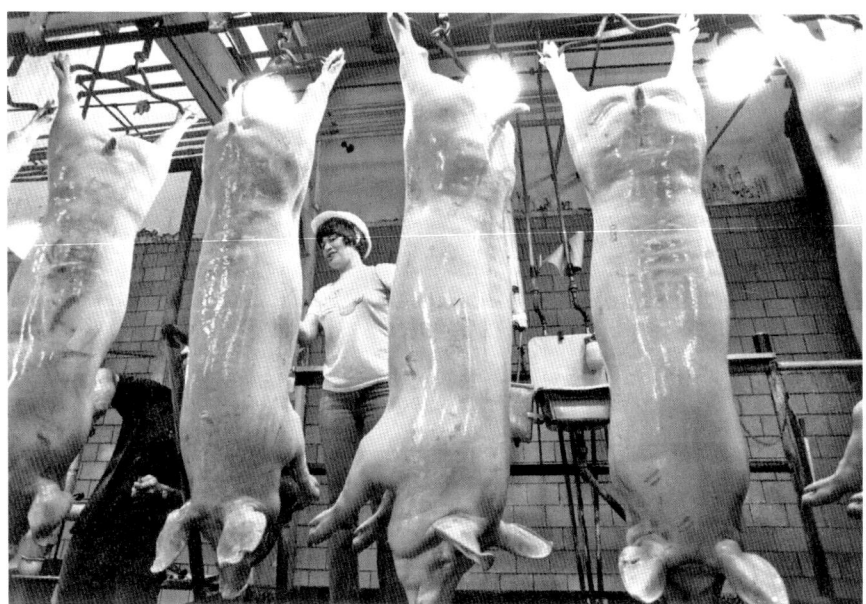

Also on the east side of the river, the CSPS hall was sold into private hands in 1976, following the ZCBJ Hall that had been sold more than a decade earlier when the Western Fraternal Life Association moved in 1959 to new quarters along First Avenue Northeast in Cedar Rapids.

In addition, the $2 million elevated and four-lane wide Twelfth Avenue Bridge opened in December 1974. That took traffic off the Sixteenth Avenue Bridge by offering a faster way to cross the Cedar River in the neighborhood. Highway 218 had long been rerouted to avoid the stop-and-go required to negotiate stoplights and bridges on the South Side.

Organizations Key Development

Despite all this—and the death of many other Czech traditions and organizations—a resurgence had begun in the 1970s with the formation of three new organizations.

The Czech Village Association, made up of business owners and associates, formed in 1972, its goal to revitalize the Sixteenth Avenue business district with renovated storefronts, added parking and a small park with a bandstand.

The Czech Heritage Foundation (1973) promoted interest in Czech ancestry, heritage and culture by raising money, publishing the newsletter *Nase Deske Dedictvi* three times a year and acting as a liaison between the Czech Village Association and the Czech Fine Arts Foundation.

The Czech Fine Arts Foundation (1974) set as its goal the establishment of a Czech museum and library. It arranged concerts by Czech artists, dance groups and orchestras.

Even though doubt surfaced, these groups would realize the fruits of their labors with a resurgence in tourist traffic by the 1980s.

"While there is evidence of new interest in Czech culture, skeptics see it not as a renaissance but a temporary affinity for the old," wrote longtime *Gazette* reporter Dale Kueter in a December 21, 1975 story, "Cedar Rapids Rich in Czech Heritage." "However strong and genuine the renewed interest, many regard it as a last-chance spurt to be capitalized upon."

Opposite, bottom: Hogs are prepared for the butcher line in October 1981 at Wilson Foods in Cedar Rapids. *Courtesy of the* Cedar Rapids Gazette.

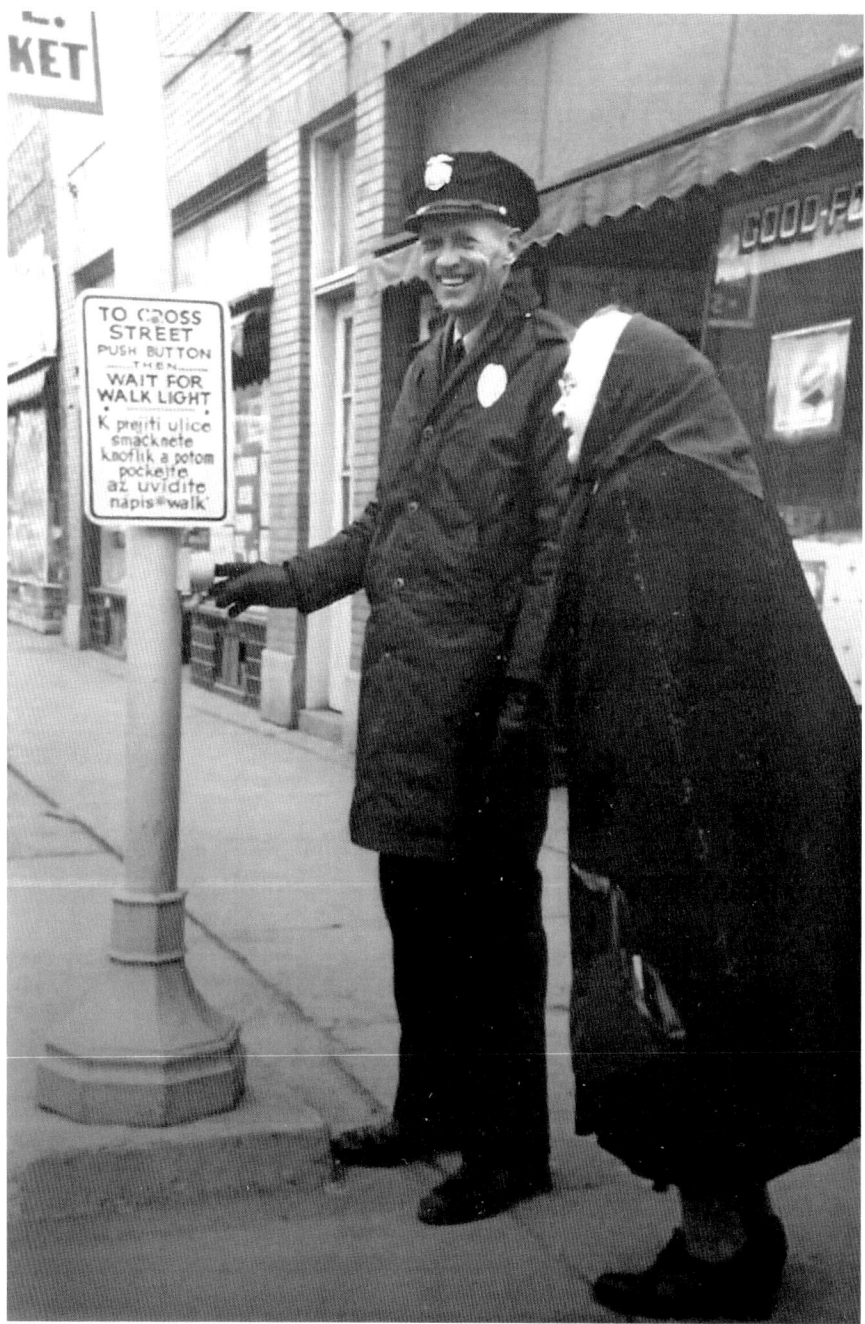

A police officer shows a pedestrian the crosswalk sign in Czech Village printed in both English and Czech. *Courtesy of the National Czech & Slovak Museum & Library.*

To emphasize his point, Kueter, a student of Czech heritage, added, "It is not uncommon for visitors to stand on Sixteenth Avenue Southwest and ask directions to Bohemie Town. You can purchase kolaches and rye bread, fresh jaternice and fine meats on the avenue. But the predominant business on the avenue today is the tavern, and 25 percent of the commerce is operated by non-Czechs."

While T.B. Hlubucek, referred to as "Mr. Czechoslovakia of Cedar Rapids," agreed with Kueter that interest in Czech culture began to wane in the 1940s, he had seen a shift in attitude. "I see a couple hundred Czechs going to Europe every year," Hlubucek said. "There is more interest in the homeland than in the '50s and '60s."

In part, they both attributed that to the United States celebration of its bicentennial heritage in 1976. But there was also concrete evidence. The Czech School, now a five-week summer session at Hayes Elementary School, had grown from 15 students a few years earlier to 70 students, 30 of whom were not Czech at all. The Sokols experienced a resurgence, too, with some classes full as membership mushroomed to 160 men and more than 200 women.

"So, where do Czechs go now?" Kueter asked.

That's not a straight line to a Bohemie joke, but a question about the future of the heritage of Cedar Rapids' major ethnic entity.

They don't sing the Prune Song anymore as they once did at Wilson high. The folk songs presented in person by old country troupes now are heard on special radio programs or infrequent trips to Chicago.

Ochotnicke Druzstvo and the ZCBJ Dramatic club act no more. The Six Bohemian Nights festival is a thing of the past.

Still, here are the Czech church bazaars, and last year there was an attempt at bringing back the St. Joseph day celebration in March to counter the Irish uprising on St. Patrick's Day.

In addition to the kolaches, the Czechs (and others) still feast on Knedlicky and Jeli, or, to translate for Germans, dumplings and sauerkraut. Christmas time heightens competition among Czech women in baking a variety of Vdolky (pastries).

Some Czech Christmas trees are still decorated with cellophane-wrapped cookies, tarts and candies, and Czech youngsters will dream of Mikulas coming down the chimney.

In conclusion, Kueter wrote, "Perhaps Czech Village will rise out of Sixteenth Avenue and be a perpetuating force of Czech heritage."

Czech Village & New Bohemia

Czech Village Establishes Itself

As Czech Village received its official designation in 1975, the Czech Heritage Foundation held public meetings in the Roundhouse to discuss improvements to the business district. As talks continued, a variety of ideas emerged. Close off Sixteenth Avenue to create a mall—after all, businesses in downtown Cedar Rapids were considering the construction of an enclosed mall on Second Street Southeast between Second and Fourth Avenues. (It never materialized.) Maybe don't close the avenue to vehicles, but make it more pedestrian friendly with a new streetscape. Upgrade storefronts to give them some Old World charm. Hold more festivals to bring tourists into the neighborhood. Hey, why not dream big, some people thought. If this Czech Village thing works, we could extend the concept across the Sixteenth Avenue Bridge into Little Bohemia.

The Czech Village Festival, kicked off in 1974, became an all-day event attended by hundreds of people in its third year. The September celebration featured demonstrations of chair caning, sand scaping, batik egg decorating and wood carving. Sokol tumblers, square dancers, Moravian dancers in

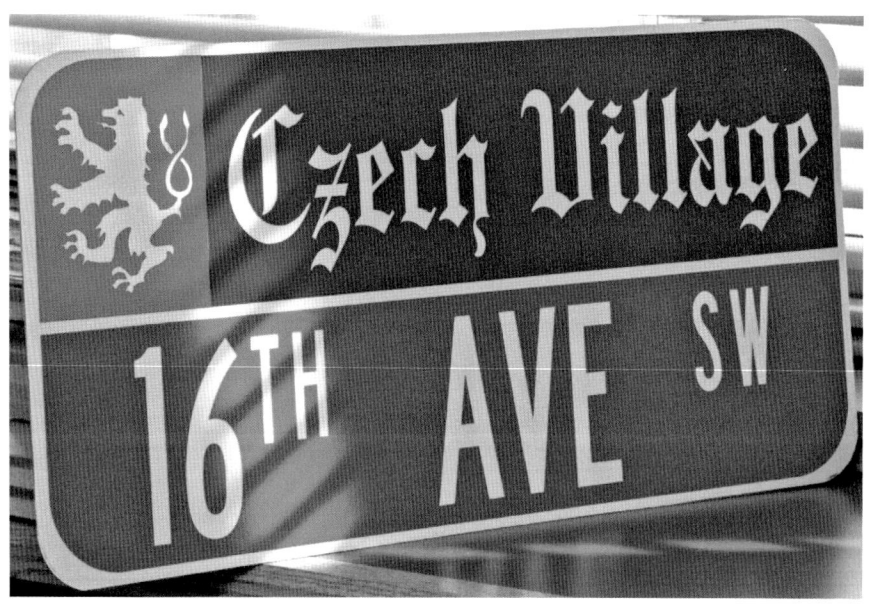

New "Czech Village" signs installed in 2002 marked eleven intersections, including those along Sixteenth Avenue Southwest, which is the Czech Village business district. *Courtesy of the Cedar Rapids Gazette.*

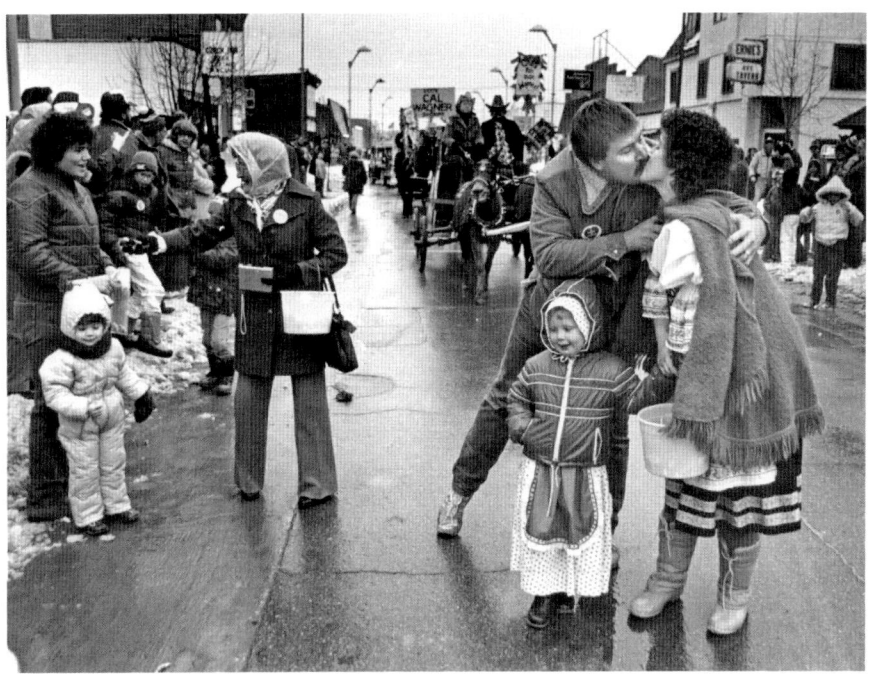

Patty Konecny (right) of Cedar Rapids gets a kiss from a parade watcher who spotted her button—"Kiss me, I'm Czech"—during the March 19, 1984 St. Joseph's Day parade through Czech Village. *Courtesy of the* Cedar Rapids Gazette.

authentic costumes and polka bands performed. By 1984, the festival included a kolach-eating contest, a carp-fishing contest and a small museum that boasted of having the largest collection of Czech costumes in the United States.

The St. Joseph's Day celebration Kueter alluded to was marching along nicely by 1978 with support from the likes of Joens Brothers Interiors, Sykora Bakery, Coast to Coast Stores, Konecny's Restaurant, Pohlena's Market, Czech Closet, Sixteenth Avenue Meat & Market, Ernie's Avenue Tavern, Olde Towne Inn, Czech Cottage, Boddicker School of Music, Bartunek's Maytag, Avenue Floral, United State Bank and Novak Heating and Air Conditioning, all on the Avenue.

St. Joseph's Day—March 19 for the past dozen centuries—celebrates Joseph, the husband of the Blessed Virgin Mary, and has been associated with the wearing of red, as opposed to the green the Irish wear two days earlier when they honor St. Patrick. In Cedar Rapids, both days feature parades to this day—the St. Patrick's parade proceeds through the central business district and the St. Joseph's Day parade goes down Sixteenth Avenue, although in 2015

Czech Village & New Bohemia

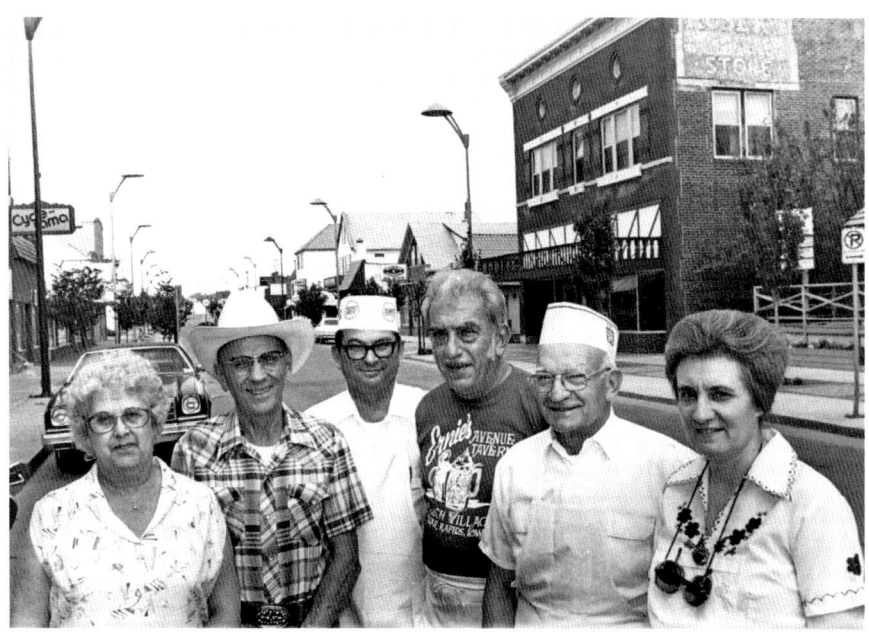

Ethnic pride helped revive the Czech Village shopping district along Sixteenth Avenue Southwest in 1982. Pictured that August are, *from left to right*, Bernadine Bartunek, George Barta, Lumir Vondracek, Ernie Hlas, Lester Sykora and Anna Kenjar of the Czech Village Association in Cedar Rapids. *Courtesy of the* Cedar Rapids Gazette.

it began on Third Street Southeast through what is now called "New Bo" and crossed the Sixteenth Avenue Bridge through Czech Village.

But in 1980, the emphasis on Czech culture in Cedar Rapids remained on the west side of the river. The Czech Village Association and other groups successfully convinced the city council to approve a new streetscape. Business owners agreed to an assessment of more than $150,000 and to spend $700,000 to renovate buildings or construct new ones.

By the fall of 1981, the Czech Village Heritage Mall opened on Sixteenth Avenue Southwest between A Street and C Street with wide sidewalks, curbs and gutters, tree planters, brick pavers and an island in the middle of the street with a place for a clock. The clock arrived soon thereafter—a pair of gifts totaling $17,000 by the time the streetscape was dedicated paid for installation of a thirteen-foot-tall clock with thirty-six-inch diameter backlit dials and Westminster-like chimes to mark each hour.

Not only was the new look well received by visitors, but it also won first place in the Iowa Community Betterment Program's neighborhood competition for its multicolored, multi-textured sidewalks. At the ceremony

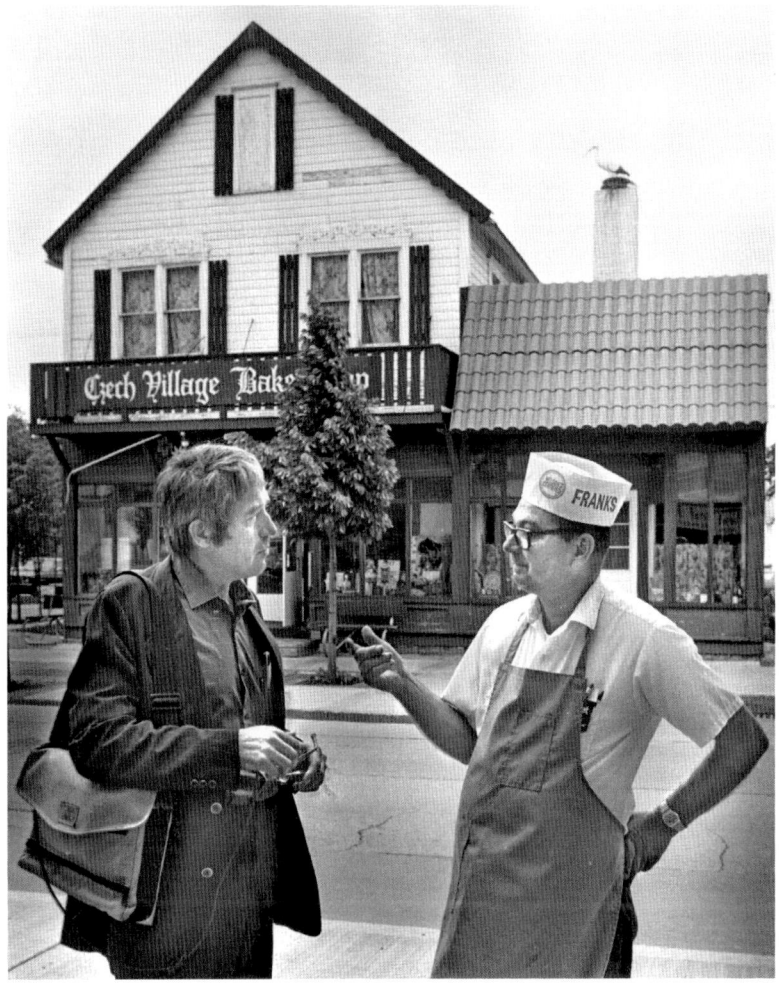

Jiri Sykora, a Czech-speaking radio reporter for Voice of America, chats with Lumir Vondracek on the sidewalk in front of Vondracek's Meat Market in Cedar Rapids' Czech Village on May 15, 1985. *Courtesy of the* Cedar Rapids Gazette.

in Iowa's capital city of Des Moines, Czech Village also won an award for community and neighborhood booth displays featuring Czech meats, baked goods, costumes, glassware and antiques, books, music and leather goods. George Joens, founding president of the Czech Village Association, accepted the awards, and the Boddicker School of Music Czech Combo and Folk Dancers entertained.

The Boddicker School of Music, founded in 1948 by Arlene Reyman Boddicker, put accordion playing back into vogue. Hundreds of students took classes, and the school spawned several music groups that performed in Cedar Rapids and around the world, winning various competitions. They included Boddicker Showcase Band, the Cedar Rapids Accordion Aces and the Polka Dots, fronted by Arlene Boddicker.

Regular music in Czech Village, revived in the 1950s by the Czech Heritage Band, received another boost in 1979 when Wes and Olga Drahozal organized the Czech Plus Band. Yes, Wes was a grandson of our Vaclav Drahozal who emigrated from Bohemia in 1909, and Olga was a Sindelar, also descended from the old country. Together, they led the band to success—Olga often out front playing her accordion and Wes either directing or simply sitting off to the side after he'd arranged the gig.

First opened in 1978 in the old worker house once owned by entrepreneur Louis Pochobradsky at 1607 C Street Southwest, the Czech Museum and Library had relocated by the early 1980s to a square brick building at 10 Sixteenth Avenue Southwest at the foot of the bridge. During the 1983 holiday season it featured twenty Czech festive costumes, homemade

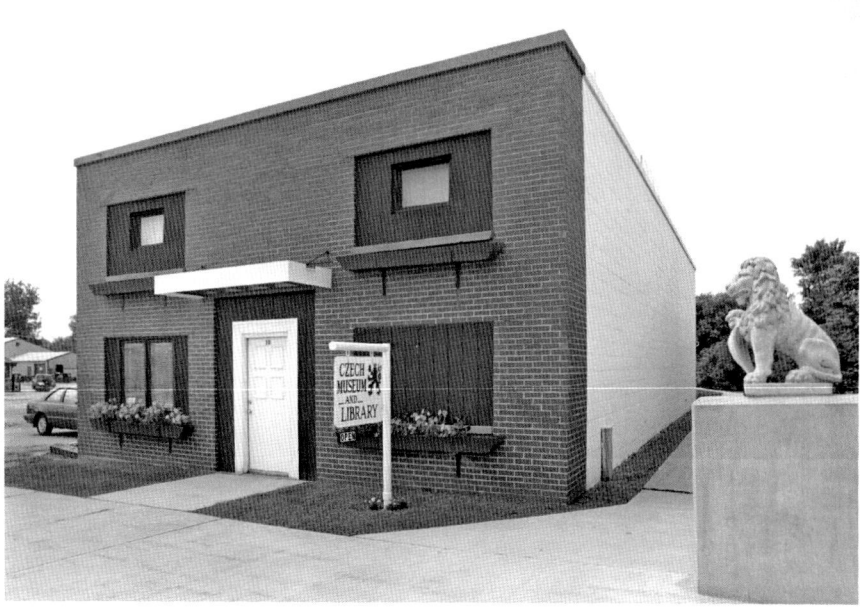

The Czech Museum and Library was located at 10 Sixteenth Avenue Southwest in 1993 before its new building was conceived. At right is one of several lions that adorn the Sixteenth Avenue Bridge. The museum's name was officially changed to the National Czech & Slovak Museum & Library in January 1991. *Courtesy of the* Cedar Rapids Gazette.

laces, cut and layered glass, musical instruments, wooden instruments and imported dolls. A special display that year had rare bronze sculptures, carved wooden items and ceramics from various regions. Admission, a suggested donation, was one dollar for adults and twenty-five cents for teenagers.

In the '80s, even if there wasn't a special event, restaurants and taverns drew nighttime visitors to Czech Village. Along the Avenue, you'd find crowds at Konecny's Restaurant, Wenceslaus Square, Ernie's Avenue Tavern, Olde Town Inn, the Red Frog and Bulicek's Bridge Villa, with an outdoor beer garden. Not far away at 229 Sixteenth Avenue Southwest was the Safari Lounge.

While a couple places on the other side of the river—namely the Velvet Feedbag, an upscale restaurant, and Dillon's Dance Hall, a nightclub on the upper levels of the ZCBJ Hall—attracted visitors from other parts of Cedar Rapids, the taverns in Little Bohemia mostly catered to "locals" and included Kacere Café, the Little Bohemia, the Pink Elephant Lounge, Don's Corner Tap and the South Side Inn.

For the most part, if you compared one side of the river to the other, Czech Village had become the prosperous entrepreneur while Little Bohemia had been relegated to the role of forgotten stepchild, some of its business owners claiming city officials completely ignored the area and let it deteriorate.

"People were scared to walk the streets after dark," said Jon Jelinek, a future investor along Third Street Southwest who politely described the nighttime atmosphere through the '80s and '90s as "seedy."

In part, neighborhood decline came about with financial struggles at the packinghouse. A strike on June 4, 1983, at Wilson Foods idled 1,750 workers in Cedar Rapids. The former T.M. Sinclair & Company packinghouse had been sold in 1913 to Sulzberger and Sons and remained Sinclair until 1935, when Thomas E. Wilson was president and the company changed its name to Wilson & Co.

The strike occurred when Wilson Foods filed for bankruptcy in April, a move that cut master union contract wages from $10.69 per hour to $6.50 per hour. Union workers had agreed to a wage freeze in 1981 that also included no annual costs of living increases until the contract opened again in 1984.

In 1982, Wilson Foods officials announced the company had made a financial turnaround. But that was only due to high inflationary times, and in 1984, the company went bankrupt. Soon, Keith Barnes of Corn Belt Meats in Albert Lea, Minnesota, organized Farmstead Foods as its successor. But Farmstead lasted just five and a half years, until March 8, 1990, when

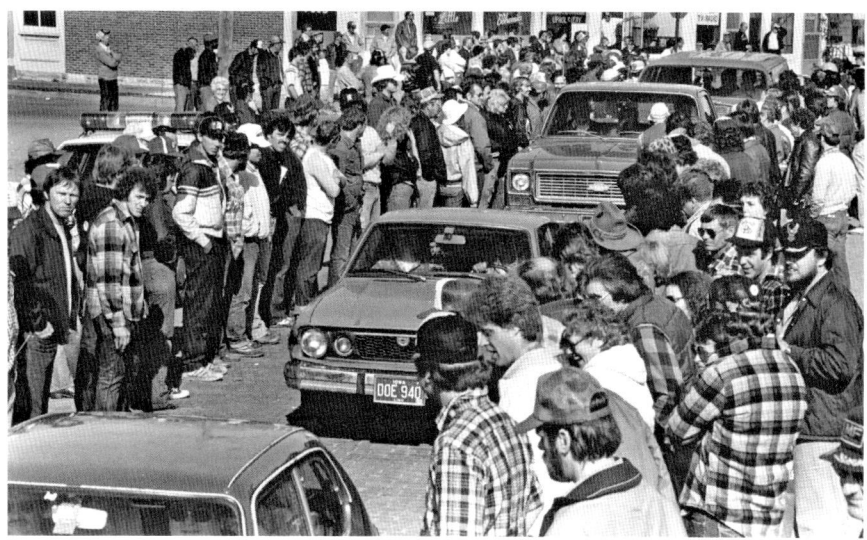

Strike demonstrators line the street on June 6, 1983, as a caravan of cars carrying Wilson Foods office workers proceeds toward the packing plant. *Courtesy of the* Cedar Rapids Gazette.

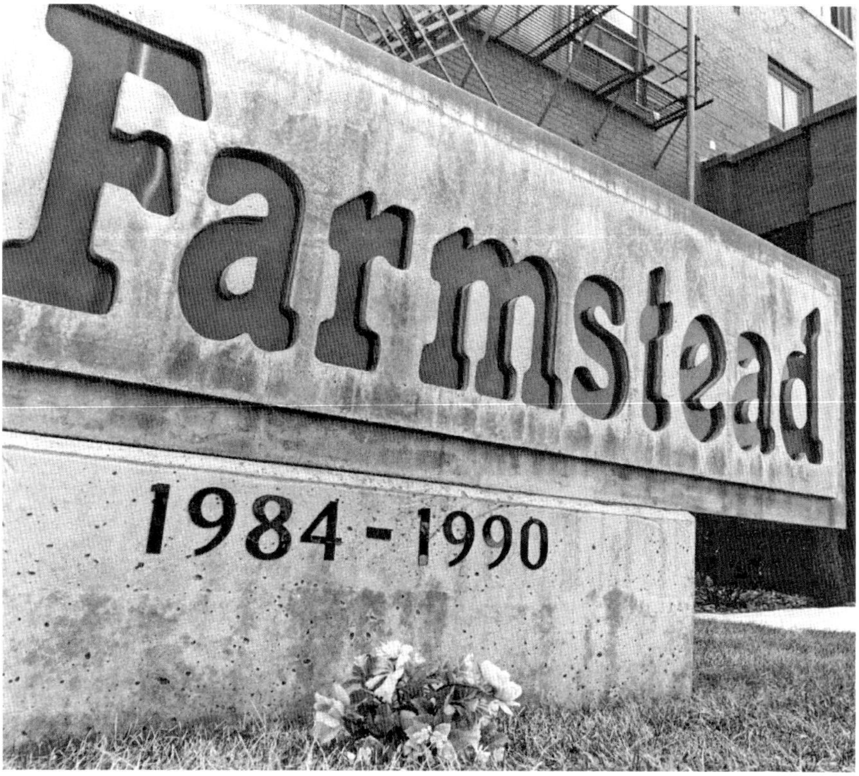

Barnes announced that it would close. At that time the packinghouse employed 1,600 people.

As the plant sat idle and officials looked for a buyer, concerns were raised about what would become of the now 19.6-acre brownfield, its buildings and its nostalgic smokestacks. Until something new happened here or along Third Street Southeast, Little Bohemia was destined to remain a lost entity.

Opposite, bottom: Artificial flowers lay in front of the tombstone-like sign at the closed Farmstead Foods on March 19, 1991. *Courtesy of the* Cedar Rapids Gazette.

9
1995

THE THREE PRESIDENTS

If somebody said it would be a cold day in—well, you know where—when a magnificent, new national museum for Czech and Slovak people would open in Cedar Rapids, Iowa, that person was right.

On October 21, 1995, an estimated seven thousand people braved windchill temperatures into the mid-twenties to witness the gathering of three national presidents for the first time in Iowa history as they stood together on an outdoor stage to dedicate the National Czech & Slovak Museum & Library. U.S. president Bill Clinton was joined by Czech president Vaclav Havel and Slovak president Michal Kovac for the nearly one-hour ceremony.

The flags of the three nations, each in red, white and blue, fluttered from flagpoles as spectators wore gloves or kept their hands in their pockets. The Czech Plus Band played traditional polkas to keep the crowd moving as one business sold T-shirts proclaiming, "Czeching it out with the Presidents." Journalists from around the country and the world covered the event, including ten from the Czech Republic.

Havel said:

> *After decades of oppression and absence of freedom, we have now reached a situation when we, too, can say in our home, "This is our land." Our respective pasts have brought us to the same or at least a similar point.*
>
> *We are united by the same ideals. We believe in the same values. And we share the desire to cherish and protect them. Part of this is best expressed in the motto of Iowa, "Our liberties we prize, and our rights we will maintain."*

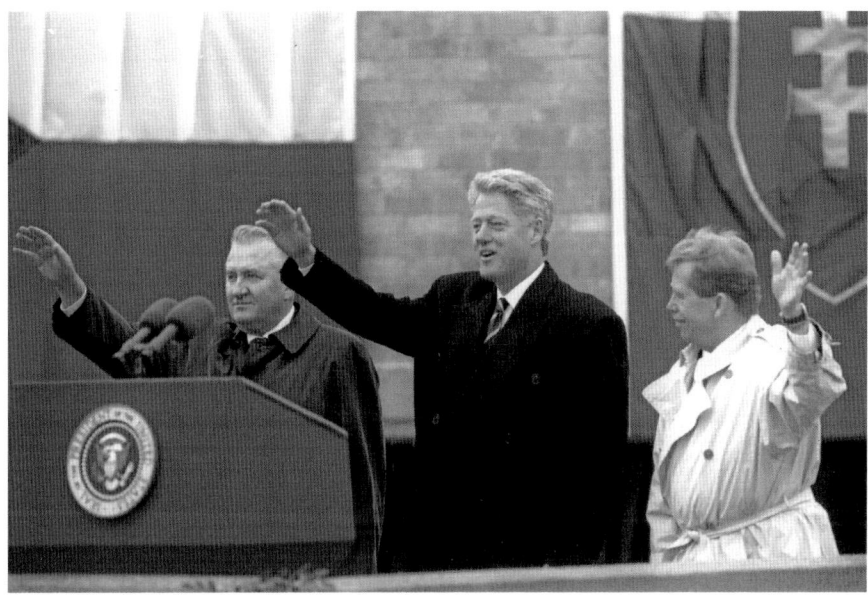

U.S. president Bill Clinton (center) is flanked by Czech president Vaclav Havel (right) and Slovak president Michal Kovac on a frigid October 21, 1995, as they helped dedicate the National Czech & Slovak Museum & Library. It was the first time three national presidents had been in Iowa at the same time. *Courtesy of the Cedar Rapids Gazette.*

Kovac talked about the positive relations between the three nations and the example the three presidents set by meeting earlier in the day. "The National Czech & Slovak Museum has embraced positive examples from the past," he said. "I am convinced that we, today's politicians, as well as our successors, will not write the pages of our common history in dark colors."

Clinton, in his remarks, recalled meeting Havel in the Czech Republic the previous year and walking across the Charles Bridge. He said a dozen eggs had been added to the mortar of the museum's cornerstone, as eggs had been added to the bridge's foundation, so that it would last as long as that bridge. He alluded to the Velvet Revolution of 1989 and recalled his first visit to Prague twenty-four years earlier.

"I remembered then all the young people I had met there a quarter century before and how desperately then they had longed for the freedom that they now enjoy."

Clinton also cited people of Czech ancestry who made significant contributions to America, including Eugene Cernan, the last astronaut to leave his footprints on the moon, and U.S. ambassador to the United Nations

Madeleine Albright, who was born in Prague and attended the museum's dedication with Clinton.

In the crowd, Pauline Jasa, eighty-five, waved her American flags during the ceremony. She'd come to the United States in her mother's womb in 1909 while her parents had nothing to their names but three boxes of belongings and the family dishware wrapped in goose-feather bedding. She said all her father wanted to do was live in a country that was free and to make a living as a painter. They came, she said, by the seat of their pants, "and the seat of their pants were threadbare."

Pauline Jasa's family settled in a home a couple of blocks from the new museum's future location and later moved to a five-acre plot where they tended a large garden, milked a cow and raised chickens.

"I was thinking, if those old-timers in the cemetery could see this, they would stand up and salute," she said.

The $2.6 million, seventeen-thousand-square-foot museum, which actually opened to the public that March, overlooked the Cedar River. The museum—designed with multiple high-pitched roofs, arched windows and a red tile roof that mimicked row houses in Czechoslovakia—dwarfed the plain thirty- by sixty-foot brick structure leased since 1981 from the city by the Czech Fine Arts Foundation that in 1989 changed its name to Czech & Slovak Museum & Library and in 1994 added the word "National."

"The barrel vault that goes down through the middle—the peaked roofs are typical," said Cedar Rapids architect Leo Peiffer, who designed the museum after extensive research. "The red roofs are typical. The color of the brick represents the stone of a lot of buildings there. It's kind of a montage of a lot of things blended in to something that we felt represented Czechoslovakian architecture."

A sixty-two-foot carillon tower on the museum grounds was designed by the Cedar Rapids architecture firm of Brown Healey Stone & Sauer to complement the museum and remind visitors of the towers they could see in Prague. The Bridge of Lions, similarly designed with its statues of lions to resemble the historic statues along the Charles Bridge in Prague, made locating the museum near the Cedar River imperative to planners.

"Sitting on the bank of the Cedar River, between the Bridge of Lions and the Twelfth Avenue Bridge, makes the setting a very Old World feeling," said interim museum director Alan Beach. "I can understand why the early Czech and Slovak settlers chose this area—it surely reminded them of home."

The museum's collections included five thousand artifacts and fifty authentic costumes from all regions of the former Czechoslovakia. The

History in the Heartland

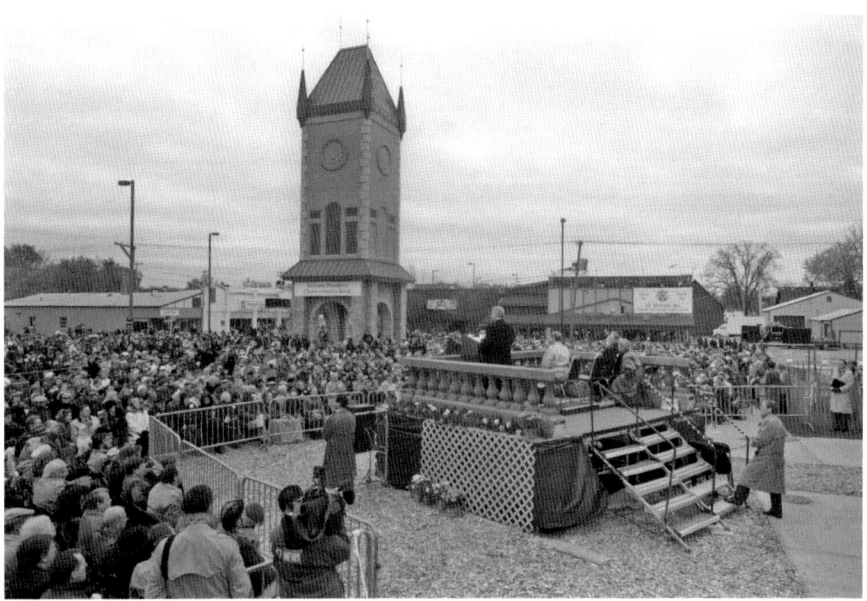

President Bill Clinton speaks to the crowd on October 21, 1995, at the dedication of the National Czech & Slovak Museum & Library. *Courtesy of the* Cedar Rapids Gazette.

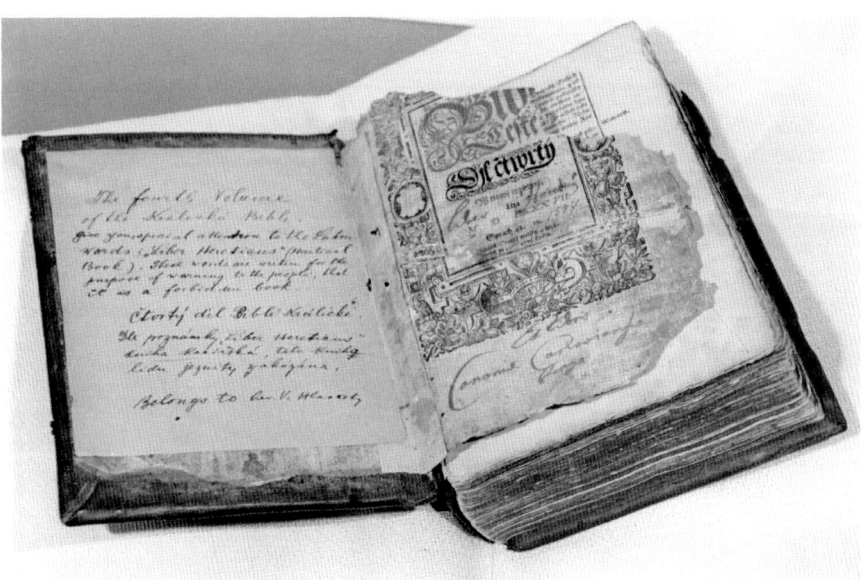

A Czech Bible, which was printed in Prague, Czechoslovakia, in the year 1587, is one of the oldest items in the collection at the National Czech & Slovak Museum & Library. The Bible was brought to Cedar Rapids in 1890 by the Reverend Vaclav Hlavaty, minister to the Czech community at Jan Hus Memorial Presbyterian Church from 1891 to 1920. *Courtesy of the* Cedar Rapids Gazette.

Czech Village & New Bohemia

oldest artifact was a Czech Bible published in 1587 and signed by the Reverend Vaclav Hlavaty, who, in 1890, became the influential leader of the Fourth Presbyterian Church in Cedar Rapids.

The large display of Czech glassware heralded back to a fifteenth-century tradition when, as legend has it, a craftsman accidentally dropped his gold pocket watch into a pot of hot liquid glass, turning the clear solution a bright red. Soon, glassmakers in the mineral-rich area added ferrous oxide to make green glass, cobalt to make blue and magnesium to make lavender. Through the centuries, they used other techniques, too, crafting colorful glassware that was embodied in the museum's collection that included cut-lead crystal, porcelain, ceramics, laces, embroidery, ethnic dolls, wood carvings and intricately decorated eggs.

The eggs, ranging in size from chicken to ostrich and some dating back hundreds of years, were examples of seven colorful and elaborate techniques. Some were created through the decades by Marj Nejdl of Ely, a descendant of early Czech settlers who still teaches the technique to adults and children in Cedar Rapids. Her eggs, presented to dignitaries across Europe, were then on display at the Smithsonian Institution in Washington, D.C.

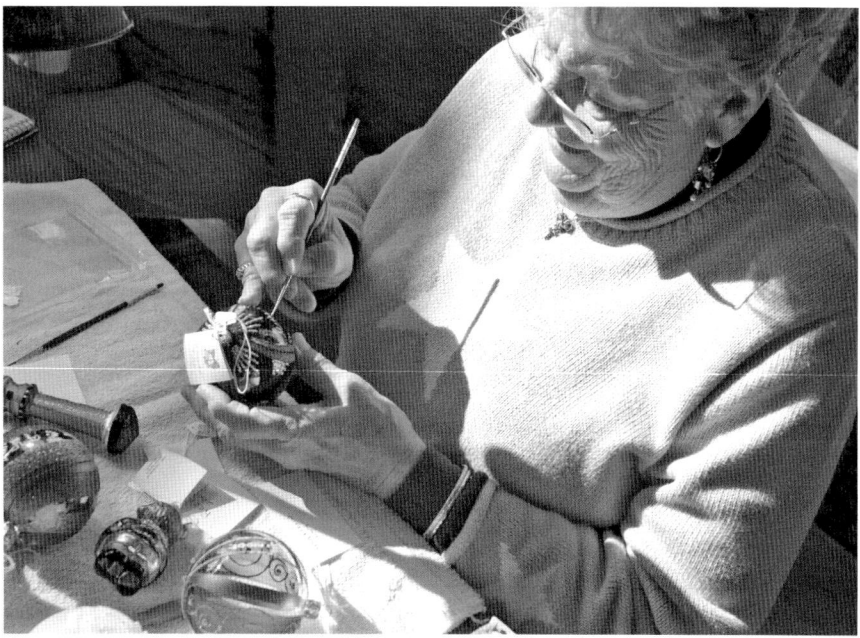

Marjorie Nejdl, a Czech folk artist from Ely, personalizes ornaments with names and dates at the National Czech & Slovak Museum & Library on November 17, 2007. *Courtesy of the* Cedar Rapids Gazette.

In addition, the Czech museum's library had ten thousand books, mostly in the Czech and Slovak languages, and there were plans to add thousands more for historical and genealogical research. While money to buy such items was tight, officials hoped that contributions would continue to expand the collections as they had done all along.

While donations for both the museum and its collections were given by thousands of people from Cedar Rapids and around the country, major financial contributions came from the City of Cedar Rapids, which leased the land to the museum for $1 per year, and the local Hall-Perrine Foundation, which contributed $2 for each $3 raised, resulting in a $750,000 donation. Other major sponsors included the Roman L. Hruska family for the grand hall, the Ray L. Jiruska family for the exhibit hall, the Lester and Ernest Buresh families for the carillon, the Western Fraternal Life Association for the Heritage Hall community center and the Tehel family for the library and cultural center. In addition, most of the books had been acquired through the efforts of Melvina Svec.

"The museum is here because the local people got behind it," said Gail Naughton, today's president and CEO. "They did it. They had the vision and they got it done."

When the museum opened in 1995, it had more than 135 volunteers, about 30 of them very active, said development director John Rocarek. In addition, it had more than 150 Czech and Slovak organizations in the United States to call upon for help and contributions.

Plans for the National Czech & Slovak Museum & Library included raising another $500,000 to organize the display area into four modules and to acquire additional items to complete collections. The first module would educate visitors on the geography, topography and social/political climate during the pre-emigration days; the second would feature kroje (costumes), glassware and artifacts from the museum's permanent collection; the third would focus on the immigration experience and life in America in the late nineteenth century; and the fourth would be space for traveling and temporary museum-owned exhibits.

On the grounds, the museum operated its immigrant home, an actual two-room Czech house that once stood in southeast Cedar Rapids donated about fifteen years earlier. The restored house was furnished to look as it did when new in the late 1800s.

"We're here to document the history of American Czech ancestry," Rocarek said. "The scope is more toward the immigrants and their experiences. This is the realization we do have something to add to the whole community—instead of catering to ourselves."

Czech Village & New Bohemia

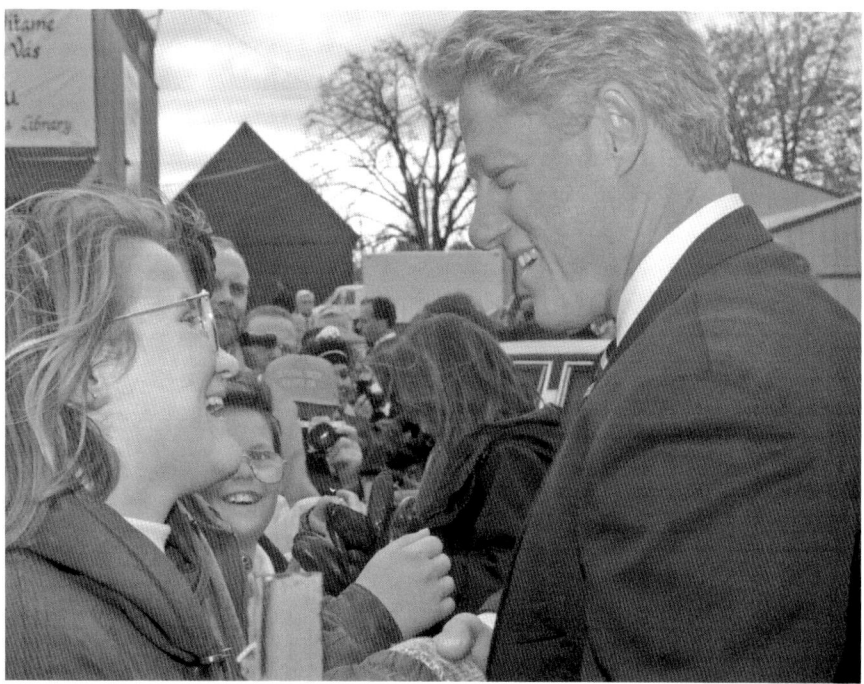

Katherine McEwien, sixteen, of Cedar Rapids waited two hours in the cold outside the National Czech & Slovak Museum & Library after it was dedicated on October 21, 1995, to shake hands with President Bill Clinton. She told him her dream was to become president. *Courtesy of the* Cedar Rapids Gazette.

A copper time capsule buried at the dedication contained names of those involved in the construction, a letter of greeting, proclamations by Havel and Kovac, uncirculated coins, newspaper articles, small flags, photographs and a ceramic hedgehog and buckeye, both believed to be good luck symbols.

In the first six months the museum was open, before the dedication, it had eight thousand visitors, more than it had the previous full year. By 1997, the international exhibition "A Thousand Years of Czech Culture: Riches from the National Museum in Prague" had attracted more than thirty thousand visitors from the United States and the world.

Many visitors who came for genealogical research also traveled up the C Street Southwest hill to Czech National Cemetery, founded in 1893, where old tombstones display diacritical marks—the hooks, slashes and circles placed above letters to indicate a special phonetic value that gradually disappeared from the spellings of so many Czech and Slovak names.

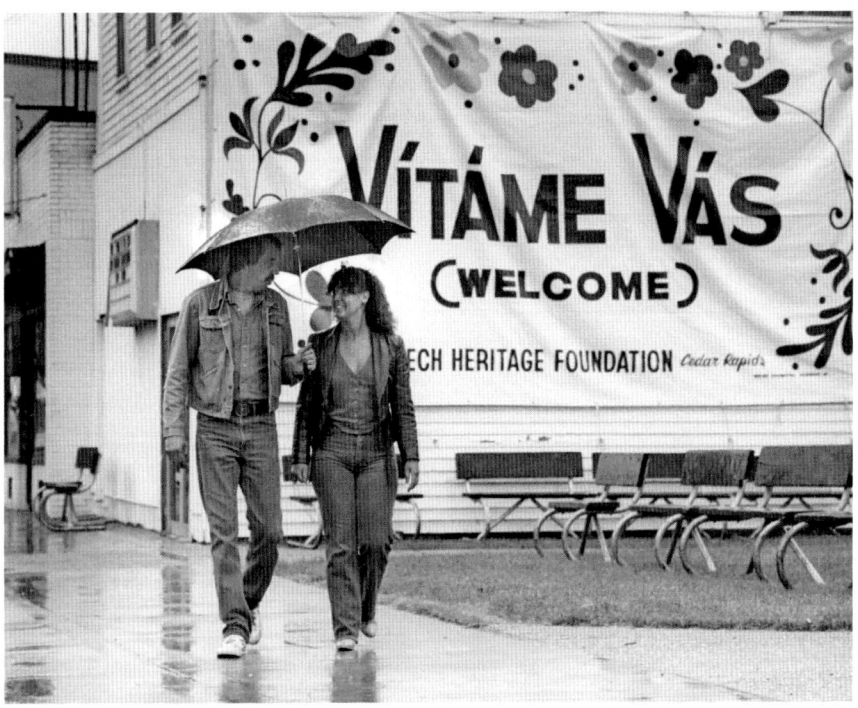

Dennis and Donna Kanke of Cedar Rapids walk down Sixteenth Avenue Southwest in the rain during the weekend Houby Days festival in Czech Village on May 17, 1986. *Courtesy of the* Cedar Rapids Gazette.

If those visitors arrived at the right time, they also might have participated in one of the annual events held in Czech Village: St. Joseph's Day (March 19), Easter traditions (the Saturdays before Palm Sunday and Easter), Houby (mushroom) Days (the Saturday and Sunday after Mother's Day), Ethnic Festival (Saturday and Sunday of Memorial Day weekend), the annual Fall Festival and St. Nicholas Day (the first Saturday in December).

The dedication of the museum and library became the most significant event in Czech Village history.

It was "one of the most magnificent things that has been done for the Czech and Slovak people in America," said the Reverend Francis Kub of St. Simon's Catholic Church in Chicago, a special guest of the White House at the ceremony.

"The fact that these three presidents are here and the fact that it happened in 1995 demonstrates the vibrancy of the awareness of the Czech and

Slovak heritages," added Robert W. Doubek of Washington, D.C, president of American Friends of the Czech Republic.

To the delight of many, President Clinton demonstrated that awareness at the dedication's conclusion when he instructed his motorcade to stop at Sykora Bakery on the way to the Eastern Iowa Airport.

"Hillary wanted an apple strudel. The president had a cherry kolach," said bakery owner Don Janda. "Everybody's on cloud nine."

10

2000

OLD BECOMES NEW

The decade-long march toward a new millennium became a time of optimistic transition in the Cedar Rapids neighborhoods where Czech immigrants settled 150 years earlier. For starters, in 1989, the yearlong project replacing the dilapidated Sixteenth Avenue Bridge connecting Little Bohemia with Czech Village culminated in the completion of the $1.5 million Bridge of Lions.

About 2,500 people attended that dedication on July 15, 1989, when U.S. senator Tom Harkin of Iowa honored the millions of immigrants who crossed the ocean to make a new home in the United States. A letter from President George Bush called the bridge "truly a monument to your civic pride and rich cultural heritage."

Ed Kuba, a local funeral home director often called "the Mayor of Czech Village," began his remarks in Czech and talked about the dream of a new bridge. As chairman of the bridge committee, Kuba had helped add eggs to the concrete a year earlier. At that time, he said, it was a seven-hundred-year-old tradition hailing back to the days of the Charles Bridge in Prague when workers ran short of mortar and issued a plea for egg whites to add to the mixture. "It adds strength to the cement," Kuba said. "It's the albumin in eggs that helps it harden."

Later in 1989, Czechs in Cedar Rapids rejoiced for the Velvet Revolution in their homeland, a peaceful demonstration from November 16 to December 29 that ousted communist rule. During the demonstrations, as many as 500,000 protestors assembled in Prague, among them a dissident playwright

Czech Village & New Bohemia

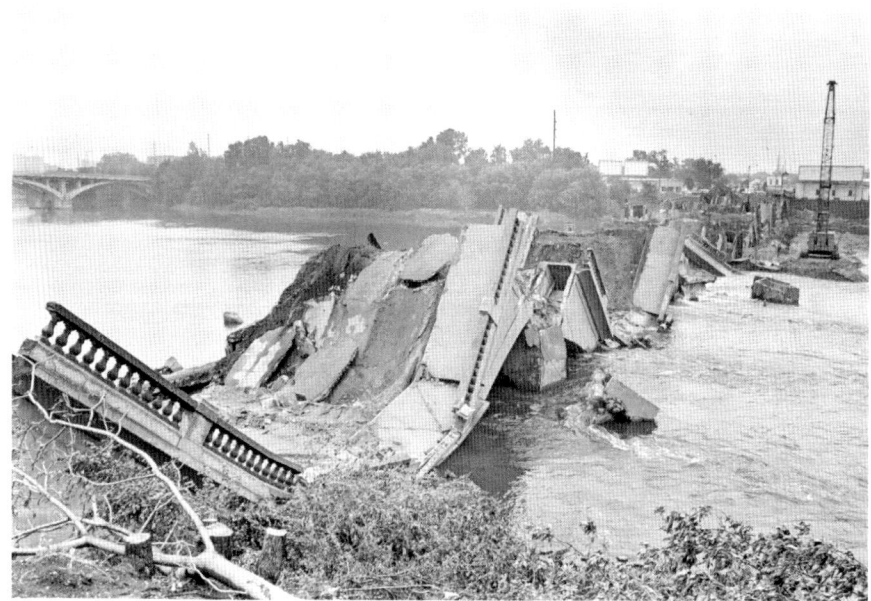

The Sixteenth Avenue Bridge became a mass of rubble on June 29, 1988, as Schmidt Construction Company of Winfield, Iowa, began demolition of the dilapidated, seventy-eight-year-old structure over the Cedar River. It had been closed to automobiles for more than a year. *Courtesy of the* Cedar Rapids Gazette.

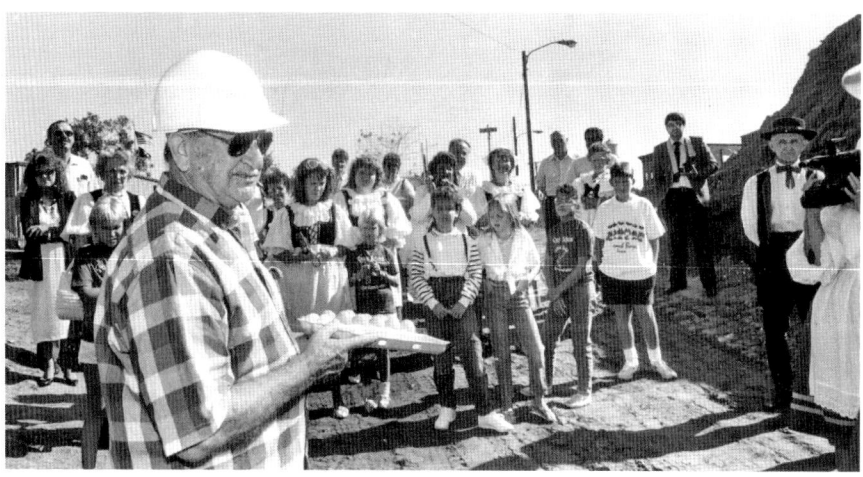

Ed Kuba, a member of the Citizen's Review Committee, holds a carton of eggs that were individually tossed into the first concrete mix for the Bridge of Lions at Sixteenth Avenue Southwest on August 24, 1988. The egg tossing procedure, Kuba said, is a Czech tradition believed to produce harder concrete. *Courtesy of the* Cedar Rapids Gazette.

by the name of Vaclav Havel, who became president. A couple years later, the Slovak republic was formed in the Gentle Revolution, bringing about the two nations: the Czech Republic and Slovakia.

In Cedar Rapids, the St. Joseph's Day parade of 1990 became a two-day celebration titled "Czech Freedom Days." Kuba, president of the Federation of Czech Groups, said it was modeled after celebrations of the past to raise money for Czech brethren. The Velvet Revolution also meant Czechs in Cedar Rapids no longer had to worry about what they wrote in letters to relatives in the homeland.

The flood of 1993 interrupted the good times, although it did minimal damage in Little Bohemia and Czech Village, seeping up through storm drains on Third Street Southeast near Twelfth Avenue and flooding the basement at Penford Products.

Flood of 1993 Tourist Attraction

As the Cedar River approached its predicted crest of more than twenty feet in early April, it became a tourist attraction rather than a worry. Improvements to the riverbank levees since the 1961 flood put the city in better shape to weather high water, so spectators gathered on the bridges to watch the river race below.

In the end, as the water crested at 19.27 feet, the city's fourth-highest flood level, the main damage seemed to be road closures, mostly in northern Cedar Rapids, and a broken water main pipe buried beneath the river.

By the time presidents from the Czech Republic and Slovakia came to Cedar Rapids in 1995 to dedicate the Czech & Slovak Museum & Library, the financial sting to the neighborhoods from industrial closures was relegated to the back burner.

Penford Products, in August 1995, celebrated the 100th anniversary of the Cedar Rapids plant that began as Douglas Starch Works. Near extinction in 1977, the plant had finished three major expansions at a cost of $85 million and employed 320 people as it became a player in specialty starch products, including a line of copolymer starches that replaced latex in paper coatings.

Across the river, Iowa Iron Works closed its doors in January 1996 after financial troubles, including an embezzlement, prompted bankruptcy and forced the layoff of twenty-two workers. Part of the plant was razed soon thereafter, while sections rusted away until additional demolition in 2001.

A fire on the packinghouse grounds engulfed the abandoned three-story main office building in October 1992 and set off a series of proposals for the 19.6-acre site. In 1993, plans took shape to develop Sinclair Industrial Park, a $20 million warehousing and industrial complex, but that idea lasted only a short while in private hands. In 1998, talk centered on a recreational complex—everything from an ice arena and an amphitheater to a farmers' market and a recreation trail, even a large water park along the Cedar River. There also was discussion about putting a casino on the site, but it remains closed and idle.

A couple of historical projects associated with the packing plant also went nowhere. Attempts to save an old brick smokestack from the early 1900s failed when it was deemed unsafe. And a row of equally historic immigrant homes built for packinghouse workers near the St. Wenceslaus Catholic Church sat neglected until flood damage in 2008 forced their demolition.

In Little Bohemia in 2005, the city purchased the former Quality Chef manufacturing plant, a series of connected buildings in the 1100 block of

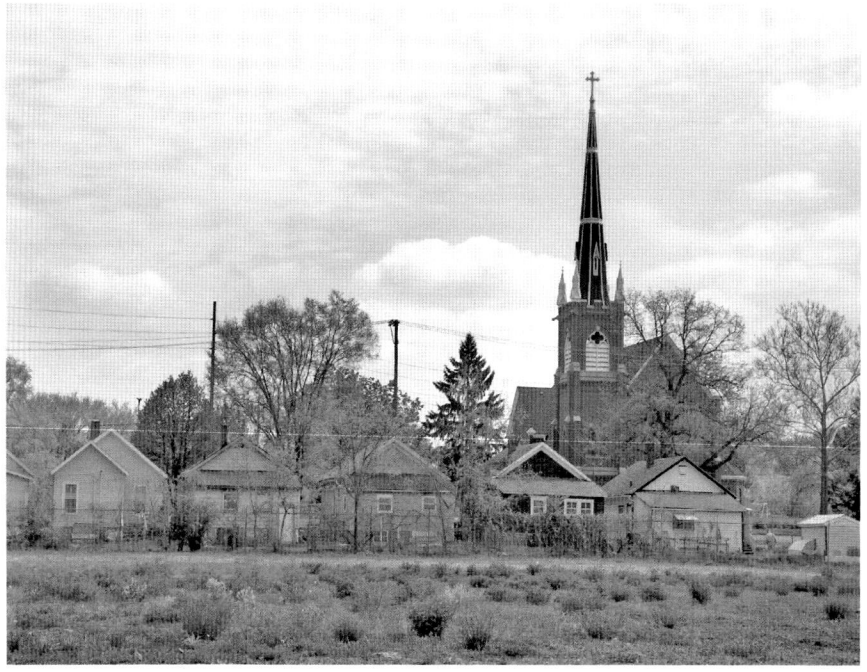

Old immigrant homes, built for workers at Sinclair Packing House near the St. Wenceslaus Catholic Church, were run-down by 2003 and considered for demolition. They still stood until after the flood of 2008. *Courtesy of the* Cedar Rapids Gazette.

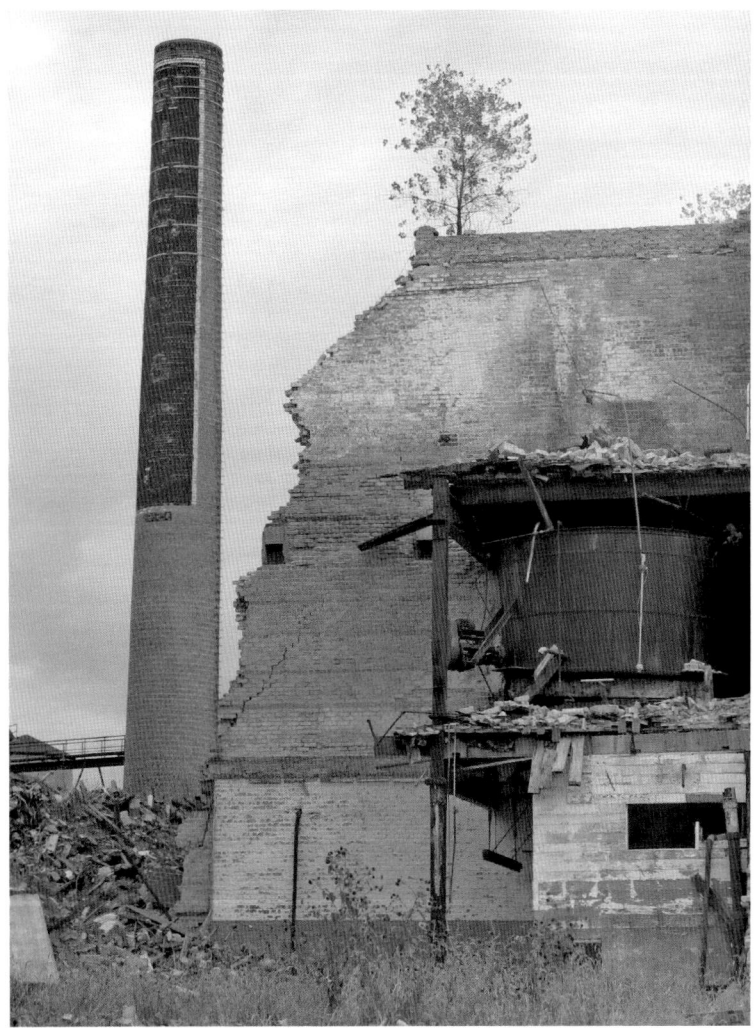

Faint letters spelled "Wilson & Co." on the old power plant smokestack that still stood in October 2005. The smokestack, dating back to the early twentieth century when the plant was T.M. Sinclair & Company was later torn down. *Photo by Dave Rasdal.*

Third Street Southeast, adjacent to Iowa Iron Works and Iowa Steel property it had bought earlier. The Quality Chef plant included a 1923 storefront, a 1930s-era building that had been J.W. Phares Wholesale Florist Co. and a late 1960s office structure once home to Richard Jones Accounting. Also in 2005, SouthSide Development Corporation investors became disillusioned with the city's lack of development on the Sinclair site and withdrew financial assistance.

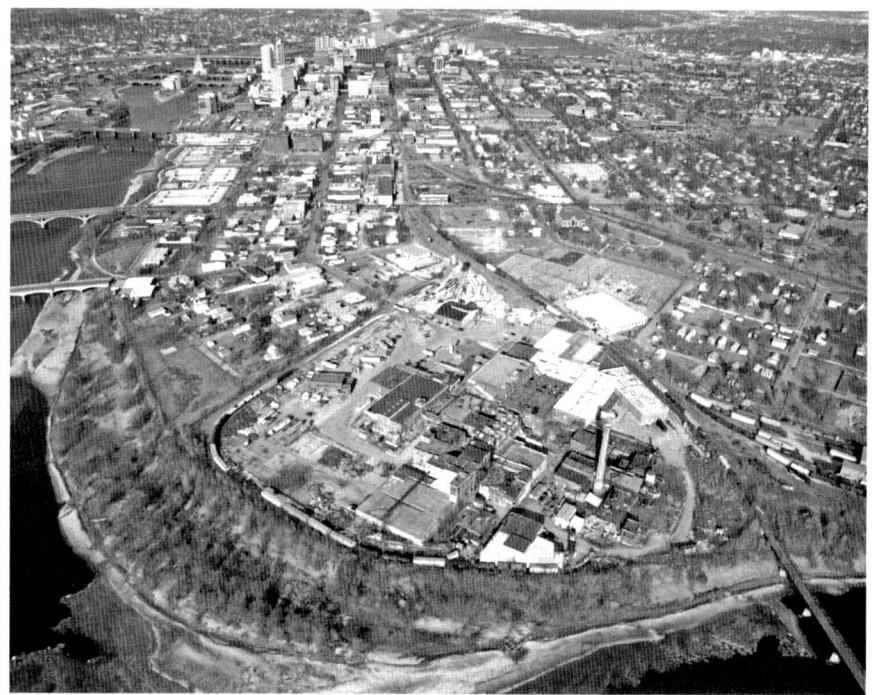

An aerial view taken on January 22, 2002, shows the old T.M. Sinclair Parking Plant site that had been considered for everything from a warehouse district to an entertainment center after Farmstead Foods closed in 1990. *Courtesy of the* Cedar Rapids Gazette.

By now, this city-owned area had been dubbed Cedar Bend, with the latest proposal being a $14.4 million indoor market, community center and space for retail shops along Twelfth Avenue Southeast from Third Street to Fifth Street. But this idea, as well as previous efforts named RiverRun and Destination Southside, with estimated prices tags up to $154 million, never came to fruition.

A couple blocks away at Tenth Avenue Southeast, though, the privately owned J.G. Cherry Building was well into transition as a center for creativity. Bob Chadima—yes, a grandson of Joseph Chadima, the founder of Chadima Brothers Ice Company that became Hubbard Ice and Coal—bought the building in 1976 as a storage facility for his plumbing supply business.

"This was an industrial area, and we were an industrial supplier," recalled Bob, now ninety. "Then everything began to close up. You could import castings from Korea cheaper than you could make them [at Iowa Iron Works] here. But the closing of the packinghouse was the big blow."

Soon, Bob said, businesses that revolved around industrial activity—a truck washing company, restaurants, taverns—closed. He sold his plumbing supply business in 1982 but kept the Cherry Building. His first major tenant, HACAP (Hawkeye Area Community Action Program), leased nearly half the 104,000-square-foot building to operate a daycare and its Meals on Wheels program for the elderly.

Artists Arrive

But the arrival of photographer Rod Bradley in 1986 changed everything. He set up his studio in a third-floor loft with high ceilings, large windows and skylights. It was perfect—so perfect that another photographer, David Van Allen, uses the space now.

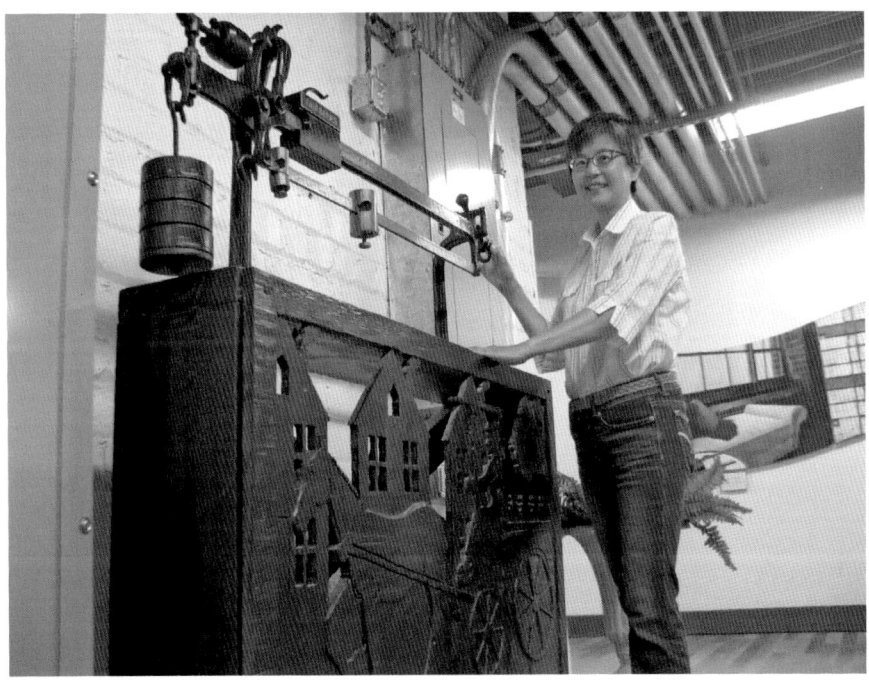

Lijun Chadima, president of Thorland Company, which owns the J.G. Cherry building, shows the original 1919 scale that can weigh up to eight thousand pounds. The scale was enhanced in the early 2000s by Native American artist Robert McIntosh to depict a horse-drawn milk truck hauling milk cans made with equipment manufactured by the J.G. Cherry Company. *Photo by Dave Rasdal.*

Over the next thirteen years, other tenants, a few of them artists, moved in and out of the building until Bob's son, David Chadima, and wife, Lijun, returned to Cedar Rapids in 1999 after a decade in Asia. David had worked for two global advertising agencies in China and Taiwan, where he met Lijun.

"When we lived in Asia, we loved the art," said Lijun, president of the family's Thorland Corporation that oversees the Cherry Building. "It's different for here, a difference between western and Chinese culture. But we saw this as potential. This was a great place to revitalize."

With one large tenant vacating warehouse space, the Cherry Building became home to a wide variety of tenants from a printing company, a couple small business entrepreneurs and a rock band renting practice space to Theater Cedar Rapids, which established its set design shop.

By June 1, 2008, the Cherry Building was full. A celebration was planned.

In 2008, Legion Arts had reason to celebrate, too. It was on the verge of buying the CSPS Hall, its home since 1990, from R.G. Prucha, who had owned the hall for decades. R.G. operated Service Press printing company on the main floor while Legion Arts used the upper two floors for art, drama and music performances. When R.G. sold his printing company in December 2007, he kept the building as rental income. That's when Mel Andringa, a founding principle of Legion Arts, asked if he'd sell.

When Prucha agreed to consider it, the 116-year-old CSPS Hall was inspected. It needed a new roof, new heating and air-conditioning systems and tuck pointing on the exterior brick. As it sat, the assessed value came in at $750,000.

"That was $700,000 more than we'd ever raised, and we were going to have this one-hundred-year-old building," Mel said. "We could never fix it up."

Still, Mel and Legion Arts founding partner, John Herbert, dreamed. They had just moved into the adjacent Hose Station No. 4 two-story firehouse, also owned by Prucha, after fixing it up as living quarters and a studio. Anything was possible. After all, they had created Legion Arts.

"In 1990, when we came here, the packinghouse was closed," Mel said. "People were afraid of the neighborhood. It hadn't been much before that. It was awful quiet. You could play an accordion in New Bohemia and hear it perfectly in Czech Village."

In the mid-1970s, Andringa and Herbert founded the Drawing Legion Company in New York City as a hybrid fine arts/applied arts organization. It moved to Amsterdam and then Iowa City, Iowa, where Andringa taught art at the University of Iowa and Herbert used his PhD knowledge in American

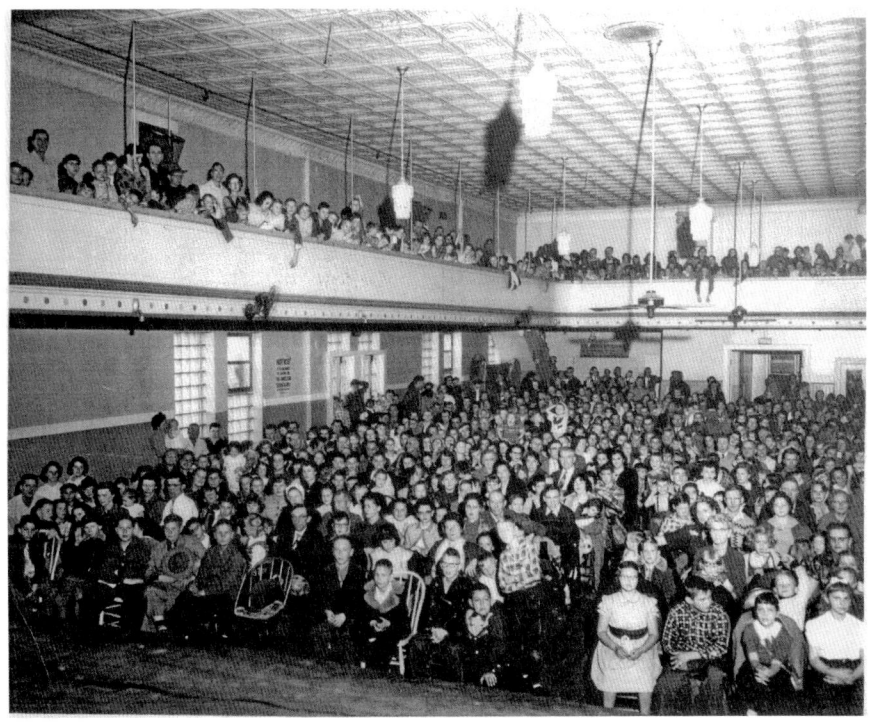

The CSPS Hall auditorium was packed, even in the surrounding balcony, for a show in the 1950s. *Courtesy of the State Historical Society of Iowa.*

studies to integrate the organization into the community. "He was the brain; I was the brawn," Mel joked.

But officials in Iowa City had other ideas and, for all practical purposes, evicted Legion Arts from downtown in favor of retail business. Andringa, Herbert, Van Allen and artist Jane Gilmore needed a new place. Gilmore recalled attending a wedding on the second level of the CSPS Building in the 1970s and heard it was available. Apparently, gymnasts had vacated the space because of its deterioration. Jane fell in love with a former bar area that she could rent for $150 a month and talked the men into looking at the space.

"R.G. drove a hard bargain," Mel recalled with a laugh. "He said it would be $600 a month for the entire second floor. John talked him down to $550. We rented the bar area to Jane for $150, so it only cost us $400."

In the early days, the rudimentary performance venue needed upgrading. To save money, Prucha turned off the steam heat when he left at 5:00 p.m. so the building would be downright chilly for evening performances.

"It was so cold," Mel said, "that we handed out baked potatoes. The audience could hold them to stay warm. We also allowed cats to wander around—they'd sit in people's laps and sometimes they'd even cross the stage. We'd also let people smoke during performances. They could bring their own alcohol if they wanted to."

Since Andringa and Herbert needed a place to live, they moved into the former dressing room tucked beneath the stage. They also quickly embraced the neighborhood with its secondhand shops, nearby Community Theater and history.

Through the decades, artists, not only those of Czech descent, had come to this neighborhood. They included painters Grant Wood and Marvin Cone (his painting of the Little Bohemia tavern is well known) and photographer/author Carl Van Vechten. Bill Heral, a Bohemian artist, lived upstairs in the Suchy building, Don Novak operated the darkly eclectic The Raven restaurant named after the Edgar Allen Poe poem and James Kern, a performance artist, was an early investor in the Velvet Feedbag in historic Tower Grove, a two-story brick mansion built in 1878 by Czech immigrant Frank Mitvalsky, before it burned in 1984.

"The Czech community had this certain outside influence for a long time," Mel said. "It was more that artists found the area interesting than they wanted to be here. It was an exotic area in Cedar Rapids."

Since its beginning, Little Bohemia had a reputation for wild parties, loose women and being dangerous at night, Mel said, which attracted artists. He likes to talk about how farmers would come to town, party, stay the night, eat breakfast and then wander home by daylight to milk the cows.

Maybe that's why Herbert's idea for live performances three or four times a month didn't fly, so it was scaled back to three or four a year. The plan was to offer alternative entertainment to "the Big Three"—Theater Cedar Rapids, the Cedar Rapids Symphony and the Cedar Rapids Museum of Art—by bringing in creative performers.

"We asked ourselves, who are the original creators in this country?" Mel said. "If they're not here, how can we bring them here?"

Soon, acoustic bands led to Celtic music, which led to performers from around the world. The audience gradually grew, particularly among the younger generation.

"If it's not being done, we'll introduce it to the community," Mel said about their philosophy. "When the community embraces it, takes it to other places, then we'll introduce something else that's new. We always wanted to be new."

Within months of relocating to Cedar Rapids, Andringa and Herbert felt a connection to the community they'd never had during their decade in Iowa City, where people wrongly associated them with the University of Iowa.

"This is a get-along community," Mel said. "That has been good for us."

The '90s was a decade where Cedar Rapids government examined the differences in its neighborhoods—from Wellington Heights to the north, Czech Village across the river and Oak Hill–Jackson, which encompassed Third Street Southeast.

"It was always a fantasy to call this an artistic neighborhood," Mel said. "Artists came up, liked what they saw, but wouldn't commit. They might live here for a year or two and then leave. Or they couldn't afford to live here."

That's also when Legion Arts began to call the immediate area New Bohemia—or "New Bo" for short.

"Some people might dispute that," Andringa said, "but I always knew it was going to be called New Bo. I'd lived in SoHo (South of Houston in New York City) and NoHo (North of Howard). I'd lived in SoHo in London, the original SoHo."

By 1993, Andringa and Herbert led an effort to gather smaller entertainment organizations together as the Cedar Rapids Area Cultural Alliance. The idea, once it grew strong enough, was to attract "the Big Three" to add clout. It was one vote per organization, no matter how big or small, and it worked so well it has become the Cultural Corridor along I-380 from Waterloo through Cedar Rapids to Iowa City.

One project that didn't work out was the 1996–97 development of the five-story brick Witwer Grocery Company building at Ninth Avenue and Third Street Southeast into OSADA, an affordable housing project that brought new immigrants from a variety of cultures into the neighborhood. Not only did these residents not become regular Legion Arts patrons as hoped, but financial difficulties prompted closure after less than a decade. OSADA was redeveloped into the Bottleworks Condominiums.

Forced to leave their home at OSADA, Andringa and Herbert moved into the firehouse and set their sights on acquiring the CSPS Hall in 2008. They knew the 1891 building's history and how the main level had been home to neighborhood businesses—a furniture store, a drugstore, a barbershop, even a mortuary—and hoped to bring in a coffee shop and similar retail businesses.

Then the flood of 2008 filled that space with ten and a half feet of water.

11

TODAY

RESURGENCE

Gold bands on Beth Chacey DeBoom's wedding ring finger reflect not only the sunshine as she sits in the living room of the Heart House she's rehabilitating in New Bohemia but also her dedication to Czech heritage. The wedding band had been worn by her maternal grandmother, Agnes Tosh, and the diamond engagement ring belonged to Agnes's older sister, Emma Cesak.

"My family decided it was probably a good thing my grandmother died a year before the flood because that would have killed her—to lose so much of her world," DeBoom said.

Agnes was in her mid-nineties when she died in 2007. She grew up the daughter of Vaclav (known as Wencil) and Bessie Melsha, who both emigrated from Bohemia. When Bessie died at a young age, Emma took over raising Agnes and became her "Ma."

In typical fashion of a Czech born in 1911, Agnes proudly wore bright red, whether that was a scarf around her neck or bold lipstick. She loved to ride around Czech Village and New Bohemia pointing out this and that as she remembered childhood landmarks. When the National Czech & Slovak Museum & Library opened, Agnes relished a stroll beneath the magnificent gold arched ceiling of its Grand Hall.

"People used to call us dumb Bohemies," Agnes would say. "Now look what we have."

The flood of 2008 threatened to take everything away. Cresting at 31.1 feet, nearly 20.0 feet above flood stage and more than 11.0 feet higher than

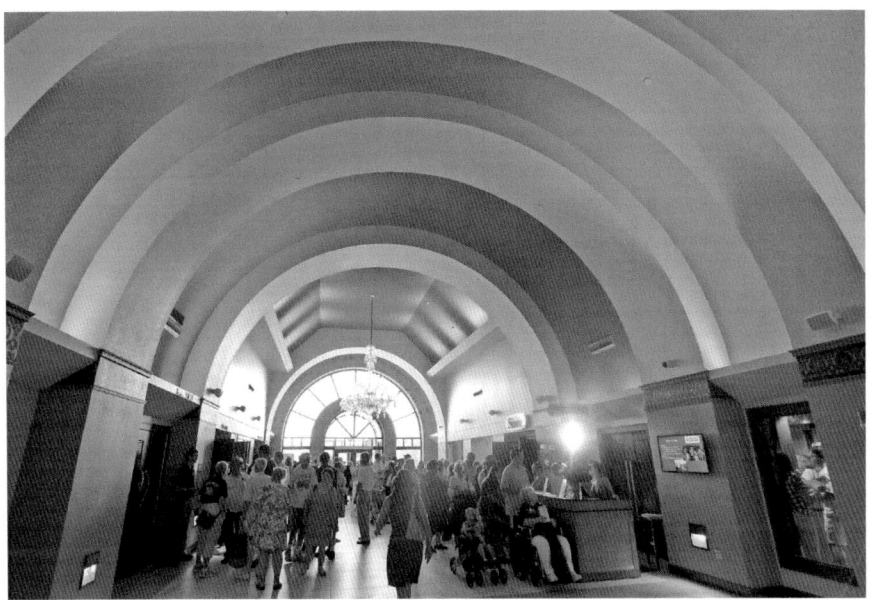

Visitors to the National Czech & Slovak Museum & Library walk through the Grand Hall during the grand reopening on July 14, 2012. *Courtesy of the* Cedar Rapids Gazette.

ever before, the Cedar River inundated the entire South Side neighborhoods settled by Bohemian immigrants. Water washed through buildings—8.0, 10.0, nearly 12.0 feet high in some cases—and left behind thick carpets of river muck and devastated walls representing historic dreams.

"This neighborhood was really interesting at that time, right after the flood," said Mel Andringa, founding partner of Legion Arts. "You saw all of the buildings stripped down to the bare walls. You could see right through them, through the bare lathe work. It was like a ghost town. You'll never see it like that again."

That's because people, like the industrious and optimistic Czech immigrants of the past, spent little time crying over what had been. Instead, they brushed away the damage and imagined what could be.

No finer example stands today than the Czech museum. Pictures of its red roof seemingly floating on floodwaters became indelibly etched in people's minds. The museum filled with at least eight feet of water in the Grand Hall. Mud and muck damaged or destroyed hundreds of artifacts. Damage totaled $11 million, and this once impossible dream had been destroyed.

So what did people do? They moved on—literally.

Beginning on June 8, 2011, in the most anticipated event of the post-flood era, Jeremy Patterson Structural Moving & Shoring of Washington,

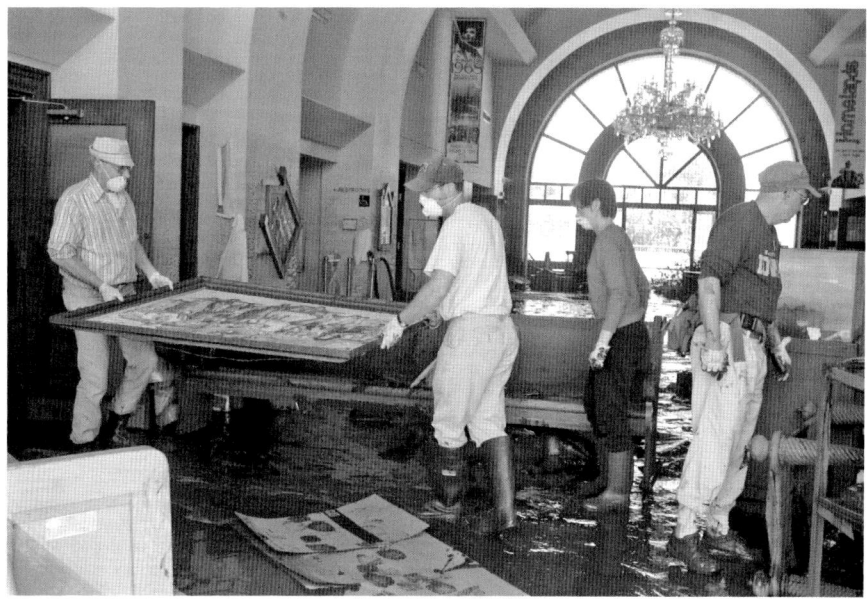

A piece of artwork is removed from the National Czech & Slovak Museum & Library by volunteer Bob Drahozal (left) and library director David Muhlena as other employees recover artifacts from the building on June 17, 2008, just days after the historic flood. *Courtesy of the* Cedar Rapids Gazette.

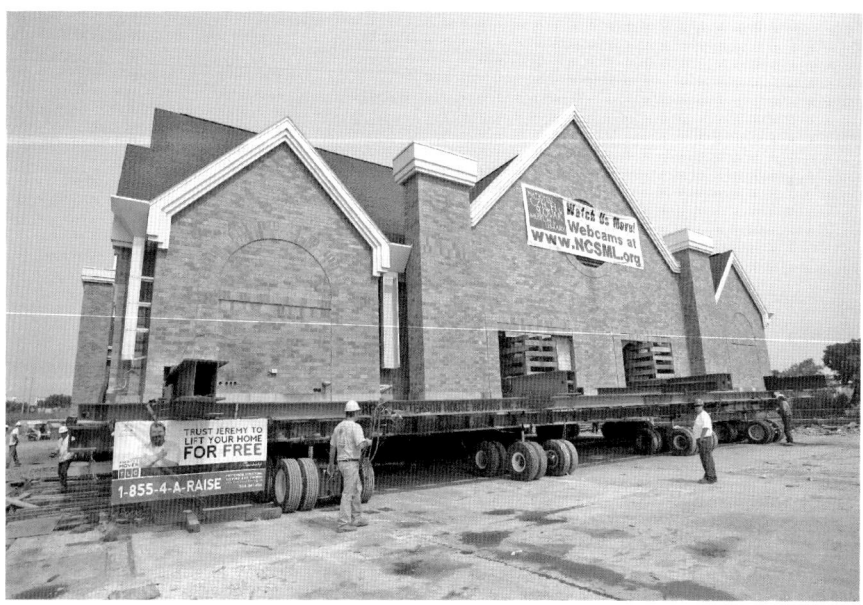

Workers monitor the back of the National Czech & Slovak Museum & Library as the building is moved to its new location on June 8, 2011. *Courtesy of the* Cedar Rapids Gazette.

Iowa, moved the original 17,000-square foot, 1,740-ton brick museum to the top of a newly constructed parking garage. The move, 480 feet across the ground and 11 feet higher, took place at a snail's pace and could be followed on Internet webcams. The start of the move drew thousands of live spectators, including media outlets from across the United States and the Czech Republic. Constant rain caused numerous delays, extending the actual move to more than a month.

The new museum, located high and dry out of the flood plain, faces the Cedar River from its perch atop a wide concrete stairway to the main entrance. The $16.5 million reconstruction brought total space to 50,000 square feet, which included a new 5,500-square-foot research library. The museum raised $25 million for flood recovery, including $10 million from I-JOBS and a $2.9 million grant from Vision Iowa Community Attraction and Tourism.

Inside the Grand Hall hangs the $10,000 crystal chandelier made in the Czech Republic originally installed in 1998. The one-thousand-piece

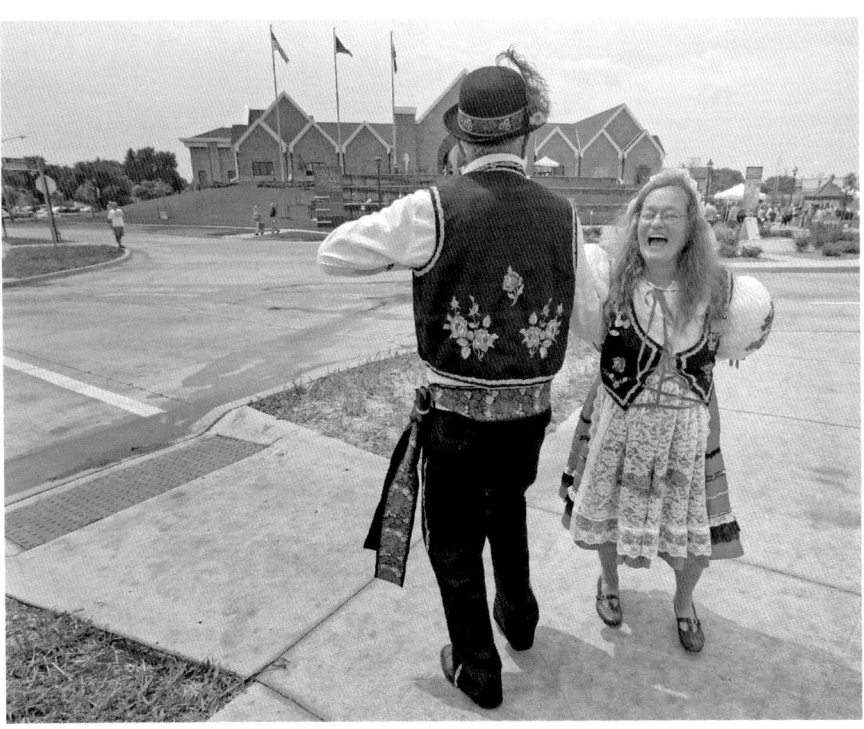

Arlene Spina laughs with her husband, Larry, as they dance to music from the Czech Plus Polka Band during the grand reopening of the new National Czech & Slovak Museum & Library on July 14, 2012. *Courtesy of the* Cedar Rapids Gazette.

chandelier survived the flood, was removed before the museum moved and then was reinstalled for the second grand opening on July 14, 2012, a much warmer day than the first dedication. The museum is now home at, appropriately, 1400 Inspiration Place Southwest.

Some Had to Leave

Alas, not everybody could return, even as a National Register of Historic Places designation helped business owners secure grants and loans.

The Saddle & Leather Shop, a staple from a century ago, when patrons rode horses and picked up supplies in horse-drawn wagons and buggies, was forced to submit its flood-ravaged building to demolition through the city's buyout program.

"There was no way financially to take on that debt and no way to recover it," said co-owner Nan Barta, the saddle shop in her family since 1946. "This has been my whole life. It has been my parents' whole life. I loved it."

Polehna's Meat Market, despite a benefit raising money for the hazardous materials cleanup of tons of spoiled meat, didn't survive. Mike Ferguson knew he couldn't afford $250,000 to $300,000 to restore the business. Moving elsewhere meant he couldn't use the surviving old brick wood-fired smokehouse that gave the wieners, ribs and jaternice (Czech sausage) their distinctive, delicious flavor. He found another job.

Others left, too, including George Joens, who operated a floor covering business, Joens Bros. Interiors, started by his brother Frank in 1959, and Greg ArBuckle, who lost his tattoo and piercing parlor at Sixteenth Avenue and C Street Southwest and his living quarters upstairs occupied since 1976.

Joens, an enthusiastic promoter of the Avenue, had fashioned his building, the former Fritz's and later Me Too food markets, into a multi-use space in 1995 called Kuncl Mall after his grandparents, Vaclav and Marie Kuncl, immigrants from Czechoslovakia in 1905. While he rebuilt after the flood, business didn't pick up as expected, so he closed in 2012.

"I had no plans of selling before," ArBuckle told the *Gazette*. "This is where I invested my whole life."

For that reason—the businesses were their lives—Anthony Vasquez wouldn't allow his mother, Connie, to close C.J.'s Sports Bar & Grill, and Andy Anderson reopened Ernie's Avenue Tavern.

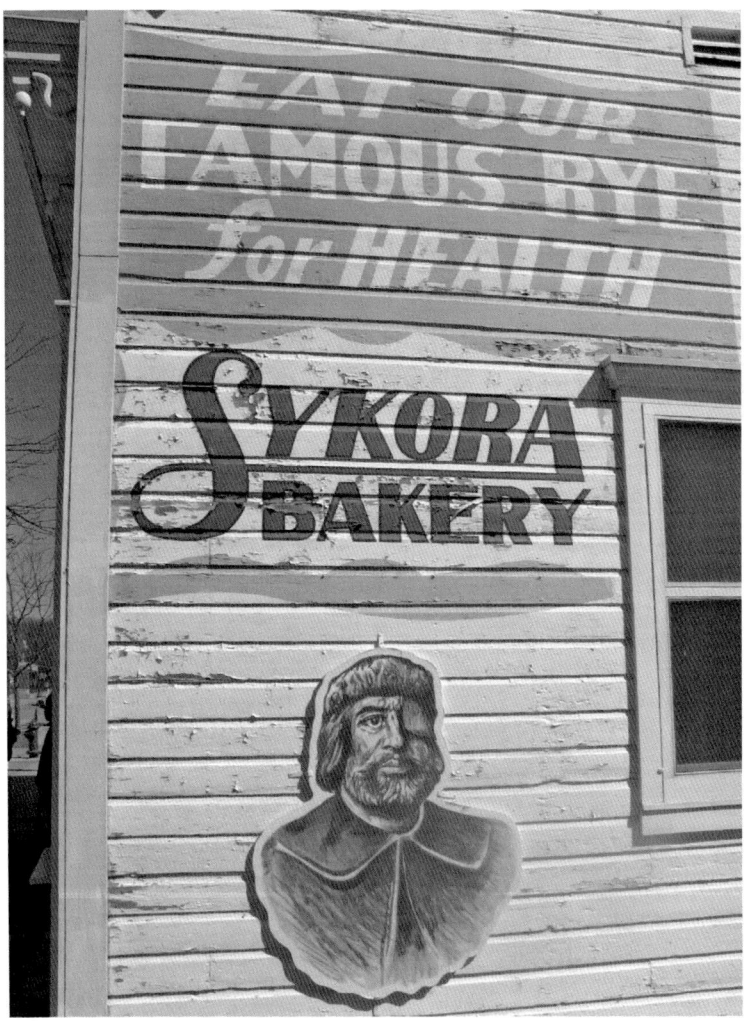

Rye bread, as advertised on the side of Sykora Bakery in Czech Village, has been a staple of Czech people for centuries. *Photo by Dave Rasdal.*

If any reopening signaled to the outside world that Czech Village was back, it was that beautiful spring day, April, 18, 2009, when Sykora Bakery flung open its doors. A bakery had operated since 1903 in this building constructed in 1900 as a saloon. Because the bakery had been closed since 2006 for remodeling, which it had to redo after the flood, a large crowd gathered. Opening-day patrons included Iowa governor Chet Culver, whose father, John, had been a U.S. senator from Cedar Rapids.

While bakery owner John Rocarek was pleased with business the next couple years, he knew rebuilding the Czech museum would be the icing on the cake. For the museum's move, he called in all available help and planned to bake nine hundred dozen kolaches for his own kolach festival.

Opportunity for Others

Even as the flood chased many business owners away from Czech Village, it opened up opportunities for others.

Lou Thompson, a Cedar Rapids native who recalled visiting the meat counter at Polehna's, returned after an absence of nearly thirty years. She had lived through Hurricane Katrina along the Mississippi Gulf Coast but didn't let the flood at Czech Village dissuade her. She pursued her dream and opened Village Meat Market & Café on Sixteenth Avenue in March 2012, with Hugh Lamont, a ten-year employee of Polehna's. The meat market not only features meats similar to those sold at Polehna's but also Cajun food and, on occasion, live music. "We went eclectic and weird," Thompson told the *Gazette* as she sat in the café surrounded by its ambiance—old Czech posters, antique musical instruments and a Victrola.

Quinton McClain, a 2000 graduate of Cedar Rapids Washington High School, brought his knack for brewing beer in Fort Collins, Colorado, back to his hometown. He chose the Joens Bros. building because it offered more than seven thousand square feet and a basement. Tax credits allowed him to take on the $1.5 million project.

"I see the preservation of our architectural and cultural history as the gateway to our city's future success," McClain told the *Gazette*. He uncovered windows boarded up for half a century, removed the false ceiling and restored glazed brick and, in early 2014, opened his brewpub, Lion Bridge Brewing Company.

John Carl Berge, son of former Czech Village Association president John Berge, eyed the Kadlec Bros. Building between the brewpub and the bridge that had been a Salvation Army retail outlet when gutted by the flood. He convinced Jim Jacobmeyer, former interim director of the Czech Village/New Bohemia Main Street District, to manage the Artisan's Sanctuary, where artists can rent studio space and hold gallery showings. The six-thousand-square-foot sanctuary, opened in November 2014, displays along its side a commissioned mural depicting patron saints of Czech and Slovak

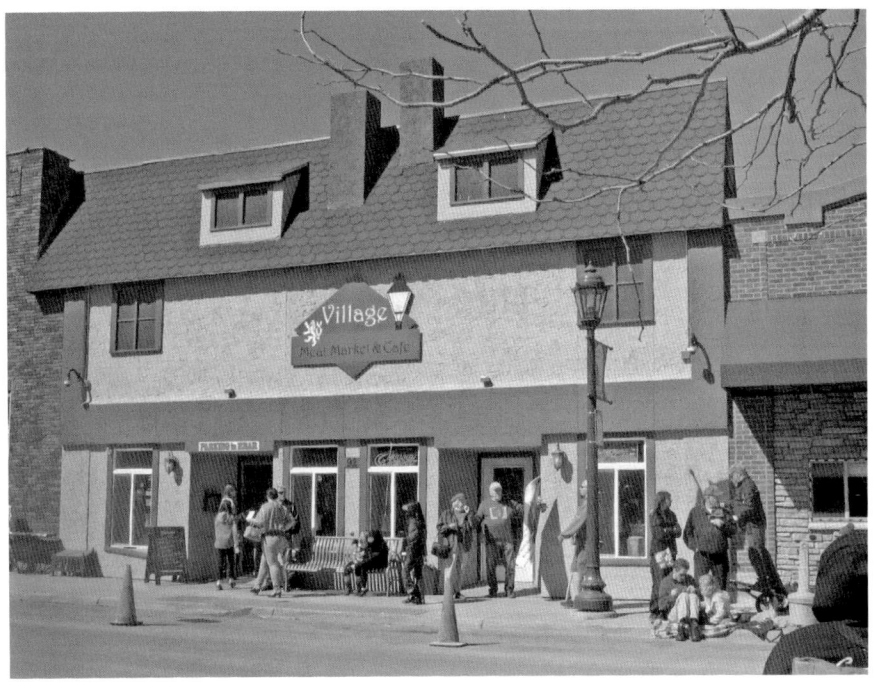

The Village Meat Market in Czech Village as it looks today once housed the Boddicker School of Music. *Photo by Dave Rasdal.*

people—St. Wenceslaus, St. Ludmila and St. John—names on the two Catholic churches and the cemetery.

St. Wenceslaus Catholic Church, inundated with floodwater, was cleaned out with volunteer help that included twenty students from the University of Notre Dame on fall break to remove contaminated soil from the basement. Just three and a half months after the flood, on September 28, 2008, the congregation held its reopening Mass.

St. Ludmila Catholic Church, razed before the flood after saving its original organ, stained-glass windows and two bells by hoisting them out with a crane, had dedicated its new $3 million church east of the old site on September 1, 2001. It stayed high and dry.

Here on these church grounds, descendants of Vaclav Drahozal, the lard renderer at the packinghouse, planted a single oak tree on June 27, 2010, to commemorate one hundred years in America.

"We will not forget the old country," said an emotional Bernie Drahozal, Vaclav's grandson, as he repeated that day the words of his ancestor. "We will still speak Czech but we will learn English. This is our country now."

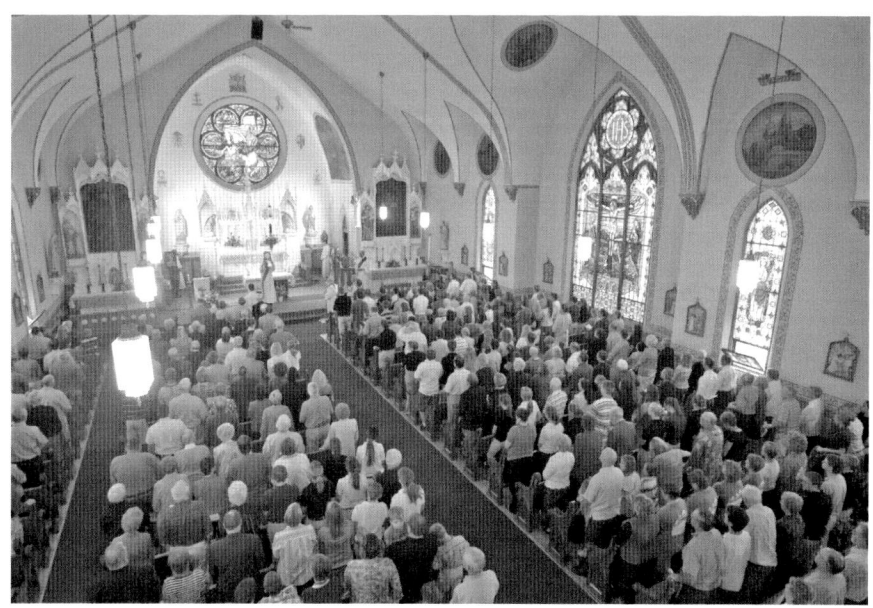

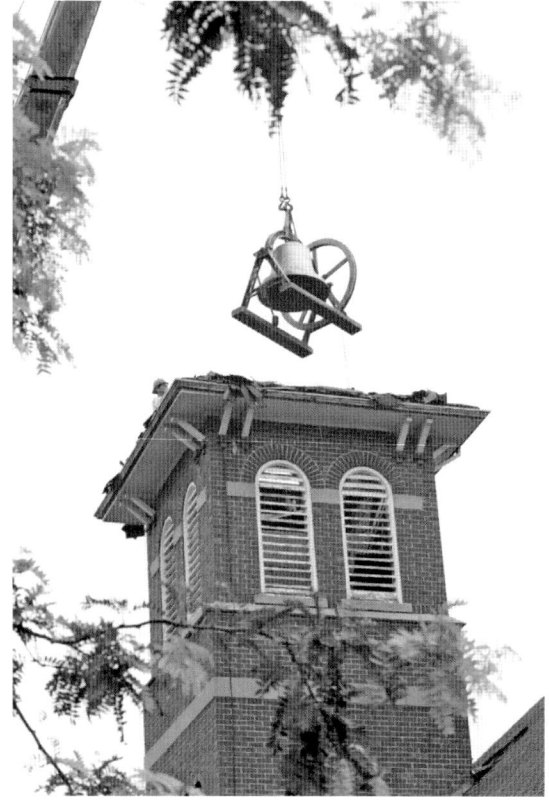

Above: Members of the congregation at St. Wenceslaus Catholic Church in the New Bohemia area worship during the post-flood reopening Mass on September 28, 2008. *Courtesy of the* Cedar Rapids Gazette.

Left: A crane from Coonrod Wrecker and Crane Services lifts the larger of two bells saved from the steeple of St. Ludmila Catholic Church on July 6, 2000, before it was torn down. *Courtesy of the* Cedar Rapids Gazette.

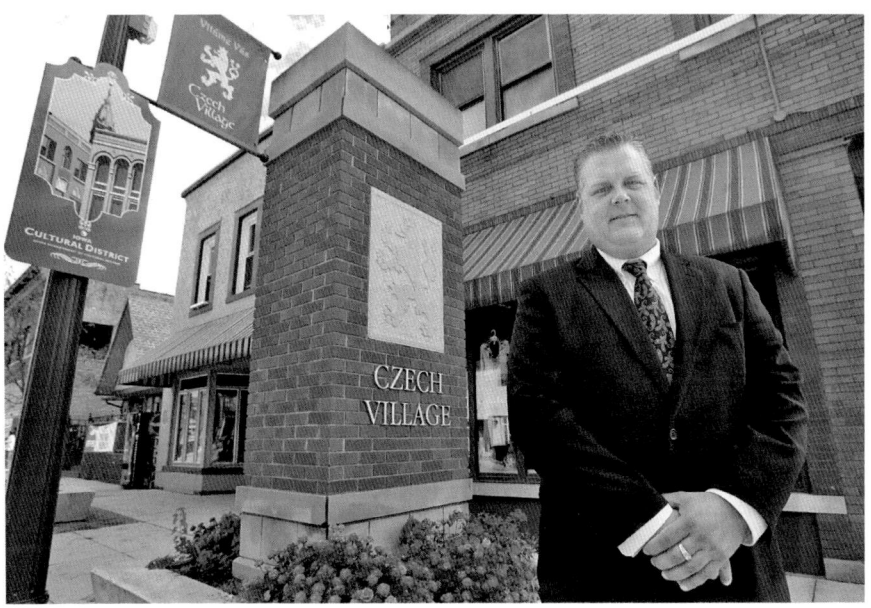

Baron Stark, who bought several buildings in Czech Village after the flood of 2008, has envisioned the area as a tourist destination similar to Galena, Illinois. *Courtesy of the* Cedar Rapids Gazette.

About that time, Baron Stark completed his acquisition of several flood-damaged properties in Czech Village. As a youngster, he'd often accompany his mother, who is half Czech, for shopping and festive events on the Avenue. He became interested in history following his father's lead of collecting antiques and war memorabilia.

"The reason why I picked Czech Village was my mom went down there constantly," he said. "We'd go down for Houby Days and to markets at the Roundhouse. I had good memories of that area. It was a historical place."

Stark hoped to restore historical value to Czech Village, as well as make it a bigger-than-ever tourist attraction.

"So many Czech people are gone from there now," he said. "That's what's sad. Some of the essence of Czech Village is gone."

In late 2006, Stark bought his first property in Czech Village to resurrect a Czech-market flavor. He liquidated the inventory of Altered Ego, a costume shop, and opened Deda & Babi's Antiques & Collectibles, playing on the names Czech children give their grandparents. He brought in fifty-five display cases and up to fifty consignees selling their wares. He hired three people to run it.

Thinking his building at 95 Sixteenth Avenue Southwest would be safe from flooding in 2008 since it was one of the last built, in 1978, and located on high ground, Stark notified vendors to remove merchandise and installed gasoline-powered water pumps in the basement as a precaution. But a week after the flood, the pumps had run dry, and the basement was full of silt and water—light bulbs floated eerily right-side up like glass bubbles. Stark cleaned and repaired to FEMA regulations, even installing a sprinkler system, and leased it as the Bohemian Café and Bakery. That worked for a while, so did Smuggler's Wharf, but for now the building wants for a tenant.

"It's not easy to attract small businesses, the mom-and-pop stores, because of the competition from the big box stores and the malls," Stark said.

But he was determined. He'd built Stark Enterprises, a grading, landscaping, lawn care, snow removal, pressure washing business in Fairfax from the ground up, incorporating in 1996. He did a lot of the early work himself. He knew what it takes to succeed.

In 2009 and 2010, Stark acquired the Czech Feather & Down (at 72–74 Sixteenth Avenue), ArBuckle's (at 77–79), Czech Quarters (at 62–67), Polehna's Meat Market (at 96) and Bartunik's Appliances (at 98). He bought the house at 1607 C Street Southwest and had two more C Street Southwest properties removed from the demolition list—1501, a former 1920s service station, and 1507, once known as Smiley's Garage—so he could buy them. They became a barbershop and Sauce Bar & Bistro, a restaurant known for using fresh ingredients.

As Stark rehabilitated, history surfaced.

ArBuckle's, in a 1910 building once home to Citizens Savings Bank, had its vault with a door dated 1898. "The guy was cheap," Stark laughed. "He bought a used vault."

Beneath the Czech Quarters tavern he discovered a "smuggler's tunnel" behind a cellar door. Inside a ten- by ten-foot limestone-walled room he found a three- by three-foot hole that led to a six-foot-tall tunnel with dirt floors and walls shored up by heavy wooden timbers. It extended toward Sixteenth Avenue and then stopped. He speculated it once led to other secret tunnels used during Prohibition. Old beer bottles, he said, were proof.

Stark's buildings required a lot of work—the Bartunik's building slid eighteen inches off its foundation, some had collapsed walls, one required removal of five layers of flooring and Pohlena's had a wall with evidence of an earlier fire. Government-backed financial incentives helped, but it will be a long time until they're worth what has been invested.

Stark's foray into Czech Village has not been without controversy. Even though he paid 105 percent of pre-flood assessed value to save buildings from the wrecking ball, some people thought he took advantage of desperate owners. And his reopening of the Czech Quarters as the Red Baron Bar & Dance Club in the spring of 2010 ignited a firestorm. To some, the name conjured up war. It didn't help that he decorated the bright red exterior with an Iron Cross.

"They think I'm German and that I'm taking over Czechoslovakia," Stark said. "Nothing could be further from the truth. Baron is my name. The Red Baron was World War I, not World War II. The Iron Cross has been around for centuries—it's not Nazi. I painted it red because that's a Czech color. I love Czech Village."

What hurt Czech Village recovery the most, Stark said, was the necessary demolition of hundreds of homes in the residential neighborhood. He hopes the city's longtime and now closed landfill—nicknamed Mount Trashmore—in the former Stumptown area downriver can finally be converted into a destination recreation area as dreamed about for decades.

"It's a slow recovery," Stark said. "We did a lot of fixing up in a short time. But I think, down the road, as we get more publicity and more people down there, it'll get better."

New Bo Emerges

Across the Cedar River in New Bohemia—people call it New Bo or NewBo—the transformation begun in the dark days of the 1990s has picked up amazing steam.

By October 2008, tenants were returning to the largely undamaged upper two floors of the J.G. Cherry Building. The main level had been cleaned up for access but still needed total renovation. Hundreds of volunteers made cleanup of the solid 1919 brick building go faster, but it had sustained more than $1 million in damage. As the owners replaced the floor and main-level windows using grants and loans but no FEMA money, they intentionally kept costs to a minimum to ensure affordable rents for artistic, creative tenants they'd attracted before and wanted to attract in the future.

About 60 percent of pre-flood tenants returned. Those that didn't were in too much shock, lost everything, didn't have the energy and/or the resources to rebuild or simply decided to relocate somewhere else. Some new tenants came from flooded buildings elsewhere in the neighborhood

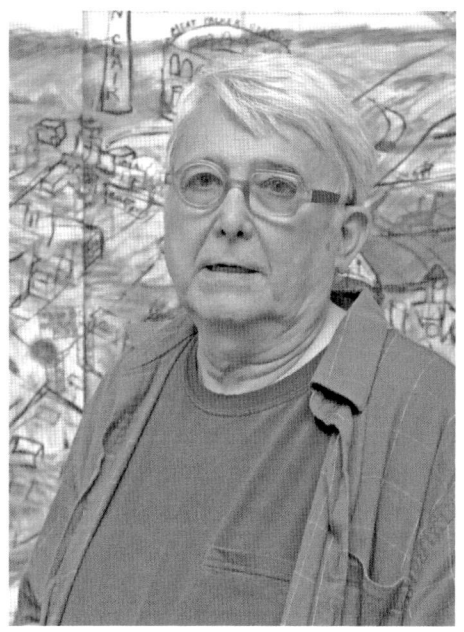

Mel Andringa, co-founder of Legion Arts, discusses the resurrection of the CSPS Hall and the New Bohemia neighborhood in his art studio in the J.G. Cherry Building. *Photo by Dave Rasdal.*

such as the Ceramic Center that had considered moving to the Cherry Building before the flood and became the first tenant on the remodeled first floor. The building is now full again.

"We have people on a waiting list to get into the building," Lijun Chadima said. "The artist, the entrepreneur, they all have this creative energy. When they come in here, they inspire each other."

Creative energy at the CPSP Hall not only brought back the first live performance on September 26, 2008 but also convinced Mel Andringa and John Herbert to push even harder to buy the building from R.G. Prucha. The Legion Arts founders had no authority to work on the first floor after the flood, but they volunteered to help anyway, as did many people in the neighborhood, even as Prucha hired immigrant workers to clean up. Then the new state I-JOBS program came along to help with flood recovery, historical preservation and job creation.

"We hit the trifecta," Andringa said. On the Register of Historic Places since the 1980s, the CSPS Hall more than qualified. The pre-flood plan expedited matters. Yet the $1 million price tag to buy and refurbish the building before the flood had mushroomed to $6 million. Still, after completing the paperwork shuffle, Legion Arts secured an I-JOBS grant, historic preservation tax credits and other incentives to accomplish the dream. It bought the CPSP Hall for $700,000 and the adjacent firehouse for $50,000 and completed what became a $7 million project for a grand opening in August 2011. And as Andringa imagined years before, the main level has its bookstore and coffeehouse.

In 2016, Legion Arts will own the CSPS Hall free and clear, just in time to celebrate the building's 125th anniversary that June. It will also be Legion Arts' 40th anniversary, the 26th in Cedar Rapids.

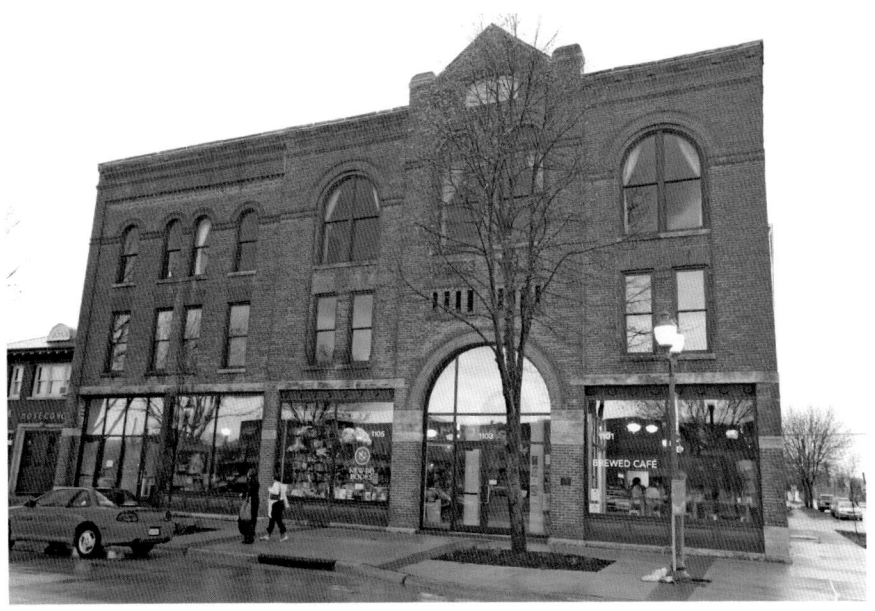

The historic CSPS Hall, home to Legion Arts in the New Bohemia district since the early 1990s, had been renovated by 2013 after it was extensively damaged in the flood. Renovation included improved performance and gallery facilities as well as retail space. *Courtesy of the* Cedar Rapids Gazette.

Yet as the neighborhood has not only recovered but also become home to shiny new buildings and $200,000-plus warehouse condominiums, Andringa feels nostalgic. "An artistic community has been achieved," he said, "but that's not without manipulation of its definition."

The recently promoted "Creative Corridor" concept that includes I-380 and Iowa City, he said, stretches the imagination to include as artists those who work at jobs or operate businesses for profit. He knows these people work hard and can be innovative in their professions, but they aren't the traditional sacrificial artists who wait tables to make ends meet while hoping something they create might help pay the bills.

"Everything became an art, so everybody is an artist," Andringa said. "Those artists can't afford to live here. Certainly no barista in a coffee shop is going to be able to afford $1,200 a month rent to live here."

But Andringa acknowledged, if there's anything constant about the neighborhood today, it is change. "We are all immigrants here. There's always a new wave."

A couple decades ago, immigrants to the neighborhood included the African American Museum of Iowa, formed in 1994 as the African

American Heritage Foundation. In 2003, the organization opened its seventeen-thousand-square-foot African American Museum near the east end of the Twelfth Avenue Bridge, rededicated in 2005 as the Dr. Martin Luther King Jr. Memorial Bridge. The grand opening unveiled "Doorways: A History of African Americans in Iowa." That permanent exhibit was soon joined by "Door of No Return," where visitors entered a slave ship in West Africa and followed the journey of black people to the United States and Iowa.

After being heavily damaged by the flood, with about $500,000 worth of exhibits lost, officials decided to remain. In fact, after the museum put $1.2 million into restoration, director Thomas Moore looked on the positive side and said the new start would give staff an opportunity to rebuild earlier exhibits better than before.

The museum reopened in January 2009, concentrated on building oral histories and featured an array of traveling exhibits in its Gayle Sayers Changing Exhibit Gallery. The permanent exhibit, "Endless Possibilities," traces the heritage of Iowa's African American citizens from Africa through slavery and the Civil War to the civil rights struggles and the contributions they make in today's society.

If there's been a staple in New Bo, it is the Little Bohemia, the longest continuously operating tavern in Cedar Rapids in the 1883 brick building at the corner of Third Street Southeast and Fourteenth Avenue, named to the National Register of Historic Places in 1998.

An iconic presence, "Little Bo" features a nearly full-length wooden bar, ceiling fans, memorabilia plastered all over the walls and the original pine floor restored after the flood. Leon "Tunnie" Melsha, who used to hang out at Little Bo, bought it in 1978. His son, Jeff, has been the manager, both before and after the flood.

When Little Bo reopened in late 2010, Jeff Melsha immediately began serving its signature goulash based on a recipe handed down from one owner to the next, although long gone from the menu were the pig's ear and snout sandwiches. Except for the flood, Little Bo had been open as a tavern since Prohibition ended in the 1930s, although rumors and police arrest records show beer was served and consumed at the tavern even when it was illegal. The tavern has operated under different names, including Puzdernick's, as far back as the 1880s.

Also in 2010 and a block away, the intersection of Third Street Southeast and Twelfth Avenue was in the midst of its post-flood transformation to become the heart of New Bohemia.

In 2003, at the southwest corner of the intersection, Village Bank & Trust had opened by turning back the clock on the vault-like gray two-story stone structure built in 1917 as the second Iowa State Savings Bank that went belly up during the Great Depression. Reorganized into First Trust & Savings Bank in 1934, the name changed in 1999 to Marquette Bank, which was later acquired by Wells Fargo.

As Village Bank & Trust, the building's "modernized" features were removed, including lowered ceilings, glass-block windows and carpet that revealed original marble floors. It was restored as much as was practically possible to the way it was.

"Because I'm Czech, I felt this was an opportunity to do two things—help revitalize the area and give us a chance to expand our market by serving this niche of customers," said Ernie Buresh, also owner of other banks and a frequent visitor to the Bohemian district since his youth in the 1930s.

After the flood, Buresh sold the bank to the nonprofit Neighborhood Development Corp. because he was nearly eighty-three years old and ready to wind down his banking career. The corporation finished flood cleanup and restoration and then sold the bank to a private entity. In March 2011,

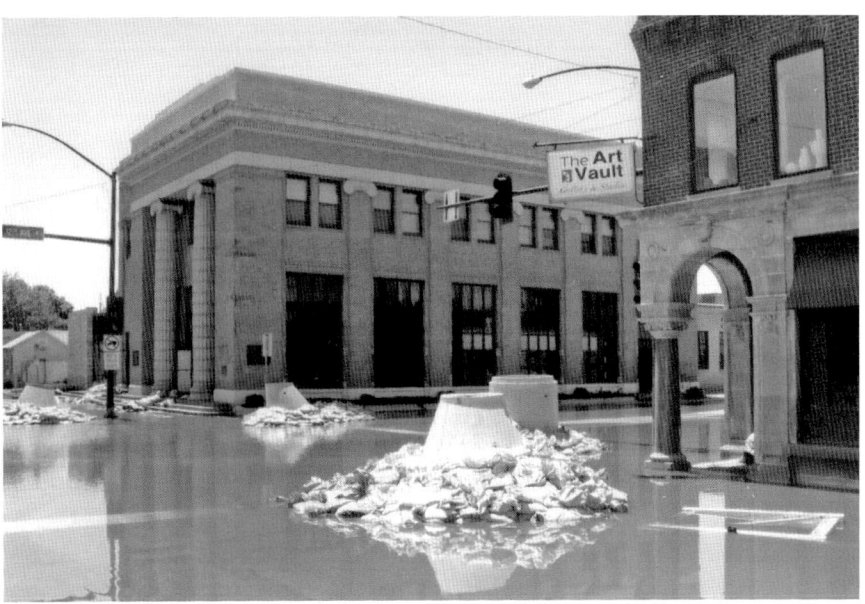

Water begins to recede from the Village Bank and the Art Vault, at the intersection of Twelfth Avenue and Third Street Southeast in the New Bohemia area on June 17, 2008. The bank is now New Bo Ale House, and the Art Vault has become Parlor City Pub and Eatery. *Photo by Mark Stoffer Hunter.*

it opened as Capone's Restaurant and Hideaway Bar, which lasted a year and a half. Today, it is the New Bo Ale House, a restaurant/tavern, with a separate business, NewBo Sushi, off to the south.

Before the flood, a handful of taverns populated the area, including the motorcycle-themed Chrome Horse Saloon & Slop House. It opened on March 13, 2004, on the main level of the ZCBJ Hall at the intersection's southeast corner, where taverns had served customers as far back as the 1960s. Upstairs, a live entertainment venue, Third Street Live, replaced earlier music venues in the auditorium-sized space with its elevated stage at one end and horseshoe balcony around the other three sides.

Both businesses reopened after the flood, but neither remain in the ZCBJ Hall, which is undergoing renovation for new office and entertainment options. Third Street Live became Third Street Saloon on December 5, 2008. The Chrome Horse, because it was on the main level devastated by the flood, took nine months to clean and refurbish. It reopened on March 13, 2009, in time for St. Patrick's Day, with a new horseshoe bar and handcrafted woodwork. A July 2014 fire forced the closure of both.

After the flood, Jon Jelinek, an investor in Third Street Live and the Chrome Horse after he was in a partnership that in 1996 purchased the ZCBJ Hall, saw opportunity cater-corner across the street in the original 1906 Iowa State Savings Bank.

No stranger to the neighborhood, Jelinek had purchased the Jacobs Building down the street, fixed it up and lived on its main level before the flood chased him out. But he had labored to build up a construction company, incorporated in 1987 and sold in 2007, so he set about cleaning the Jacobs Building and eyed the old bank occupied by the Art Vault. Jelinek said owner Dick McGowan wasn't interested in selling the building before the flood but offered it for sale the day they returned to the muddy mess. Jelinek hesitated for a couple of weeks, just long enough for the basement and main level to be mucked out, and then offered to buy the building. Not wanting to discuss a price out loud, they each wrote a number on a sheet of paper and compared. McGowan's asking price was $5,000 more than Jelinek's offer, so they split the difference. "You never saw a man with a bigger smile on his face," Jelinek recalled.

All along, Jelinek's plans were to open a bar in the space to compete with the Chrome Horse, since he'd parted with the other owners on less than amicable terms. But he needed a different theme, a unique name.

He selected Parlor City Pub and Eatery, playing off the city's historical nickname, one made famous in Carl Van Vechten's 1924 novel, *The Tattooed Countess*, which took place in the 1890s.

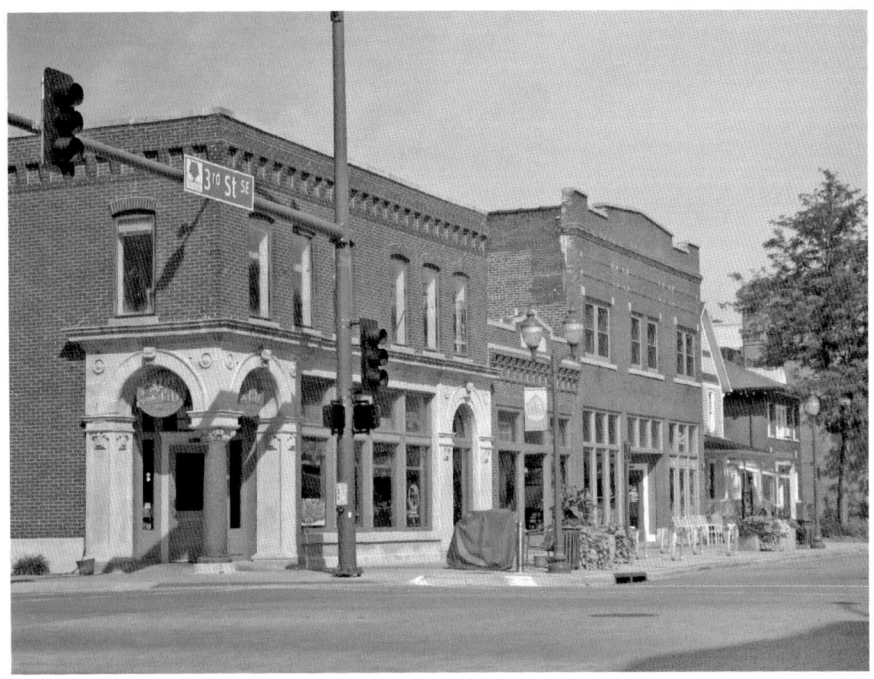

Parlor City Pub and Eatery, as it looks today at 1125 Third Street Southeast, in the New Bo district, opened on March 13, 2009, after owner Jon Jelinek bought and refurbished the flood-damaged building. *Photo by Dave Rasdal.*

"I always heard Cedar Rapids got that name because it was a friendly and clean town, that people would invite you into their parlors," Jelinek said. "Then somebody told me the town had some whorehouses and the clients would wait in the parlor. I like to believe the first reason and I think that's closer to what it was."

Jelinek restored the old bank building at 1125–27 Third Street Southeast, added artifacts and old photographs of Cedar Rapids on the walls, offered several dozen beers on tap and opened on March 13, 2009—the thirteenth a significant date in the Chrome Horse's history. Business has been so good he's expanded Parlor City twice, including a large courtyard flanked by one-hundred-year-old concrete sidewalk advertising signs salvaged in 2012 when the ZCBJ Hall sidewalk was redone.

"I never had any interest in history until the flood," said Jelinek, who is approaching his sixtieth birthday. "Then I saw all the stuff the city was tearing down and it was time to do something. I realized every day is history."

He also comes from good Czech stock—his great-grandfather Jelinek who died in 1938 came from Bohemia—and is proud that "the Czechs were a big influence on Cedar Rapids. People who come down here can see that every day."

In 2012, he received a $50,000 challenge grant from Main Street Iowa and set about restoring two houses between the Jacobs Building and the firehouse/CSPS Hall complex. With another $200,000, he turned the tiny fourteen- by eighteen-foot laborer's house at 1113 Third Street Southeast, built in 1875 by Albert and Anna Herda, into a cute green one-room bed-and-breakfast and redid the two-story circa-1900 house at 1117 Third Street into a bright yellow commercial space and walkup two-bedroom apartment.

Lest you think he'd stop there, Jelinek, with invaluable assistance from his family—four children, Nick, Maddie, Ben and Sam (deceased), and Nick's wife, Stephanie, who manages Parlor City—plans restoration of the old Cedar Rapids Carriage Works that has its manual wagon lift inside and an old butcher shop that faces Second Street Southeast with an adjacent brick house that's home to Nick and Stephanie. He hopes the businesses can be passed from generation to generation, which is why he also bought the old Ideal Theater building on Fourteenth Avenue Southeast to open as a reception hall.

"It's cool," Jelinek said. "You have to understand, with history, that old buildings are going to flood because that's where they built them in those days, along the rivers. You need to preserve them. You can't build a new one-hundred-year-old building."

Jelinek feels fortunate—the right place, the right time—to watch the neighborhood develop around him with new construction integrated into the old look and no chain operations of any kind.

"The flood was the best thing that could have happened to New Bo if it was to become what it is today," he said. "With the way it was down here before that time, it would have taken twenty years or more to get things really moving."

NewBo City Market

Paramount to the progress was the city's $3.1 million streetscape along Third Street Southeast completed in 2011 and, directly across from Parlor City, the opening of the NewBo City Market in 2012.

The streetscape—half paid by the city and half paid by property owners—dressed up Third Street Southeast from Eighth Avenue to Fourteenth Avenue with a new concrete street, sidewalks, lights and planters.

An overflow crowd of two thousand people streamed through the doors when NewBo City Market opened on October 27, 2012. Customers bought out bread, cupcakes, flowers, coffee, ice cream, popcorn, fresh vegetables and other goods offered by twenty-five vendors who had set up shop inside the converted eighteen-thousand-square-foot warehouse. And they just keep coming.

"I think it will revolutionize the town and it's already revolutionizing the neighborhood," Kurt Friese, director of healthy food and advocacy at the market, told the *Gazette* in 2012. He predicted it could draw 300,000 visitors or more annually.

The $5 million NewBo City Market, based on ideas planted at least a decade earlier, rose in a salvaged warehouse of Iowa Steel and Iron. Once pale green, it had holes punched in it for windows and was painted a brick red. A green tractor-riding rooster became part of the new logo while in front of the building a landscaped green space and sidewalks hosted outdoor farmers' markets, musical entertainment and even yoga classes.

Diagonally across the Eleventh Avenue Southeast intersection with Third Street, Michael Richards restored the two-story brick Matyk building that his family bought in 1999. He spent $100,000 on restoration, including the tedious removal of the pre-flood whitewash to reveal red brick and native Stone City limestone. He hoped additional work, including tuck pointing the brick, would add another one hundred years of life to the 1893 building erected by Czech immigrants who operated a dry goods store on the main level and lived upstairs through World War II before it became Midwest Distribution in the '50s. Richards operates Soyawax International (soy-based candles) out of the building and uses the main level for neighborhood gatherings. Active in the Oak Hill–Jackson neighborhood and an advocate of the NewBo City Market from the beginning, Richards told the *Gazette* in 2013 that "we're heading toward the vision."

Down the street, in Frank Suchy's old jewelry store building, Anthony and Nick Bata, father and son, also saw a future in the neighborhood and opened their upscale yet comfortable restaurant, Bata's, in 2012.

Today, New Bo is bustling, even though the Sinclair site has yet to be developed. New construction is a constant with a five-story condo/business complex rising just north of NewBo City Market, new condominium developments set to open east and west of the main corridor and the recent

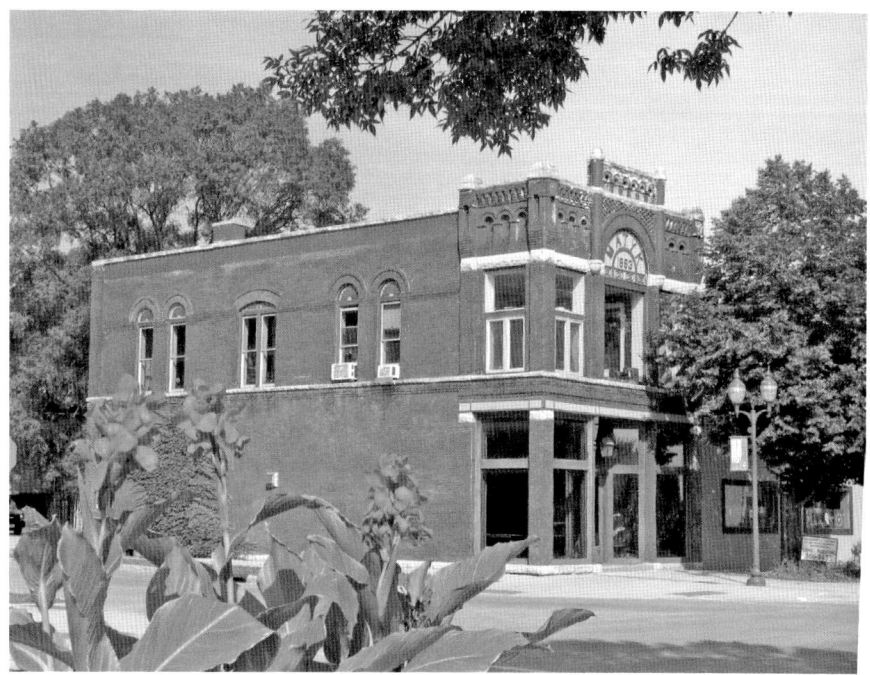

The exterior of the Matyk Building, an 1893 dry goods building at 1029 Third Street Southeast in the New Bo district, has been fixed up by owner Michael Richards since the flood of 2008. *Photo by Dave Rasdal.*

completion of a new building for Geonetric, a website developer. A $20 million, four-building complex across the street and just east of NewBo City Market will add office, retail and residential space.

The transition has, in just a few short years, brought regular bicycle traffic all week long, Friday night crowds to the taverns where sheer numbers provide a safe environment and weekend visitors to vendors and special events at the NewBo market. The inaugural New Bo Music Fest sold 2,900 tickets in August 2015.

September 2015 saw everything from an accordion flash mob surprising visitors at Czech Fest to the opening of Czech Deli in the NewBo City Market by recent Czech Republic immigrant Thomas Slepicka, who specializes in open-faced sandwiches and kolaches. The annual five-day Landfall Festival of World Music centered on the CSPS Hall featured such groups as the musical and dance Zedashe Ensemble from the Republic of Georgia. And the city of Cedar Rapids agreed to transfer ownership of the NewBo City Market to the nonprofit group operating it.

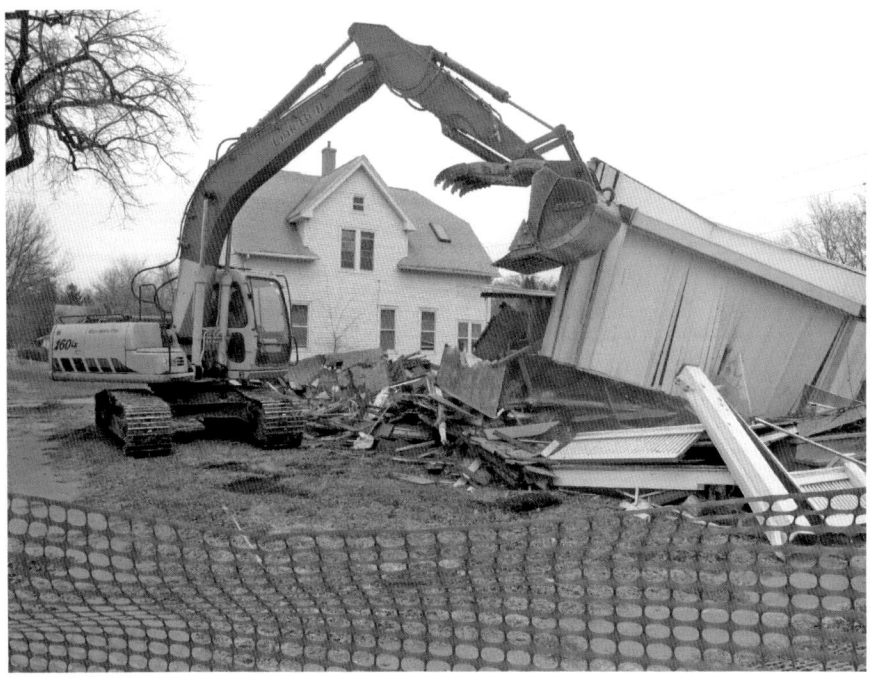

Demolition crews finish off the first round of house demolitions from the flood of 2008 in Czech Village on November 18, 2010. *Courtesy of the* Cedar Rapids Gazette.

The future seems wide open. For one, business owners in Czech Village/New Bo have asked the city council to allow them to tax themselves as a self-supportive municipal improvement district to use the revenue for beautification and marketing.

Front-burner projects include enhancing a thirty-five-acre green space in Czech Village, where houses once stood, into a parking area with room for reinstallation of the Roundhouse, disassembled after the flood. The washed-out CRANDIC railroad bridge could be replaced with a lighter trail bridge atop the same pillars in a $2 to $3 million project to give pedestrians and bicyclists on the Cedar River Trail a loop around Czech Village and New Bo when combined with the Bridge of Lions. And scheduled for Grant Wood's 125th birthday in 2016 is an art festival centered on the NewBo City Market.

Czech Village & New Bohemia

Historical Challenges

Still, not every dream could be realized, including rescuing historic flood-damaged structures. One disappointment—the old Wencil Martinek hardware store, built about 1890 and used in the early 1900s as Globe Grocery at 131 Fourteenth Avenue Southeast—was damaged beyond saving in a November 2012 fire. Another was the 113-year-old P. Hach building across Fourteenth Avenue Southeast at Second Street. It succumbed to the wrecking ball on May 12, 2014, despite rescue attempts by Save Cedar Rapids Heritage.

Last known as the South Side Tap, which closed years before the flood, the two-story wood-frame P. Hach building was a landmark to people crossing the Bridge of Lions from Czech Village. It once had a bowling alley and survived the Great Depression, but the flood of 2008 was too much. In 2009, Leon "Tunnie" Melsha, owner of the adjacent Little Bo tavern, paid $35,000 for it and considered restoration as a tavern or office building. Memorable to Tunnie as the first bar he'd visited at age six or seven, he told *Gazette* columnist Todd Dorman in 2010, "Big fish bowls of beer. Man, that really stuck in my mind. They wouldn't let women into the bar, but they let children in."

Left untouched since the flood, the building was planned for demolition in 2013. When word got out, Beth Chacey DeBoom, president and founding member of Save Cedar Rapids Heritage, tried to save it. The process was too far along, however, and estimates of $500,000 to $1 million for restoration made it unfeasible.

"I shed a tear for the place," said Allan Hach, great-great-grandson of Peter Hach, on the day of demolition. "But what I noticed when they tore it down, there was not a decent piece of lumber in the whole place laying there. Especially the base floor. The cross members and the floor boards were all just rotted out."

"Something will be built there someday," said a disappointed DeBoom, "but there's no way you can reconstruct what was lost today."

With another bit of history gone, DeBoom could stroll diagonally across the block to her Heart House at 1301 Third Street Southeast. She'd become acquainted with the house in 2012, when city officials asked Save Cedar Rapids Heritage to evaluate several flood-damaged homes. An "Ewww" at first sight turned into hesitant affection. An inspection proved the house a worthy, but costly, candidate for restoration. At auction, DeBoom paid $3,000 for the ugly duckling and promised to rehabilitate it into at least a not-so-ugly duck.

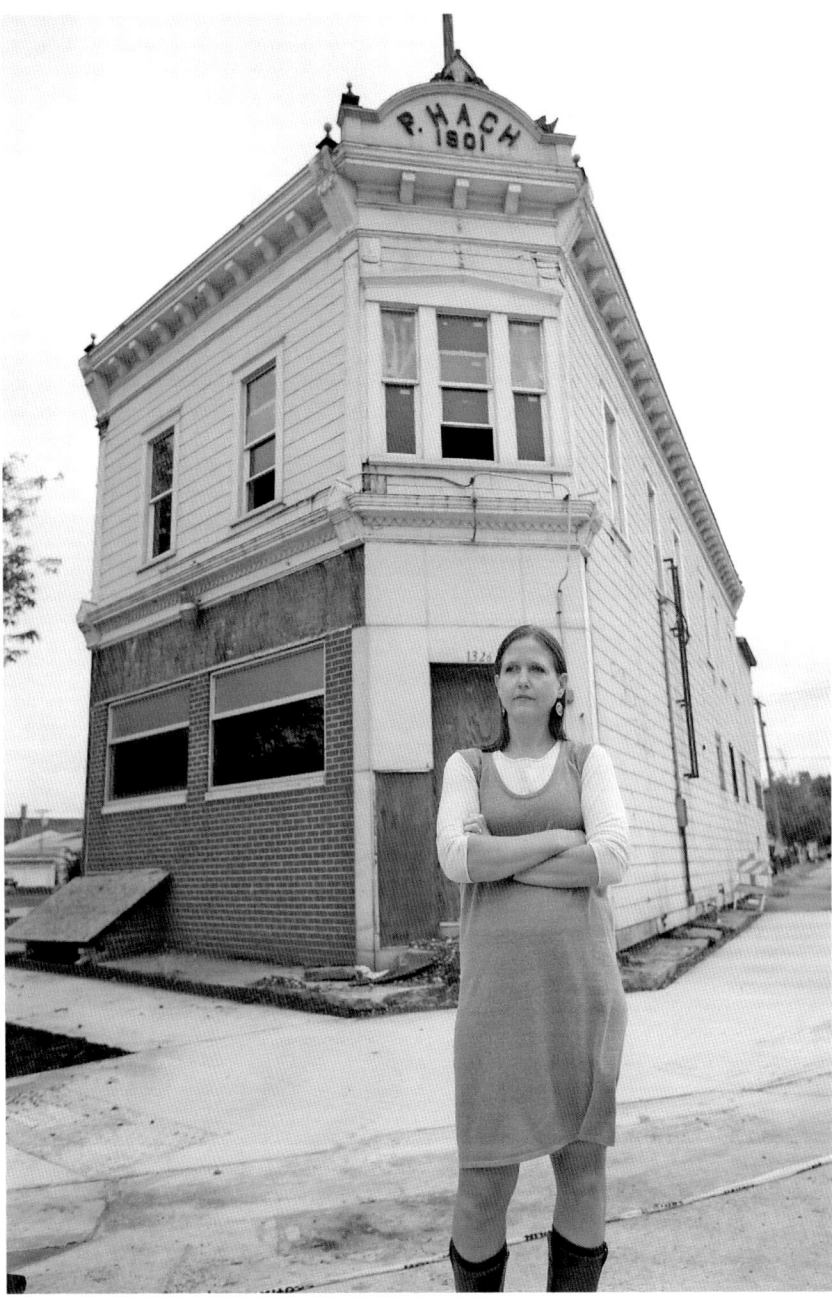

Beth Chacey DeBoom stands in front of the P. Hach building, built in 1901 at the Sixteenth Avenue bridge entrance to New Bohemia, which she and other preservationists hoped to save from demolition on September 16, 2013. The building was later torn down. *Courtesy of the* Cedar Rapids Gazette.

Built in 1885 by thirty-year-old delivery driver Vaclav Novotny and his wife, Antonia, a seamstress, the house remained in the same family until 1951. It began as one story, with the second floor added about 1910 to provide room for a daughter and her family. A barn out back, large enough for two cars today, was the stable for Vaclav's horses and wagon. Later, Elmer and Hilda Medinger, who worked at the nearby packinghouse, converted the upstairs into an apartment. It remained a two-family house until the flood.

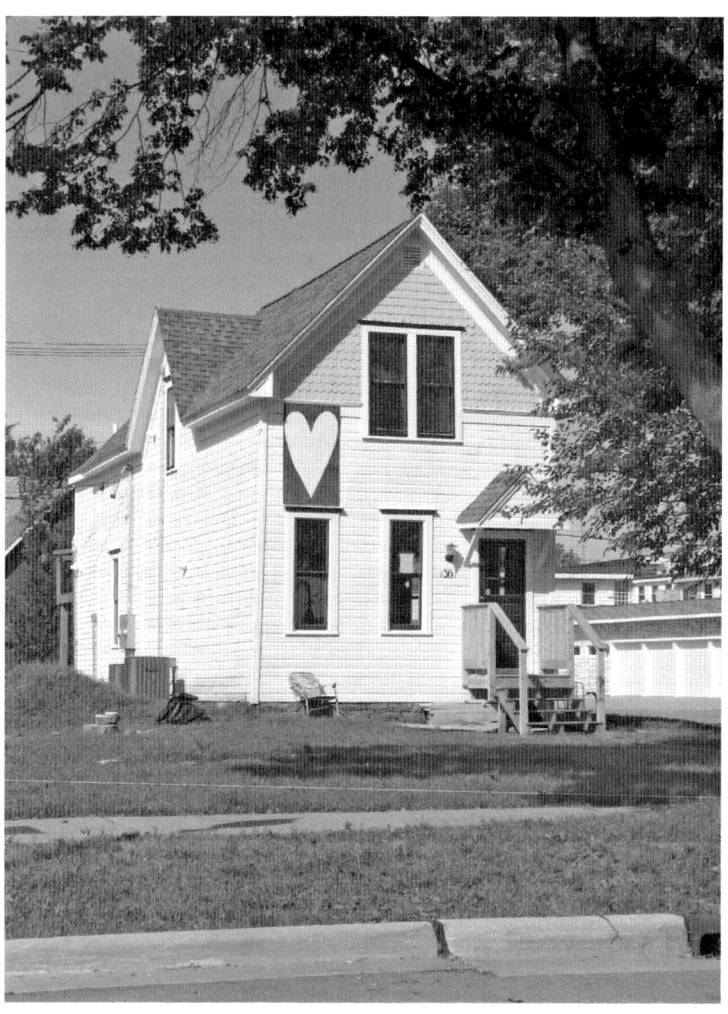

A new front stairway had just been added to the Heart House when this photo was taken in July 2015. Owner Beth DeBoom had completed renovation of the second floor into an apartment and planned to open Little House Antiques on the main level in the fall of 2015. *Photo by Dave Rasdal.*

Inside, DeBoom pointed to a line on a stairway railing support where floodwaters peaked nine feet above the main floor. She heard elderly upstairs residents were rescued by boat, leaving everything behind. As DeBoom began cleanup and restoration, she fell in love with the house. On a whim, on the outside second level visible to passersby, she mounted a large white heart.

"It was supposed to be temporary," she said, "but I'm not taking it down. It has become part of the house."

After elevating the 1,600-square-foot structure seventeen inches to be out of the flood plain, as required by the city, DeBoom and her husband, Tom, and their children, Finn and Frankie, embraced the project that includes a second-floor apartment with a claw-foot bathtub. "Every extra penny we've had has gone into this house," she said.

Resourcefulness, a Czech trait, has served her well, even as bills mount for new electrical wiring, plumbing, furnace and air-conditioning and energy-efficient windows. While most of the original hardwood floor and siding have been preserved with only a few new boards, she's also used pieces from eight other houses and a church.

A scavenger at heart, DeBoom has salvaged and recycled for years—hence the first floor of the Heart House became Little House Artifacts. She scours auctions, flea markets, houses being torn down and even roadside ditches for old sinks, light fixtures, chairs, doorknobs, doors—you name it. She has adopted the slogan "Everything has a story."

Inside the Heart House, DeBoom works with the windows open so the soothing sound of the chimes from the Czech museum's clock tower drift in from across the Cedar River. "That music keeps me on my toes," she said. "I hear it at noon, I know it's time for lunch."

The house is ideally located on Third Street Southeast, midway between New Bo's busy Twelfth Avenue intersection and the Little Bo tavern. Standing in the Heart House regularly reminds DeBoom of her Czech heritage. She'll remember her deceased mother, Jacqueline Chacey, who was "mortified" when her class at Wilson Junior High sang the school song in Czech. She'll laugh at her father, Al, who lives in Minnesota and claims to be all English even though his mother, Vlasta Dlask Chacey, was Czech. She'll fondly recollect the stories from Grandma Agnes about growing up in "the Flats" just east of New Bo in a house with no running water into the 1930s.

"My Czech heritage is more important to me than any nationality mixed in my blood," she said. "The reason why? I saw it through the eyes of some really lively, feisty women who embraced their heritage. I saw the culture as very vibrant, very much alive."

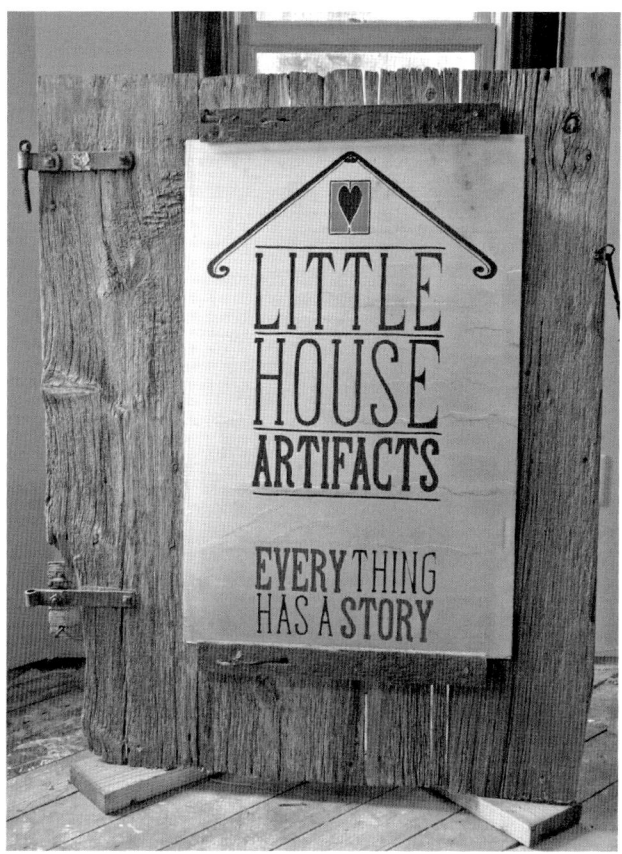

The Little House Artifacts sign that Beth DeBoom used to advertise her new business at early sales rests inside the living room of the Heart House. *Photo by Dave Rasdal.*

Soon after her Heart House quest began, DeBoom opened the door to Evelyn Medinger Swanson, a daughter of former owners, who feared it would be demolished. Overjoyed at the news of restoration, Swanson became a regular visitor, cheerleader and historian.

DeBoom, forty-seven, knew she was on the right path even as she was saddened by Swanson's death on September 4, 2015, at the age of eighty-three. For in this one house—in everything that has been preserved in the New Bohemia and Czech Village neighborhoods—one generation after another will continue to see and experience the role Czech immigrants played in the creation of "the Heartland" of America.

Appendix

EAT LIKE A CZECH

Donna Merkle, half Czech and half German, met her late husband, Guenter, who was born in Germany, at International Folk Day in Houston, Texas. They sampled Czech food and fell in love.

"It was the day that we both embraced the Czech culture and Guenter fell in love with Czech cooking," Donna said.

In 1999, they made their first of many visits to the National Czech & Slovak Museum & Library and by 2007 had moved to Cedar Rapids. Even though Texas has a large Czech population, the Merkles enjoyed being close to the museum, where Donna volunteers and has become president of the museum guild. She welcomed me into the world of Czech food at the museum's annual Taste of Czech and Slovak.

From Czech goulash, Slovak meatballs and dumplings with pork gravy to sauerkraut salad, rye bread and kolaches, we sampled more than a dozen dishes catered by Dostal Catering of Czech Village, a staple in Cedar Rapids since 1924.

Czech food encompasses so many tastes—from sweet to sour, from spicy to rather plain—that everyone can find something to like. As proof, Donna gave me a copy of the cookbook *Czech and Slovak Heritage: Family Stories, Traditions, Recipes* produced by the museum guild in 2007. It seems that whenever Czech people talk about their history they mention food.

Hermina Unzeitig Trejtnar's memories of her log cabin days in Cedar Rapids not only include recipes handed down from the late 1800s but also an explanation of how her family processed meat.

Appendix

"Every winter, probably twice during the cold months, my father would select a fat pig to butcher," Hermina recalled.

> *This would be another exchange job. My aunt and uncle would come to help. A fire was built outdoors and a big iron kettle would be filled with water. As the hog was butchered the blood was caught and saved to use in making jelita later in the day. The boiling water was poured into a large wooden tub that looked like a bath tub. The hog was dipped into this to loosen the hair. After the hog was clean inside and out it was hung up outside to cool well.*
>
> *Then my mother and aunt took over. The head was boiled and the meat from it, the heart, the liver, cooked barley, and loaves of dry bread were used for stuffing the jaternice. Stuffing the jaternice and jelita (sausages) was interesting to watch. Dad stuffed them a certain length and someone helped tying them off. Dozens were made and then placed in some outdoor building to freeze. That way they were kept for several weeks.*

Hermina described how her mother cut pork roasts and placed them into a large crock with grease and hot lard to be cooked. By covering the pork, it could be kept all summer.

> *Finally there was the chore of cutting up layers of fat to render the lard. We would cut the fat in pieces about one and a half inches square and place these in a big kettle to heat and fry. As the fat fried, mother poured off the hot grease into 4 gallon size crocks. When solid we had our lard for baking kolaches, pie baking, rye bread and cookies. The bits left from the fried down fat we called skvarky* [cracklings]. *A looked forward to treat was warm, fresh rye bread and skvarky.*

Since you can fill a book with recipes—that's what cookbooks are for—I'm limiting recipes here to a handful. If you really want to eat like a Czech, pick up the museum guild's *Czech and Slovak Heritage: Family Stories, Traditions, Recipes* or any number of Czech cookbooks available today.

Here's a *gulas* (goulash) recipe from Marj Nejdl in that book and four tasty recipes from Hermina and her daughter, author Marianne Klinsky:

APPENDIX

Gulas (Goulash)

1½ pounds beef (cubed)
2 pounds pork (cubed)
⅔ cup onions (chopped)
2 stalks celery (chopped)
ground caraway seed
paprika
garlic powder
pepper
seasoned salt
½ cup Italian dressing
1 cup chicken broth
½ cup tomato sauce

Bake beef for about an hour (might add a little water), half the time with lid on and half the time without the lid to brown. Add the pork and bake another hour. Add onions and celery (to taste), sprinkle with seasonings and add the liquids. Stir and bake another hour or until meat is tender. You can then sprinkle with flour (to make desired thickness). I make a sauce by shaking 3 tablespoons flour and 1¼ cup water and stir gradually into gulas. (I sprinkle a little sugar to bring out the taste and take a little of the sharpness out.) Serve over dumplings, noodles or mashed potatoes. This recipe can be made according to taste by adding and/or deleting spices.

Kolaches

2 packages dry yeast
½ cup warm water
2 teaspoons sugar
1 cup flour

Mix and let stand about 15 minutes, then add:

1 egg, plus 2 egg yolks
½ cup shortening, melted
½ cup sugar

2 teaspoons salt
1½ cups milk, warmed
¼ teaspoon mace
grated lemon rind

Once combined, add about 6 cups of flour. Beat well, grease top and let rise about two hours. Shape into small balls the size of a walnut. Brush with melted lard or oil and let rise until doubled in size. Kolaches need to be kept warm during the rising. Press down centers and fill with prune, poppy, apricot, cottage cheese or fresh fruit. Let rise again, bake in 400-degree oven about 10 minutes until deep golden brown. Remove to a rack to cool.

Sulc (a type of head cheese)

1 pound pork hock
1 pound pork cheek
1 beef heart
1 veal shank or knuckle
1 onion, chopped
1 cup chopped celery
1 teaspoon pickling spice
1 clove garlic
2 teaspoons salt, plus to taste
2 quarts water
1 cup vinegar
pepper
gelatin
parsley

Cook the meat, vegetables and spices in water until the meat is tender. Remove the meat from the liquid and cut into cubes. Strain the liquid. Add about 1 cup of vinegar to 3 cups of liquid. Add salt and pepper to taste. Soften gelatin in cold water and dissolve it in the hot liquid using the amount of gelatin as specified on the package for the amount of liquid that you wish to gel. Pour over the meat. Stir once or twice as the mixture congeals. May unmold and garnish with parsley.

APPENDIX

Rye Bread

2 packages dry yeast
1 quart warm water
1 tablespoon sugar

Mix and let the above stand about 15 minutes, then add:

4 cups white flour
3 tablespoons lard or oil, melted
3 tablespoons sugar
2 tablespoons salt
rye flour, as required (Old Doc if available)

Add enough rye flour to make a stiff dough. Grease the top, and let rise about two hours. Knead, and shape into loaves. Let rise ½ hour before baking. Bake at 350 degrees about 45 minutes depending on size of loaves.

Christmas Houska

2 packages yeast
½ cup warm water
1 tablespoon sugar
1 cup milk, warmed
½ cup sugar
½ cup shortening
6 cups flour
2 eggs
1 teaspoon salt
1 teaspoon mace
1 teaspoon vanilla
1 teaspoon anise
lemon rind
½ cup nuts
½ cup white raisins
1 cup candied fruit

Dissolve the yeast in warm water and sugar. Add remaining ingredients through lemon rind and enough flour to make a bread dough consistency (about 6 cups). Let rise until doubled in bulk. Stir in ½ cup nuts, ½ cup white raisins and 1 cup candied fruit.

Make into 8 rolls. Braid three for the bottom layer, another three for the second layer and twist the remaining two rolls and place on the top. Let rise 15 minutes or until light. Bake at 350 degrees for 45 minutes. When cool, the houska may be iced.

BIBLIOGRAPHY

Armstrong, Mary Helen. "The Cechs in Cedar Rapids." Bachelor of arts thesis, Cornell College, Mount Vernon, January 1950.

Brewer, Luther A., and Barthinius L. Wick. *History of Linn County Iowa from Its Earliest Settlement to the Present Time.* Illustrated. Vol. 1. Chicago: Pioneer Publishing Company, 1911.

Epic Surge: Eastern Iowa's Unstoppable Flood of 2008. Cedar Rapids, IA: Gazette Communications, 2008.

The History of Czechs in Cedar Rapids. Vol. 1, *1852–1942*, and Vol. 2, *1942–1982*. Cedar Rapids, IA: Czech Heritage Foundation, n.d. Revised 2012.

The History of Linn County, Illustrated. Chicago: Western Historical Company, 1878.

Hrbkova, Sarka B. "Bohemians Have Done Much for Cedar Rapids." *Cedar Rapids Republican Semi-Centennial Magazine Edition.* June 10, 1906.

Iowa Board of Immigration. "Iowa, Home for Immigrants." 1870. Reprinted in *Iowa: The Definitive Collection.* Edited by Zachary Michael Jack. North Liberty, IA: Tall Corn Books, 2009.

Jungman, C.A. "Chuck." Sixteenth Avenue Commercial Club. History paper, copyright 2005.

Rudis-Jicinsky, John. "Bohemians in Linn County." *Linn County Atlas*. Davenport: Iowa Publishing Company, 1907.

Newspapers

Cedar Rapids Evening Gazette, 1883–1981.

Cedar Rapids Gazette, 1981–2015.

Cedar Rapids Republican, 1874–1915.

Cedar Rapids Tribune, March 1929.

Family Histories

Chadima, Kathryn L. *A History of the Thomas & Anna Chadima Family of East Bohemia, Czechoslovakia and Cedar Rapids Iowa. Immigrated about 1866.* N.p., January 1986.

Klinsky, Marianne T. *Hermina: Her Recollections from Her Log Cabin Days, 1899 to 1992.* As told to Marianne Klinsky by Hermina Unzeitig Trejtnar. N.p., December 1991.

Svec, M. Melvina. *The Family History of Frank Svec and Rose Kvetensky, 1865–1984.* Cedar Rapids, IA: Lilly Printing Company, 1984.

Websites

Bicha, Karel D. "The Czechs in Wisconsin History." http://www.mfr-eng.com/rumreich/czechs-in-wisconsin-history.pdf.

"Czechoslovak History." Encyclopedia Britannica. http://www.britannica.com/topic/Czechoslovak-history.

Bibliography

"Early Temperance Activity in Iowa." Iowa Pathways. http://www.iptv.org/iowapathways/mypath.cfm?ounid=ob_000094.

National Register of Historic Places Continuation Sheet. Preservation Iowa. http://www.preservationiowa.org/downloads/bohemianhd_2.pdf.

"The Odyssey of the Czecho-Slovaks." http://nortvoods.net/rrs/siberia/czecharmy.htm.

"Teaching With Documents: The Homestead Act of 1862." National Archives. http://www.archives.gov/education/lessons/homestead-act.

INDEX

A

African American Museum of Iowa 159
Albright, Madeleine 128
Andringa, Mel 39, 142, 147, 158
ArBuckle, Greg 150
ArBuckle's 156
Artisan's Sanctuary 152
Art Vault 162

B

Ballon, Father Thomas 81
Barta Building 86
Barta, Frank 101
Barta Saddle & Leather 107, 150
Bartunik's Appliances 156
Bata's Restaurant 165
Beach, Alan 128
Belle Plaine 49
Benesh Mounted Band 56
Benes, President Eduard 105
Berge, John Carl 152
Bever, S.C. 34
Big Barn Livery Stable 107
Bily Lef (the White Lion) 101
Boddicker, Arlene Reyman 121
Boddicker School of Music 119, 121
Bohemain National Alliance 103
Bohemian Athens of America 68
Bohemian Brass Band 46, 52
Bohemian Dance Hall 31
Bohemian National Alliance 74
Bohemian Relief Society 74
Bohemian Savings and Loan Association 59, 89
Boies, Horace 56
Bridge of Lions 13, 14, 34, 37, 128, 135, 167, 168
Brown Healey Stone & Sauer 128
Buckhalter, Reverend Dr. Edward R. 72
Buresh, Ernie 161
Buresh, Lester and Ernest 131
Burian, Jacob 43
Bush, President George H.W. 135

Index

C

Capone's Restaurant and Hideaway Bar 162
Carmody Foundry 113
Carmody, J.T. 85
Cedar Rapids and Iowa City (CRANDIC) interurban railway 63
Cedar Rapids and Marion City Railway Company 63
Cedar Rapidske Listy 62
Cedar Rapids Restoration Club 90
Ceramic Center 158
Cereal City 63
Cernan, Eugene 127
Cesak, Emma 146
Ceska Beseda 58
Chadima, Bob 69, 140
Chadima Brothers Ice Company 68, 69, 140
Chadima, Joseph 69
Chadima, Lijun 41, 142, 158
Chadima, Thomas 68
Charles Bridge 13, 14, 127, 128, 135
Chelsea 49
Chmelar, Father Francis 60
Chrome Horse Saloon & Slop House 162
Citizens Savings Bank 80, 83, 90, 156
City of Five Seasons 28, 112
Civil War 14, 23, 24, 26, 54, 160
C.J.'s Sports Bar & Grill 150
C.K. Kosek bakery 79
Clifton Hotel 83, 84
Clinton, U.S. president Bill 126, 134
Clutier 49
Coe Camp 76
Cone, Marvin 144
Council of Higher Education 59

CRANDIC railroad bridge 36, 110, 167
Creative Corridor 159
CSPS Hall 39, 47, 55, 56, 57, 64, 74, 78, 94, 98, 142, 145, 158, 164, 166
Culver, Iowa governor Chet 151
Czech Alliance 95, 97, 100, 101
Czech Deli 166
Czech Feather & Down 156
Czech Fine Arts Foundation 115, 128
Czech Heritage Foundation 115
Czech Home Guard 98, 99
Czech National Alliance 97, 101
Czech National Cemetery 105, 132
Czech Plus Band 122, 126
Czech Quarters 156, 157
Czech Reformed Church 61
Czech Republic 13, 14, 126, 127, 134, 137, 149
Czech School 46, 58, 59, 74
Czech Village Association 115, 120
Czech Village Heritage Mall 120

D

Damska Matice Skolska 47
DeBoom, Beth Chacey 146, 168, 171, 172
DeCastello, Reverend R.N. 62
Deda & Babi's Antiques & Collectibles 155
Destination Southside 140
diacritical marks 132
Douglas Starch Works 51, 67, 78, 81, 82, 83, 84, 113, 137
dracky 100
Drahozal, Bernie 153
Drahozal, Bob 43, 45, 91, 107, 108
Drahozal, Frank 91
Drahozal, Olga 122

INDEX

Drahozal, Vaclav 43, 59, 91, 107, 122, 153
Drahozal, Wes 122
Dr. Martin Luther King Jr. Memorial Bridge 160

E

Ely, John F. 34
Ernie's Avenue Tavern 119, 150

F

Farmstead Foods 123
Faye Brothers Lumber Company 58, 69
Federation of Czech Groups 104, 137
Ferguson, Mike 37, 150
Fiala, Vince 39
Filip, Frank 101
First Trust & Savings Bank 161
Fisher Concertina Orchestra 99
Five-in-One Bridge 112
flood of 1929 87
flood of 1961 110, 111
flood of 1993 137
Flying Squadrons 75
Ford, Henry 94
Free Thinkers 31, 32
Friendly Service Station 94
Fritz's Food Market 107
Fulton, Park J. 94

G

Gatto Building 86
Geonetric 166
George Cervenka's orchestra 100
Gilmore, Jane 143
Globe Grocery 76, 77, 168
G.M. Olmstead Soap Factory 64, 78
Grand Hall 146, 147, 149

Great Depression 83, 87, 90, 94, 161, 168

H

Hacha, Czech president Emil 96
Hach, Allan 168
Hach, Peter 66, 77, 94, 168
Hall, Howard 85
Hall-Perrine Foundation 131
Harkin, Iowa U.S. senator Tom 135
Harold Fine Foods 86
Havel, Czech president Vaclav 126
Hayes Elementary School 98, 117
Heart House 146, 168, 171, 172
Heral, Bill 144
Herbert, John 142, 158
Herda House 164
Hickenlooper, Iowa senator Bourke B. 109
Hitler, Adolf 95
Hlahol Society 53
Hlavaty, Vaclav 61, 130
Hlubucek, T.B. 117
Holubova, Jaroslava 100
Hoover, Herbert 83, 90
Hose Station No. 4 78, 142
Houby Days 133, 155
Hruby, Reverend Francis 87
Hruska, Roman L. 131
Humoroisticke Listy 62
Hurricane Katrina 152
Hus Memorial Presbyterian Church 72

I

Ideal Theater 77, 78, 94, 164
I-JOBS 149, 158
Industrial Club of 16th Avenue West 107

INDEX

Iowa City 19, 49, 62, 63, 112, 142, 143, 145, 159
Iowa Iron Works 137, 139, 140
Iowa Manufacturing Company 85, 102, 113
Iowa State Savings Bank 66, 76, 83, 84, 90, 161, 162
Iowa Steel 139, 165
Iowa Steel and Iron Works 85, 108

J

Jacobmeyer, Jim 152
Jacobs Building 77, 162, 164
Jakoubek, Vaclav 110
Janda, Vaclav 101
Jan Hus Memorial Presbyterian Church 60, 103
Jan Hus Methodist Church 74, 81
Jansa, Ben 100
Jasa, Pauline 128
jaternice 117, 150, 174
Jednota Tyrs 53, 54
Jelinek, Jon 37, 123, 162
jelita 174
Jeremy Patterson Structural Moving & Shoring 147
J.G. Cherry Building 41, 64, 113, 140, 157
Jiruska, Ray. L 131
jitrnice 75, 100
Joens, George 121, 150
John Hus Methodist Church 61
John Krejci 76
Jungman, Chuck 107
Junior Falcons 98
J.W. Phares Wholesale Florist Co. 139

K

Kadlec Brothers 80, 152
Karban Building 78

Karla Masaryk Chorus 99, 100, 103, 105
Kern, James 144
Killian, A.L. 105
King, David W. 21
Kingston 21, 34
Klinsky, Marianne 92, 174
Kohout, Joseph 32
Kolach Festival 86, 87
Komensky Society 75
Kopecky, Father Frank 60
Korab, Thomas 17, 18
Kosek, Ernest 101
Kouba, Frank 52, 101
Kouba, Jan V. 59
Koubat, Vaclav 52
Kovac, Slovak president Michal 126
Krejci Blacksmith 78
Kuba, Ed 135
Kucera, John N. 86
Kuncl Mall 150
Kun, Reverend Frank 28, 60

L

Lamont, Hugh 152
Legion Arts 39, 142, 143, 145, 147, 158
Lesinger Block 66
Lidice, Czechoslovakia 99
Lindale Mall 112
Lindale Plaza 104, 111, 112
Lion Bridge Brewing Company 152
Little Bohemia tavern 38, 66, 94, 107, 110, 123, 144, 160
Little House Artifacts 171
Lzicar Building 79

M

Maid of Iowa, The 21
Martinek Hardware 78, 168

INDEX

Martinek, Wencil 66
Masaryk, Jan 95, 96, 97
Masaryk, Thomas 47, 95, 96, 98, 103
Matyk building 66, 165
Matyk, Peter 64
McClain, Quinton 152
McGowan, Dick 162
Medinger, Elmer and Hilda 170
Mekota, Frank 99
Melsha, Jeff 38, 160
Melsha, Leon "Tunnie" 160, 168
Melsha, Vaclav 146
Merkle, Donna 173
Military Road 19, 20
Minerva Society 59
Mitvalsky, Frank 59, 144
Modern Bakery Building 86
Monroe School 51, 60
Moore, Thomas 160
Mount Trashmore 157
Muzik Cigar Manufacturer 107

N

National Czech & Slovak Museum & Library 14, 39, 126, 131, 146, 173
Naughton, Gail 39, 131
Neighborhood Development Corporation 161
Nejdl, Marj 130, 174
New Bo Ale House 162
NewBo City Market 164, 165, 166
North Star Oat Meal Mills 30
Novak, Don 144
Novak, Rudolf 54, 55, 98
Novotny Tavern 86
Novotny, Vaclav 170

O

Oak Hill–Jackson 145, 165
OSADA 145
Oxford Junction 49

P

Paidar, Rose 98
Parlor City 43, 52, 62, 68, 83, 111
Parlor City Pub and Eatery 162
Pazdernik, Louis 66, 77, 94
Peiffer, Leo 128
Penford Products 137
Penick & Ford 84, 113
Peremsky, Frank 17, 23, 24
P. Hach building 66, 168
Pirkl, Frank 52
Pisney, Frank 91
Pisney, Mary 91
Pochobradsky, Louis 67, 80, 122
Poe, Edgar Allen 144
Pokrok 32, 62
Polehna's Meat Market 37, 150, 156
Polehna's Meats 107
Prague 13, 14, 25, 33, 44, 47, 49, 55, 58, 72, 73, 74, 78, 94, 95, 96, 98, 105, 127, 128, 132, 135
Praha Rebekah Lodge 58
Prokop Velky Lodge 55, 56
Protovin 49
Prucha, R.G. 142, 158

Q

Quaker Oats 26, 30, 51, 63, 69, 83, 113
Quality Chef 138

R

Racine, Wisconsin 18, 25, 32, 62
Raven, The 144

INDEX

Reading Society, the 31, 33, 52, 53, 54, 58
Red Ball Route 85
Red Baron Bar & Dance Club 157
Renchin, Frank 23
Richard Jones Accounting 139
Richards, Michael 165
RiverRun 140
Riverside 49
Riverside Park 51, 68, 75, 78, 84, 109
Rocarek, John 131, 152
Rose Dale Country School 92
Roundhouse, the 108, 118, 155, 167
Rudis-Jicinsky, Dr. John 49, 54, 74

S

Salvation Army 89, 152
Sauce Bar & Bistro 156
Save Cedar Rapids Heritage 168
Severa, W.F. 59, 101
Shepherd, Osgood 19, 20
Shueyville 24
Sibrinky 54, 100
Sinclair Industrial Park 138
Sinclair, T.M. 26, 27, 28, 42
Sirowy & Novak Service Station 107
Sixteenth Avenue Commercial Club 107, 111
skvarky 174
Skvor and Tichy Druggist building 79
Slets 55, 75, 98, 105
Smid, Frank J. 66, 78
Smid Hardware Store 66
Smiley's Garage 156
Sokol Hall 54, 58, 89, 97
Sokol Park 68
Sokols, the 53, 54, 97, 109, 117
Sommer, Joseph 33
Sosel, Joseph 19, 22

South End Business Men's Club 67, 76
South Side Commercial Club 76, 84, 94
SouthSide Development Corporation 139
South Side Tap 94, 168
Spevacek, Alice 100
Stark, Baron 38, 155
Stark Enterprises 156
Star Wagon Works 30, 51
Stepanek, William 101
Stepan, John C. 47
St. Joseph's Day 119, 133, 137
St. Ludmila Catholic Church 81, 87, 153
St. Luke's Hospital 59
St. Mikulas 71, 112, 117
stock market crash 89, 91
Stoffer Hunter, Mark 27
Stumptown 111, 157
St. Wenceslaus Catholic Church 42, 45, 59, 81, 85, 109, 138, 153
Suchy, Frank 66, 94, 165
Sulek, Anton 23
Sutter's Mill 20
Svec, Frank 17, 24
Svec, Melvina 24, 131
Svec, Rose 24
Svoboda, Charles B. 101
Svrdlik, Reverend Florian 60, 81
Swanson, Evelyn Medinger 172
Sykora Bakery 79, 119, 134, 151

T

Tahlee Society 52
Tama 49
Tehel family 131
The Light Guard Band 52
Third Street Live 162
Thompson, Lou 152

INDEX

Tlapa, Josef 52
Tlusty, Anton 101
T.M. Sinclair & Company 27, 29, 35, 36, 43, 61, 63, 64, 68, 123
Tosh, Agnes 146
Town and Country Shopping Center 104
Trejtnar, Hermina Unzeitig 92, 93, 173
Trejtnar, Joe 93
Trejtnat, Hermina Unzeitig 92, 93, 174
Tucek, Marie 45

U

Union Station 43, 62, 93, 102
United State Bank 90, 119
Unzeitig, Frank 93
Urban, Joseph 32

V

Van Allen, David 141
Van Buren School 51
Vane, Vaclav 101
Van Vechten, Carl 144, 162
Vcelky 74, 102
Velvet Feedbag 123, 144
Velvet Revolution 127, 135, 137
Vic Holets Potato Chip factory 107
Viktor Building 79
Viktor, John 79, 81
Village Bank & Trust 161
Village Meat Market & Café 152
Vision Iowa 149

W

Wellington Heights 145
Westdale Mall 112
Western Bohemian Fraternal Association 57, 58, 101, 102
Western Fraternal Life Association 58, 115, 131
Whiting's Foundry 51
Wilson Foods 108, 113, 123
Wistein, Dr. Rose 96
Witousek, Frank 101
Witwer Grocery Company 145
Woitishek, Frank 24
Wood, Grant 92, 144, 167

Z

ZCBJ Drill Team 101
ZCBJ Hall 57, 76, 110, 115, 123, 162, 163
Zdrubek, Frank B. 32, 62
Zika, Louis 101
Zlata Kniha 97

ABOUT THE AUTHOR

Dave Rasdal is a retired newspaperman. For over three decades, he worked as a columnist at the *Cedar Rapids Gazette*. He also maintained the blog Ramblin' with Rasdal. In 2011, the newspaper published *Ramblin': Reflections of Hidden Iowa*. Rasdal is a graduate of the University of South Dakota.

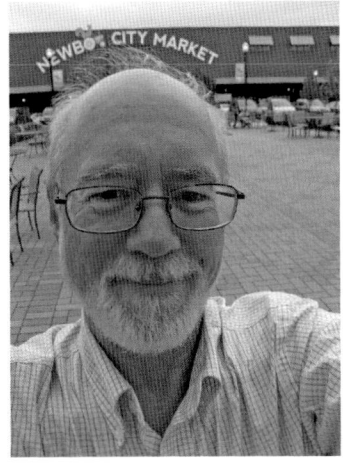

Visit us at
www.historypress.net

This title is also available as an e-book